Managing IP Addresses

How to Number Your Network for Growth and Change

Bill Dutcher

Wiley Computer Publishing

John Wiley & Sons, Inc.

NEW YORK · CHICHESTER · WEINHEIM · BRISBANE · SINGAPORE · TORONTO

Publisher: Robert Ipsen
Editor: Carol Long
Managing Editor: Marnie Wielage
Text Design & Composition: Publishers' Design and Production Services, Inc.

Designations used by companies to distinguish their products are often claimed as trademarks. In all instances where John Wiley & Sons, Inc., is aware of a claim, the product names appear in initial capital or all capital letters. Readers, however, should contact the appropriate companies for more complete information regarding trademarks and registration.

This book is printed on acid-free paper. ⊗

Published by John Wiley & Sons, Inc.

Published simultaneously in Canada.

This publication is designed to provide accurate and authoritative information in regard to the subject matter covered. It is sold with the understanding that the publisher is not engaged in professional serves. If professional advice or other expert assistance is required, the services of a competent professional person should be sought.

Library of Congress Cataloging-in-Publication Data:

Dutcher, Bill, 1946–
    Managing IP addresses : how to number your network for growth and change / Bill Dutcher.
       p.   cm.
    Includes bibliographical references and index.
    ISBN 0-471-25484-3 (pbk. : alk. paper)
    1. TCP/IP (Computer network protocol) 2. Internet addresses.   I. Title.
    TK5105.585.D88   2000
    004.6′2—dc21   99-049094

Printed in the United States of America.

10 9 8 7 6 5 4 3 2 1

Contents

Acknowledgments   **xi**

Introduction   **xiii**

Chapter 1   What's an IP Address?   **1**

The IP Protocol   3

IP Addresses and Classes   5
Class A Addresses   7
Class B Addresses   8
Class C Addresses   9
Class D and E Addresses   9

Making Life Easier for Binary-Challenged Humans   10
Identifying a Type of Network Address   11

The Working Classes   13

Hosts and Interfaces   13

Summary   14

Chapter 2   The Politics of IP Address Delegation   **17**

What Is Delegation?   18

IANA   19

Expanding the Task   20

Winding It Down   22

IRs and the ISPs   24

The ISP Viewpoint   25

The Future of IRs   26

Summary   28

Chapter 3   Global Internet Routing   **31**

Routing   32
Example of Internet Routing   34

It Takes a URL	36
To Connect or Not to Connect	37
Top-Level Routing	40
IP Routing Principles	41
Routing Tables	42
The Hop Count	44
Link Weight	45
Inside, Outside	45
Interior and Exterior Routing Protocols	47
ASes and CIDR	49
CIDR	50
Simplifying Routing	51
An Imperfect World	52
Managing the Load	52
CIDR Masks	53
Groups of Cs	54
Enforcing the Rules	58
Summary	59

Chapter 4	**Why Renumber?**	**61**
	Reasons for Renumbering	62
	Internal Factors	63
	Cleaning Up Legacy Routing	63
	Documenting Incomplete Networks	63
	Joining Networks with Business Partners	64
	Outgrowing Address Space	64
	Moving to Private Address Space	65
	Virtual LANs (VLANs)	65
	External Factors	66
	Changing ISPs	66
	Provider-Independent Address Space	67
	Aggregating Several Small Networks into Large	
	CIDR Blocks	68
	Nonunique Addresses	68
	Swampland Reclamation	69
	Network Expansion	71
	Ipv6	71
	Drawbacks of Renumbering	72
	Summary	72

Chapter 5	**Making the Business Case for Renumbering**	**75**
	The Business Case	76
	What's in a Business Case?	76

Composing the Business Case   78

Justifying an Address Space Request   79
IP Address Space Value   80
Apply Yourself   81
Current Address Usage   81
Future Address Usage   82

Summary   84

Chapter 6   Diagrams and Documentation   85

Dependencies   86

Preparing the Surface   86
Site Plans   86
Existing Networks (LANs and WANs)   87
Routing   88
External WAN Links   89
Current Addressing Plan   90
    Types of Addresses in Use   90
Unaggregated or Unaggregatable Addresses   91
Private Address Space   92
Subnetworks   93
Business Partner Address Ranges   93
Network Expansion Plans   94
Available Address Ranges   94
ISP Connections   95
Router Layout and Connectivity   95
Interior and Exterior Routing Protocols   96
Firewalls and NAT   97
Intrusion Detection Systems (IDS)   98
Proxy Servers   98
Dial-Up Access or Remote Access Service (RAS)   99
Domain Name Service (DNS)   99
Applications   100
Hosts and Printers   101

Summary   102

Chapter 7   Subnetworking   103

Less Wasted Space   104

The Basics of Subnetworking   106

IP Addresses and IP Routers   107

Subnetworks and Addresses   108
Stockpiling Subnets   111

Masking   112
Misleading Masks   113

Beneath the Byte Boundary   114
    Subnetwork Masks   117
Class C Subnetworks   117
All-Zeroes, All-Ones   121
Variable Length Subnetwork Masking (VLSM)   122
Summary   124

Chapter 8   Network Address Translation   127
The Need for NAT   128
NAT Basics   128
Why NAT?   129
    NAT for Security   130
    NAT for Proxy Services   131
    NAT for Private Address Space   132
    NAT for Routability   132
    NAT for Business Partners   133
How NAT Works   134
    Only by Proxy   136
Positioning NAT   137
NAT's Dark Side   137
NAT and TCP   138
    That TCP Port Thing   138
    TCP Ports   139
    Establishing the Connection   140
    Back to the Ports   142
    To Connect or Not to Connect   143
Summary   145

Chapter 9   DNS Considerations   147
The DNS Database   148
DNS as a Network Service   149
DNS Services and Domains   150
Name Resolution at Work   151
DNS Resource Records   154
    A Records   157
    CNAME Records   157
    NS Records   158
    MX Records   158
    PTR Records   159
DNS Zones   159
Summary   160

Chapter 10 **Provider-Aggregated and Provider-Independent Address Space**   **163**

    Independent and Aggregated   164
        Provider-Aggregated Address Space   164
        Provider-Independent Address Space   166

    Private Address Space   167

    Maybe You Can Take It with You   168
        I Want My PI   169

    The New PI Rules   170

    Do I Need an Autonomous System Number?   171

    Getting PI   172

    Summary   173

Chapter 11 **Host Considerations**   **175**

    A Host Is a Host   176

    HOSTS File   176

    WINS and NetBIOS   177

    Unix System Configuration Files   178

    Readdressing with Configuration Files   179

    DHCP   180
        DHCP Server, Where Are You?   180
        DHCP Scope   181
        Displaying DHCP-Assigned Address Information   182

    Configuring a PC to Use DHCP   182

    Hosts with Multiple Interfaces   183

    Ethernet Switch Problems   184

    The DHCP Downside   185

    Summary   186

Chapter 12 **You and Your ISP**   **187**

    Stub Networks   188

    Multiconnected Networks   190

    Multihomed Networks   192

    Primary and Backup   193

    Sharing the Load   195

    Transit Networks   196

    BGP and Transit Networks   198

    Summary   199

Chapter 13	**You as ISP**	**201**
	Drawing the Line of Demarcation	202
	Address Space	203
	Route Aggregation	204
	Static Routes	205
	Multihoming	206
	Autonomous Systems	207
	DNS	210
	Documentation	214
	Summary	215
Chapter 14	**Renumbering Routers**	**217**
	Router Interfaces	218
	Serial Ports	219
	LAN Interfaces	222
	Secondary Addresses	222
	Additional Network Addresses	223
	Separated Addresses	223
	Transition from Bridged Networks	224
	Loopback Address	225
	Terminal Ports	225
	Dial-Up Port Pools	226
	DHCP Services	227
	DNS Implications for Router Renumbering	227
	Authentication Server Access	228
	Summary	230
Chapter 15	**Renumbering Steps**	**231**
	Process Steps	232
	Plan Renumbering Effort	232
	Get Address Allocation Assignment	233
	Establish Current Address Usage	234
	Determine Address Usage	235
	Get Address Assignments	237
	Update and Upgrade DNS Servers	237
	Changing NS Addresses	238
	Changing the SOA	239
	Start Renumbering Rollout	240
	Enable Routing	241

Update DNS and Test   243

Complete Rollout   245

Reset DNS Services   245

Do Administrative Cleanup   246

Summary   246

Chapter 16   Small Network Case Study   247

Situation   248

Scoping the Project   249

Project Plan   249

Preparing for Renumbering   251

Addressing Rollout   251

Administrative Cleanup   252

Future Growth   253

Summary   254

Chapter 17   Medium Network Case Study   255

Situation   255

Scoping the Problem   258

Project Plan   259
   DNS   261
   DHCP   261

Preparing for Renumbering   261

Addressing Rollout   263

Administrative Cleanup   264

Future Growth   265

Summary   265

Chapter 18   Large Network Case Study   267

Situation   268

Scoping the Problem   271

Project Plan   272

Preparing for Renumbering   274

Addressing Rollout   275

Administrative Cleanup   276

Future Growth   276

Summary   277

Chapter 19 The Future of IP   **279**

The Trouble with IPv4   279
Killing Me Softly with New Apps   280
Feelings of Insecurity   281

Once and Future Solutions   281
Quality of Service   282

The Version 6 Solution   285
That Security Thing   286
IPv6 and QoS   288
IPv6 and DNS   288

Getting There   289

Why Me?   291

Bibliography   **293**

Index   **297**

Acknowledgments

Writing a book has given me a new insight into how all of those stacks of titles in the bookstore actually get there. Those books represent not only the work of the author and the publisher, but also all of the editors, compositors, proofreaders, printers, distributors, packers, shippers, shelvers, and booksellers who play a role in that long trail from the word processor to the reader. Books are words on pages, but they also represent the lives of all of the people involved for the time it takes to write, edit, and produce a book.

I must thank Carol Long, my editor at John Wiley & Sons, who first approached me with the idea for this book. Her encouragement, direction, and sense of humor have been invaluable in making this book happen. And somehow I get the feeling from the other terrific people that I have worked with at Wiley—Christina Berry, Emilie Herman, and Marnie Wielage—that I'm not the first author they've had to threaten and cajole to get drafts and edits on time.

I also want to thank a number of other people who have played roles both large and small in this project, including Don Telage, David Graves, Faith Rodman, Bob Senesi, Bill Casey, and Dave Kosiur. I am also very grateful to Ralph Droms, known to me as the patron saint of DHCP, for his patient and careful review of my manuscript, and his many helpful corrections and comments. My greatest debt is to my wife and son, Anne and Greg, for their forbearance during this project, and for enduring lengthy exposure to more than they ever wanted to know about IP addressing.

Introduction

What's in This Book

Used virtually throughout the computing world, the IP protocol is the technical underpinning of the global Internet, but it was neither intended nor designed to be the foundation of universal computing. It has become that because it works, and because something that works, and that is also in effect free, is accepted, standardized, and universally applied.

The goal of this book is to illuminate the dark corners of this key communications protocol, the Internet Protocol, commonly referred to as IP. Along with other protocols that work with it, such as the Transmission Control Protocol (TCP), the IP protocol makes the Internet work.

The IP protocol, invented more than two decades ago to foster communications across relatively unreliable, long-distance communications networks, has continued to amaze and confound its creators. Its current-day users, the unruly, unwashed masses of Internet citizens do not consider it at all. To them, it's part of the internal machinery that makes the Internet work, and, like a balky accelerator pedal that they might have to futz with once in a while, most users seldom think about IP or worry about their IP addresses any more than they do their telephone numbers.

Unlike users, network administrators must deal with the workings of the IP protocol, and with IP network addressing, more than occasionally. They are the mechanics of the Internet, and it is for them that books like this are written. The goal of this book is to be a readable, logically thought-out account of how IP works, addressing the hows and whys of changing IP addresses, from both technical and management perspectives. The chapters of the book, arranged to carry out this logical flow, are as follows.

Chapter 1: What's an IP Address?

An IP address is a unique identifier for a computer attached to the Internet. Chapter 1 introduces the fundamental concepts of IP addressing, including the different classes, or types of IP addresses, and how they are used by computers to identify the source and destination of information flow in the Internet. The purpose of this chapter is to lay a foundation in the function and use of IP addresses for Internet and other network communications.

IP addresses are used by the IP protocol, which governs addressing in TCP/IP networks like the Internet, so Chapter 1 also discusses some of the functions of the IP protocol. IP identifies the computer from which Internet communications originate and, more important, where that communication is supposed to end—at a file server, another computer, a Web site, or something else. Greater numbers of potential destinations, such as streaming video sites, IP telephones, and other, more exotic applications, are being dreamed of and, in some cases, implemented, every month.

Chapter 2: The Politics of Address Delegation

IP addresses are like telephone numbers or Social Security numbers. Everyone needs them, but unless you're concerned about having an easy-to-remember telephone number or a commercially unique number, it doesn't really matter too much what they are. They only have to be unique. Likewise, nobody else can use the same IP address, or the whole system starts to break down.

Because there are potentially millions and millions of IP addresses, someone has to become master of IP address assignment, to make sure that everyone's address is unique. It's a logical part of the operation and governance of the Internet, which only seemingly operates by itself, and which seems to resist any effort to govern its millions of users. Now, however, address assignments that were once controlled by U.S. government-sponsored agencies are being turned over to private, not-for-profit companies.

This chapter discusses the intertwined histories of IP address assignment and Internet governance, with an emphasis on the roles played in the past, present, and future by agencies such as the American Registry for Internet Numbers (ARIN) in IP address assignment. Other players, such as Network Solutions (NSI), and the other companies that register domain names, and the new Internet Corporation for Assigned Names and Numbers (ICANN), also have roles in the sometimes convoluted issues of assuring IP address uniqueness and establishing Internet identities.

Chapter 3: Global Internet Routing

In Chapter 3, we ascend out of the murky worlds of politics and business into the complex world of IP routing. IP routing is the process by which IP routers in networks and the global Internet deliver addressed packets of data, called IP datagrams, across the Internet. This chapter looks at the processes by which a simple URL typed into a Web browser is transformed into a message with an IP address and how it is delivered across the Internet.

As this chapter illustrates, delivering an IP datagram on demand to any other destination on the Internet depends on a remarkably complex set of interactions and coordination among many individually controlled parts of the Internet. Routers from several providers, such as local, national, and global Internet service providers (ISPs) must know about the existence of other networks, as well as ways to route traffic to those networks. The process depends on different types of routing protocols, such as interior and exterior routing protocols, to share routing tables that match IP network addresses to destinations.

The rapid growth of the Internet has threatened the capability of the Internet's top-level, or *core* routers, to keep track of all of the IP networks in the world. As a result, methods such as Classless Inter-Domain Routing (CIDR), to make more efficient use of routers as well as IP address space, have been employed to keep the Internet from falling apart. This chapter also examines CIDR, and its intended and actual effects on global Internet connectivity.

Chapter 4: Why Renumber?

One of the basic premises of this book is that companies and organizations will be undertaking a project to reassign IP addresses or renumber their networks and hosts. Presumably, they have good reasons to do so, and Chapter 4 discusses what some of those good (as well as not-so-good) reasons might be.

As this chapter illustrates, sometimes renumbering is forced on an organization, such as when it switches its Internet connections to a different ISP. Renumbering is sometimes a consequence of such a step, which might be taken to get better service, to lower Internet access costs, or to gain some other advantage, such as better security or a Virtual Private Network (VPN) service.

In other cases, renumbering is required when a company decides to move out of "private" address space, and into routable, "public" address space, or when private addressing causes problems with key business applications or with certain types of network or security systems.

Chapter 4 concludes with circumstances that may force renumbering, such as the release of the next version of the IP protocol, IPv6, and efforts to simplify Internet routing with CIDR addressing. While it is being implemented on a voluntary basis for the time being, Internet engineering organizations like the Internet Engineering Task Force (IETF) want to reclaim in-use address space in order to "drain the swamp" of the 192 address block and to consolidate those addresses into larger CIDR blocks.

Chapter 5: Making the Business Case for Renumbering

Renumbering a network isn't a task that a network manager or administrator undertakes casually. It's a project. It's simpler than building the Panama Canal but more difficult than changing your default Microsoft Word settings; in short, it's not to be undertaken without a lot of forethought.

Renumbering could involve some degree of disruption and interruption of vital network services, and it might force users to reconfigure their PCs manually. It has literal costs as well, and Chapter 5 discusses some of these costs, as well as how they can be justified as an operational expense.

In summary, the network manager who has concluded that renumbering is necessary may have to justify the decision to IT or to general corporate management. In addition, the network manager may have to quantify the benefits to management.

Chapter 5 also discusses the issues surrounding justifying a request for IP address space, either to an address assignment authority or to an ISP. Now that IP address space is no longer free to ISPs, they need justification for the address space requested by network managers to carry out a renumbering project.

Chapter 6: Diagrams and Documentation

In Chapter 6, we move into some of the mechanics of a renumbering project. Renumbering an existing network is like planning a construction project. The network manager must know precisely which addresses and network numbers are being used, as well as which addresses, if any, have been allocated but are not in use. The network manager may find it useful to have site plans of the buildings in which the renumbered network will be located, in order to determine how and if the networks can be broken into new subnets.

This chapter also identifies some of the other planning elements that must go into a renumbering effort, including planning the renumbering to achieve different design goals, such as efficient use of address space, route summarization, and aggregated address blocks.

Changing the addressing in a network must also take into consideration the effect of new addresses on other network services. For example, records in network and the Internet Domain Name Service (DNS) may have to be changed to reflect renumbered networks, as will address ranges assigned by servers running the Dynamic Host Control Protocol (DHCP). Router connections to ISPs may also be affected by renumbering. Finally, ways to hide the changes wrought in the renumbering effort from other networks, such as the Internet, are discussed in a section on firewalls and network address translation (NAT).

Chapter 7: Subnetworking

Using address space most efficiently means subdividing address space beyond its "natural" IP class boundaries. In Chapter 7 we discuss some of the techniques of subdividing IP address space into subnetworks, both on byte and on bit boundaries.

As networks have grown beyond the IP address space originally allocated for them, most network managers have become familiar with subnetworking. It's a key survival tool for large, complicated networks, and it's essential for using most any kind of IP address space efficiently. As Chapter 7 emphasizes, subnetworking allows a network manager to tailor IP address space to the configuration and topology of the organization's networks.

Chapter 7 concludes with a discussion of handling the "heels of the loaf," the leftovers of subnetworking—the all-zeroes and all-ones subnets. In some renumbering projects, where there is an emphasis on using absolutely every available address, even these normally unusable network addresses come in handy.

Chapter 8: Network Address Translation

One of the complications of using private address space, discussed in Chapter 4, is that private addresses must be translated to routable, public addresses to be sent across the Internet. Systems that do this, such as routers and firewalls, do network address translation, or NAT, to transform unroutable addresses to routable ones.

As this chapter suggests, NAT can be a relatively straightforward, one-for-one address substitution process. Networks that are readdressed into private address space can use this strategy to pass traffic from the privately numbered intranet to the public Internet. However, NAT can become much more complicated if the router or firewall that does NAT substitutes only a single address, which is that of its external Internet interface, for any internal address. That requires the NAT device to track TCP port numbers and to maintain an application port translation table, to direct incoming traffic from the Internet back to the appropriate inside source address.

This chapter also addresses the implications of NAT on network security and on firewall and router performance. As you'll learn here, hiding internal addresses can be a helpful security measure, but it may also incapacitate certain applications and network management software.

Chapter 9: DNS Considerations

The Domain Name Service (DNS) is a key network service for Internet usability. DNS servers all over the Internet, as well as in private intranets, work together transparently to translate host names and Web site URLs to IP addresses. DNS services simplify using the Internet by allowing users to specify destinations with familiar, easy-to-remember text names, rather than IP addresses.

In this chapter, we cover the effects of network renumbering on DNS services. In most cases, the greatest impact falls on local DNS servers, rather than the Internet's root zone servers. Local DNS host name-to-IP address records must be updated to reflect new host, server, and router IP addresses. In addition, the records of any secondary or backup DNSes must also be changed. As this chapter indicates, dynamic DNS services, which are automatically updated by DHCP servers, aren't necessarily foolproof methods of updating DNS records.

Primary and secondary DNS services work together to keep their records synchronized. When a network is renumbered and changes are made to the records in the primary DNS, the timing of secondary DNS updates must be changed, so that the new host name-to-IP address records are propagated as quickly as possible to secondary DNSes. This chapter also discusses the mechanics of forcing secondary updates relatively quickly during renumbering programs, so that DNS services continue to work without interruption.

Chapter 10: Provider-Aggregated and Provider-Independent Address Space

Many network managers who undertake a network renumbering project view it as good experience—and a great one to add to their resume; nevertheless, it's something they'd prefer to avoid in the future. Chapter 10 discusses one of the more common, but not always guaranteed, ways to avoid renumbering if the network moves to a different ISP. An organization that has provider-independent (PI) address space may be able to change ISPs and not have to renumber, because its address space is not associated with a specific ISP.

Most other organizations, particularly smaller organizations and companies or those that have relatively new networks, have provider-aggregated (PA) space. The difference, as Chapter 10 describes, is that networks with PA can keep that space as long as they don't change ISPs. Moving to a different ISP means moving outside the larger block of address advertised by the ISP. In order to be "found" on the Internet, the network may have to renumber into a new ISP's address block.

The chapter concludes with a discussion of one of the solutions to the PA-PI dilemma, which is to use private address space and network address translation (NAT). However, private addressing can pose its own set of problems: NAT doesn't necessarily work with all applications, and NAT can bog down a firewall with extra processing chores, affecting the speed of Internet access.

Chapter 11: Host Considerations

Readdressing isn't just a matter of assigning new addresses and rebooting PCs. As Chapter 11 points out, most of the systems that will get new IP addresses in a readdressing project will be hosts. That general-purpose term includes PCs, workstations, servers, minicomputers, and mainframes. The problem is that each may have a different type of configuration file or a different method of keeping and discovering its IP address.

This chapter also covers some of the tools that can make host renumbering easier to do and easier to maintain. For example, DHCP servers can assign IP addresses dynamically. If DHCP address assignments are linked dynamically to a dynamic DNS, the DNS records can be updated automatically when DHCP assigns a host a new address.

DHCP is a great tool, and it simplifies the readdressing problem significantly, but at the conclusion of Chapter 11 we discuss some problems that may arise when using DHCP through Ethernet switches. In addition, network management systems, such as those that use the Simple Network Management Protocol (SNMP), may rely on systems that have specific IP addresses, not those that are assigned dynamically by DHCP.

Chapter 12: You and Your ISP

Renumbering networks may not change much about the internal routing in an organization's networks, but as Chapter 12 explains, it may have a more profound effect on connectivity to the Internet through the organization's ISP. We will examine what local and national ISPs may have to do to accommodate changes in the addressing used within an organization's networks.

Most of the changes involve route announcements, which are the network addresses and address ranges that ISPs advertise to other ISPs. Top-level, or national, ISPs, in turn, advertise routes to the networks maintained by the customer of lower-level ISPs. If the addresses in use in an ISP's customer networks change, the route advertisements by that ISP must also change.

This chapter also addresses some of the complications that may arise when organizations' networks are connected to the Internet through two or more ISPs. Usually, the reason is to provide a backup circuit in case the primary circuit fails. However, some companies and organizations want to balance the load of Internet traffic between two ISP links. As Chapter 12 observes, this is often harder to do than it seems, and may lead to asymmetrical routing complications that are unhealthy for everyone concerned.

Chapter 13: You as ISP

Many network managers think of themselves as providing Internet access for their organizations, but today's customer-driven network service focus, even in IT departments, may cast those same network managers in the role of an Internet service provider for their internal, captive customers.

Chapter 13 addresses the issues that IT departments may have to face if their internal customers come to regard them as a service provider. The organization may have a single, real ISP that provides Internet access for the entire organization, whereas the IT department may have to deal with routing, network service, and service-level agreements to its subsidiary organizations. The result will be that the IT department will have all of the disadvantages of being a real ISP and none of the advantages. It's a consequence of the decentralization of authority in some large companies and of the transformation of IT departments into cost and profit centers.

Much of the focus of this chapter is on the technical issues that the IT department may have to manage if it is to provide Internet connections for a decentralized organization. For example, the IT department may have to run its own internal routing protocol, establish an Autonomous System (AS), and run DNS services. It may also have to resolve issues with multihoming, static routes, and route aggregation to provide Internet access services for its customers.

Chapter 14: Renumbering Routers

IP routers are key connectivity components for IP networks, both at the organizational and the global Internet level. Network renumbering may change the relationship between an organization's routers and ISP routers. At the least, router interfaces to networks that have been renumbered must be changed, and the new networks advertised properly to other routers.

This chapter discusses many of the router configuration and management issues that the network manager must control when renumbering networks. Routers may have several different types of network interfaces, such as those for serial links and LANs, some or all of which may have to be reconfigured in a renumbering program.

To ease the transition between the old and new network addressing plans, some router interfaces may bear two or more network addresses or support secondary addresses to separated subnets. Renumbering may affect authentication for dial-up systems, which may enter the network through ports controlled by routers for back-end authentication systems.

Finally, this chapter describes the effects of router interface renumbering on other network services, such as DNS records that may reference router host names and addresses.

Chapter 15: Renumbering Steps

The previous chapters have served as the background for understanding the scope and implications of a renumbering project. In contrast, Chapter 15 details a cookbook approach to actually executing a renumbering project. The specifics of an organization's renumbering project may vary, but the basic steps will be the same. This chapter outlines the sequence of steps required to renumber a network, starting with planning and justifying the project, through changing DNS records and documenting the final network numbering plan.

As this chapter emphasizes, most of the work in a renumbering project lies in the preparation process; relatively little effort is involved in the actual assignment of new addresses to host and network devices. (This assumes that address assignment and address management tools such as DHCP can be and will be used in the renumbering program. Sometimes they cannot, or should not, be used, such as in giving servers and other devices that must have fixed addresses their unique IP addresses.)

This chapter also lists the sequence of steps to take to enable DNS services to know about changes in the addressing structure. Also covered is the key issue in managing DNS updates during renumbering: propagating DNS resource record changes from the primary DNS to the secondary DNSes as soon as possible. This chapter stresses that renumbering is not so much a problem of fixing new addresses; rather, it is a challenge to make sure that the right network services and Internet routers know about it so that the new addresses can be reachable from other networks and the Internet.

Chapter 16: Small Network Case Study

To illustrate how organizations of different sizes might conduct renumbering programs, Chapters 16, 17, and 18 present case studies of renumbering programs in networks of different sizes and different levels of complexity. In each case, the conditions and the goals of the renumbering project are different, as they would be in real life and in real companies.

The first case study in this chapter describes the process of renumbering a relatively small network, consisting of only a few hundred hosts in one office. This study has been structured to emphasize the renumbering process and the goals the network manager is attempting to achieve.

As for the other case studies, the renumbering solution described in this chapter is not the only way that the network could be renumbered, nor is it the only way to achieve the stated objective. In the small network case study, the objective of renumbering is to reorganize the network to achieve better route summarization, because the company is changing ISPs.

Chapter 17: Medium Network Case Study

This chapter continues with the pattern established in Chapter 16 with the small network case study, but addresses the renumbering problem in a larger network, one that is spread over three locations. In this case study, the objective is to integrate existing networks in three different locations into a single network that has more efficient internal routing, not just more efficient routing to the Internet.

The objective of renumbering in this case study is to reorganize the company's internal networks into an Open Shortest Path First (OSPF) network, to make the network respond to routing changes more quickly and efficiently. Certainly, Internet routing will benefit from route summarization, but in comparison to the case study in Chapter 16, the goal of this larger network renumbering project is to make the internal workings of the network more efficient and more robust.

Chapter 18: Large Network Case Study

The last network case study, in Chapter 18, addresses a large network composed of several thousand hosts in several different locations. The premise of this case study is that the parent company is acquiring the networks of another, smaller company, and the larger company wants to integrate them into its network infrastructure. However, for business organizational reasons, the parent company only wants to integrate the networks to a certain degree, so that the acquisition's networks are held at an arm's length from the parent company. The acquisition's networks use private address space, and they must be renumbered into new, public address space, then integrated into the parent company's larger routing scheme.

As with the two previous case studies, the solution presented and the objectives achieved are not the only ones that would work for a company of this size or a network organized in this fashion. As for the small and medium-sized network case studies, this example also integrates the steps outlined in Chapter 15.

Chapter 19: The Future of IP

Throughout the book, we've examined many facets of IP addressing in conjunction with the many issues that must be addressed in renumbering networks into new address space. In this, the final chapter, we examine where IP addressing seems to be headed in the foreseeable future.

IP's history has been a long, strange journey from its origins in military communications systems to the lingua franca of the Internet. As this chapter points out, we are likely to see even more TCP and IP in all kinds of new, Internet-enabled devices, such as cable television set-top boxes, robots, and all sorts of new Internet-enabled computing appliances.

The IP protocol has proven itself to be remarkably resilient and adaptable, but it's unlikely that it can continue to be so forever. Or can it? The telephone system has had unprecedented staying power; it's only recently that we are seeing developments such as ISDN and DSL bringing the advantages of digital technologies all the way back through the local loop.

The most immediate change that may affect IP addressing is IPv6, the newer, bigger, better, and faster version of IPv4. In this chapter, we discuss some of the characteristics of IPv6, specifically with respect to addressing, that will prolong its usefulness and enable a more comprehensively connected world in the future.

What's an IP Address?

The rapid growth of the Internet has led to the widespread acceptance of the TCP/IP protocol as the one protocol to have if you're not going to have more than one. So it's not surprising that practically everyone who has a computer that is attached to a network—even the most technically unversed or digitally challenged—has gained at least a passing familiarity with IP addresses.

An IP address is a number that uniquely identifies a computer to the rest of the world. The rest of the world is, in today's environment, the other computers on the Internet; but it could be the other PCs, servers, and computers on a LAN or on any other network that uses TCP/IP. To a computer, an IP address, such as 125.38.127.12, is its network identity, even though it may be better known by a more human-friendly and thus memorable title, such as www.bigco.com, Camembert.BigCo.com, or My_PC.

An IP address is like a phone number. It's the Internet's way of identifying a specific computer on a specific network, as illustrated in Figure 1.1, just as a phone number identifies a specific phone on a specific phone system. Want to call a coworker at the office in California? Dial the number and the phone will ring. Want to get to the home page of the BigCo Web site on the Internet? You'll need its IP address—though you might get to the Web site without it, by typing only its URL on the

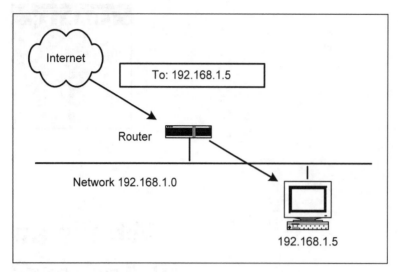

Figure 1.1   An IP address identifies a destination computer system.

Location line of your Netscape Web browser, or by picking a reference to it from your list of bookmarks. Assuming everything works properly, the URL will be translated for you to the IP address in the background by the Domain Name Service (DNS). The operation of DNS is another story entirely, but its key role is to hide the mechanics of determining the correct IP address for a Web site or Internet host from end users.

That IP addresses are familiar does not necessarily mean that everyone understands them. Nor does everyone have to. Though it's somewhat helpful for the average user to understand what that IP address means in the Windows Control Panels...Networking window, it's not essential. It is essential, though, that the network administrator or the network manager understand IP addressing, as well as how to subdivide IP address space into subnetworks, how to manage IP address space with DHCP, and how to maintain assigned addresses with IP address management tools.

Similarly, the router administrator may have to understand IP addressing and subnetworking even more thoroughly than the network administrator, to maintain proper connectivity with an ISP or with other parts of the enterprise.

The IP Protocol

Communications protocols, such as TCP/IP, SNA, NetBIOS, and others, are sets of rules or agreements that govern communications between computers. Two computers that communicate, such as a Web browser and a Web server, must use the same sets of rules, or protocols, for these simple reasons:

- They must be able to understand each other.
- They must control the flow of information reliably.
- They must have ways to handle and to recover from errors.

The full array of functions that two devices must perform to communicate is described in the dreaded seven-layer ISO Model, depicted in Figure 1.2. The ISO Model isn't as difficult to understand as most people believe—it's just that most explanations of the ISO Model are more confusing than the model itself.

ISO is a model because it's an idealized structure, and few protocol *suites* follow it exactly. TCP/IP, for example, has four *layers*, and IBM's SNA has eight. But remember that its purpose is to describe the functions that two devices have to perform when they communicate over a network, not how they perform them. It's like saying that people have to speak on the telephone to communicate, but there's nothing about the telephone "protocol" that specifies the language in which those people speak.

TCP/IP is a shorthand method to describe a set of other protocols that are usually implemented along with them. Though they are the main

TCP/IP	ISO Model	Translation
Application (HTTP, FTP, etc.) Transport (TCP) Internetwork (IP) Physical (LAN, X.25, ATM, etc.)	• Application • Presentation • Session • Transport • Network • Data Link • Physical	• Application and interface • Data format and code set • Transaction binding • Reliable delivery of data • Addressing • Packet packaging • Signaling on wire

Figure 1.2   The seven-layer ISO Model specifies communications functions.

protocols of the Internet, Internet users rarely encounter IP, and never see the functions of TCP. The IP protocol, which is less well-known by its real, full name, the Internetworking Protocol, is most widely associated with its companion protocol, the Transmission Control Protocol (TCP).

The main components of the TCP/IP protocol suite are:

Applications protocols. Protocols that control useful applications, such as FTP, HTTP, Telnet, and SMTP, sit at the top of the TCP/IP protocol suite. They allow users to access applications, and give them an interface to specify the Web site to which they want to go, the files they want to transfer, and so on.

Transport protocol. TCP is concerned with delivering data and user requests reliably across a network. It is referred to as a transport protocol because its purpose is to control and manage the flow of data between two computers, so that it arrives reliably at its destination.

Addressing protocol. IP is an addressing protocol. Its purpose is to specify the computer from which the data originated and the computer to which the data is destined.

Network protocols. The network protocols control the transmission of digital signals across wires or other communications media, such as LANs, ATM networks, serial links, and so forth. The Ethernet protocol, X.25, and ATM protocols are good examples of network-level protocols. These protocols have no idea what the bits they are transmitting mean, nor what application they are performing. They are concerned only with creating a digital signal and getting that signal across a communications path.

So IP and, by implication, IP addressing, has a limited, but crucial role in Internet communications. IP is a set of rules that govern only a few of the functions that have to be performed for devices to communicate.

The most important functions that IP controls are:

Identifying the sender and receiver with a numeric IP address. An IP address is like a phone number, in that it gives each computer a unique identity on a network, such as the Internet. The IP address identifies a specific computer on a specific network, just as a 10-digit phone number identifies a specific phone in a specific area code.

Routing traffic to its destination. IP routers use IP to interpret IP addresses and to forward traffic to its eventual destination. IP routers use routing protocols, such as the Border Gateway Protocol (BGP) or the Open Shortest Path First protocol (OSPF), to govern how they work with other routers.

Maintaining the integrity of IP datagrams. As they traverse a complex network like the Internet, IP datagrams may have to be broken down into smaller-sized blocks of data, in order to traverse a specific network. If that happens, IP provides a means to maintain the integrity of each IP datagram so that it is assembled back together properly. A datagram is a block of data that has an IP header on it that can be transmitted by a TCP/IP network. Sometimes datagrams are called *packets* or *frames*, but a block of data with an IP header is called a *datagram*.

Collecting and discarding lost packets. IP routers in the Internet identify IP datagrams that have gone through an excessive number of routers as "lost," and they delete them. This Internet "garbage collection" frees the Internet from the hazards of unnecessary "space junk."

A more important aspect of IP is that IP routers use IP addresses to determine where and how to route IP datagrams across the Internet. Routers examine the IP address in the datagram header, consult a routing table, and determine where to forward the datagram so that it will eventually reach its destination.

IP Addresses and Classes

IP is mainly concerned with establishing a unique identity for networked computers, which is the IP address. IP addressing was formally described in Request for Comment (RFC) 760, which was published in January 1980. *RFCs* are documentation of the Internet, describing Internet protocols and standards, as well as proposed new standards and practices, such as an updated version of IP, called IP version 6. A catalog of RFCs is available at www.isi.edu. Like most of the hardware and software infrastructure of today's Internet, IP was devised by computer scientists working on advanced and experimental networking projects for the U.S. Department of Defense.

The author of RFC 760 was Jonathan Postel, a legendary figure in Internet development. Along with other Internet luminaries, such as Leonard Kleinrock and Vinton Cerf, he developed IP and other protocols. Developing the protocols described in the RFCs was a government-sponsored group effort to devise the software infrastructure for distributed computer systems to communicate over a network that could tolerate outages and instability.

Two decades ago, the computing landscape looked markedly different from the way it appears today. Remarkably, the design of the IP protocol and the other protocols of the Internet, such as TCP, FTP, SMTP, and others, have proven resilient.

Postel, Cerf, and the other people who devised IP and its addressing and numbering conventions had three major goals for it:

- Establish a system to identify network hosts.
- Accommodate growth of the network.
- Allow for unforeseen changes in networking.

Establishing a numeric identifier for hosts fulfilled the first two goals. They used a 32-bit binary number for both the source and destination IP address. This fixed the IP address space at 2^{32} separate addresses, or more than 4.3 billion possible numbers. It would seem, and certainly it did from the perspective of 1980, that this would allow plenty of room for future growth.

To fulfill the third goal, they devised separate *classes* of addresses, which were later referred to as Class A, B, and C addresses. Each was devised to meet the perceived needs of a specific type of networking environment. Creating different classes of addresses was not part of the original design of IP addressing. Initially, there was to be only one kind of IP address, which was equivalent to the Class A address. RFC 760 was replaced in January 1981 by RFC 791, which specified the three classes of IP networks.

Keep in mind that at the time that this class system was devised, there were relatively few networks and not that many computers. The invention of the PC was still neither technologically nor economically feasible, but the first minicomputers, such as the DEC PDP-11 were starting to appear. So the number of computers was expected to grow, but the number of networks was not.

Figuring that it might be wise to identify specific computers on specific networks, rather than placing them into one, huge block, the protocol pioneers subdivided the 32-bit IP address number into two parts, which are still used today (see Figure 1.3). The two parts are:

Network. Called a network identifier, or net ID, the first part of an IP address is a binary number that identifies the network to which a computer is attached.

Host. Called a host identifier, or host ID, this is another binary number that identifies a specific host on the network specified by the network ID.

Even though there are really two parts to the number, an IP address is expressed as a single decimal number. All IP addresses look like a single number, subdivided into four component numbers. That single number of the IP address contains within it the network and host identifiers.

Class A Addresses

To accommodate the networking environment of 1980, which, as noted, had relatively few networks and relatively few computers compared to today, Postel and company established the first class of IP address, the Class A address.

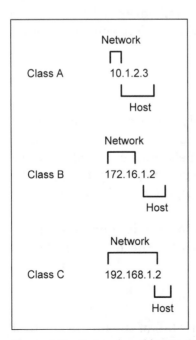

Figure 1.3   Network and host parts of an IP address.

In a Class A address, the first byte of the 4-byte IP address identifies the network, and the second, third, and fourth bytes identify specific hosts on that network. A Class A address, then, looks like this:

10.103.17.235

Since there are only 8 bits in the first byte, there can only be 2^8, or 256 Class A network addresses. However, the first bit in a Class A address is always a 0, which leaves only 7 bits for Class A network addresses. Making the first bit a 0 helps identify the address as a Class A address. Consequently, there are only 127 possible Class A network addresses, which run from Network 1.0.0.0 (00000001) through Network 127.0.0.0 (01111111).

Another convention that is still used today is to express the network ID part of an address with trailing zeroes in the positions of the numbers that are used for host IDs. Therefore, Class A Network 127 is expressed as 127.0.0.0, even though the last 3 bytes are used for host IDs. That the numbers are all zeroes indicates that this is a network ID, and not the ID of a host on that network.

The rest of the bits in the Class A address space were left to identify individual hosts on each of the 127 possible Class A networks: 3 bytes (2^{24}) allowed for about 16 million hosts on each Class A network. It was thought unlikely that any Class A network would ever be home for this many hosts, but the Class A address space surely left enough room for growth.

Class B Addresses

Recognizing that the future would probably bring about the development of many smaller networks, Postel and his colleagues had to accommodate potential future changes in networking, specifically the development of a number of smaller networks. So, using the same 32 bits of IP address space, they created a second class of addresses, the Class B address.

Class B addresses use the first 2 bytes of the 32-bit address space for the network identifier, and the last 2 bytes for the host identifier. A Class B address looks like this:

172.25.86.4

Since Class Bs use 16 bits for a network ID (all of the bits in the first 2 bytes) there could be 2^{16}, or 65,536, Class B network addresses. However, Postel fixed the first 2 bits of the first byte of every Class B address at 10, which meant there could be only 16,536 (2^{14}) Class B networks. The last full 2 bytes of the Class B address space are used for the host ID, which allows for as many as 65,536 (2^{16}) hosts on each Class B network.

Class C Addresses

The developers of the IP addressing scheme also had to anticipate the invention of some completely new and unforeseen technology that would foster a large number of smaller networks. To that end, they devised a third class of IP address, the Class C address.

In fact, they were not completely unaware of new networking technologies. Furthermore, the development of new technologies that would lead to the creation of numerous smaller networks was not at all unforeseen. They were all aware of the work going on at the Xerox Palo Alto Research Center (PARC) in Palo Alto, California, on an experimental network for local computing called Ethernet, and on packet-switching technologies that Xerox and other companies had devised.

Class C addresses use the first 3 bytes for the network ID, and the lone, last byte for a host ID. A Class C address looks like this:

192.168.25.88

Following the convention established for the Class A and B networks, the IP developers set the first 3 bits of the first byte of a Class C address as 110. This allowed for (2^{21}) separate Class C network IDs, but only 256 (2^8) separate host IDs per Class C network.

Class D and E Addresses

The group also created Class D and E addresses. Each Class D address begins with 1110 and identifies a multicast group, which is a group of computers or network interfaces. The idea of Class D addresses is to allow an IP datastream to be broadcast to a number of devices at the same time. The normal model of IP communications is between just two devices, but Class D addresses identify hosts or interfaces that are part of a multicast group.

Class D addresses are used today on the experimental MBONE multicast network, a broadcast network on the Internet that is composed of several thousand hosts that use Class D addresses. However, many IP routers aren't configured to handle Class D addresses, and multicast can have severe impacts on server and network loading. Multicast networks that use Class D addresses work best over networks that have been engineered for multicast applications.

Despite these problems, there is a great deal of interest in using IP for multicast applications, such as videoconferencing, IP conference calling, and streaming audio and video. Today, most of these applications use standard Class A, B, and C addressing, with special servers around the Internet to which several users connect at the same time.

Class E addresses, the first byte of which begins with 1111, are intended to be used for experimental purposes.

Making Life Easier for Binary-Challenged Humans

Though IP addresses are always binary numbers, most people find it hard to remember, let alone type accurately, a unique string of 32 ones and zeroes. So, to make life a little easier for binary-challenged humans, by convention, the 32 bits of any IP addresses are separated into four 8-bit bytes, and each byte is set off with decimal points, or periods. The human-friendly way to express the number is to translate each byte back to its decimal equivalent.

The resulting four decimal digits may still not be memorable, but they're a lot easier to work with and remember than their binary (or hexadecimal) equivalents. For example, this binary IP address:

00011010000001010000000000000010

can be separated into four, 8-bit bytes, set off with periods, as:

00011010.00000101.00000000.00000010

and then each byte can be translated into its decimal equivalent, which is:

26.5.0.2

Note that because there are only 8 bits in each of the 4 bytes of the IP address, and there are never more nor less than 8 in each byte, the value of each of the four *dotted decimal* numbers in the decimal version of the IP address byte must be a decimal number from 0 to 256. IP addresses are referred to as dotted decimal numbers because they are the decimal representations of the original binary numbers, with decimal points—or dots—added to separate the four decimal values of each 8-bit byte.

When we discuss subnetworking in Chapter 7, we will combine bits from adjacent bytes to make subnetwork addresses. But even then, the same binary-to-decimal conversion rule will apply. IP addresses are always translated to their decimal equivalents by translating these same 8-bit bytes back to their decimal equivalents.

Identifying a Type of Network Address

There's a simple way to determine whether an IP address is a Class A, B, or C. Though it's not precisely what routers do when they evaluate an IP address to determine where the network part of the address ought to be, it accomplishes the same objective. The rules are simple, and they all apply to the number in the first of the four fields of the IP address:

- Class A addresses have values from 1 to 127 in the first field of the IP address.
- Class B addresses have values from 128 to 191 in the first field.
- Class C addresses have values from 192 to 223 in the first field.

Therefore, an IP address of 192.112.36.5 is the address of host 5 (actually, 0.0.0.5) on Class C network 192.112.36.0. How did we determine this? The number in the first field of the address is 192, and 192 falls in the range of 192 to 223, so it's a Class C address.

At least that's what it appears to be. As we will see when we discuss subnetworking in Chapter 7, this could be the IP address of a host on a subnetwork or a finer division of the Class C address space for network 192.112.36.0. As Chapter 7 reveals, subnetworks are, for the most part, invisible to routers, as well as to anyone else who looks at an IP address. They can only be deciphered with the help of a key, called a *subnet mask*. The mask indicates which bits of the IP address are being used for the network address.

The first number of the decimal version of the IP address is a key to the class of network address because the binary IP addresses force the numbers into those ranges. As we discussed earlier, the first bit of the first 8-bit byte of a Class A address is, by the design of IP, a 0. Since that's the position for the eighth power of 2 (2^8), which is 128, the highest value that can appear in the first byte of any Class A address is:

01111111

This number translates to a decimal as 127, so it would be the first byte of network 127.0.0.0.

Conversely, the lowest binary value that can appear in the first byte position of an IP address is:

00000001

This translates back to 1, and is the first byte of the IP address for network 1.0.0.0. This distinction belongs to the Bolt, Beranek, and Newman Corporation (BBN), which did enough work on the formation and foundation of the Arpanet, the predecessor to the Internet, to have a legitimate claim to Network 1.

Class B networks always have the binary digits 10 in the first two of the bit positions of the first byte of the binary version of the address. So, the first 2 bytes of the first valid Class B network address are:

10000000 00000000

and the first 2 bytes of the last valid Class B network address are:

10111111 11111111

These binary values translate back to the decimal values 128.0.0.0 and 191.255.0.0, which are, respectively, the first and last network addresses in the Class B address range.

Class C networks always have the binary digits 110 in the first three bit positions of the first byte of the binary version of the address. So, the first 3 bytes of the first valid Class C network address are:

11000000 00000000 00000000

and the first 3 bytes of the last valid Class C network address are:

11011111 11111111 11111111

These binary values translate back to the decimal values 192.0.0.0 and 223.255.255.0, which are, respectively, the first and last network addresses in the Class C address range.

The Working Classes

What we think of today as IP addresses are referred to as *classful* addresses, because they adhere to the traditional (RFC791-compliant) Class A, B, and C address ranges. In Chapter 3, we will discuss new and more flexible ways of managing IP address space, specifically *classless* addressing, and Classless Inter-Domain Routing (CIDR).

For reasons we'll discuss more completely in Chapter 3, the trend today is to use the same IP address notation of 32 bits divided into four 8-bit bytes, or octets, but to eliminate the distinctions of Class A, B, and C addresses. With classless addressing, Internet hosts still get unique IP addresses, and those hosts are still on uniquely identified networks. However, eliminating classful addresses can help reduce the scope of the routing and connectivity problems caused by the number of IP addresses in use on the Internet, as well as help Internet service providers (ISPs) better manage the address space they have.

"CIDR-ized" and classful IP addresses will both be around for quite some time, although at the ISP level and above, the trend is clearly to migrate as much of the IP address space to classless addressing.

Hosts and Interfaces

We most frequently associate IP addresses with computers, but in fact, an IP address actually refers to a network interface, or the connection of a computer to a network. That is, an IP address actually identifies not a computer itself, such as your PC or the host computer that maintains the BigCo Web site, but either of those computers' connections to their respective networks. It is, after all, called an IP address, not a host identifier, just as a phone number identifies the endpoint on a telephone network, not the phone or fax machine or modem connected to the line.

Anything with a network interface, or a connection to a network, can have an IP address. Computers with several network connections can have several IP addresses, each of which identifies a specific interface to a specific network. For example, a host computer or a server that runs a multiuser application, such as a billing or inventory control system, may be connected to more than one local area network (LAN), and it may have a separate, leased line connection to a wide area network (WAN), through which it communicates with a central mainframe, a

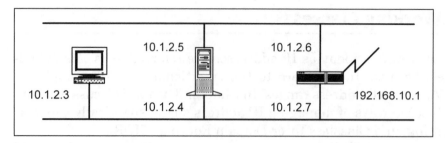

Figure 1.4   IP addresses identify network interfaces, not necessarily computers.

credit bureau, or some other system. If the computer uses the TCP/IP protocols, each of its network interfaces or connections will have a separate, different IP address. That may sound redundant, but it's necessary, to identify a specific interface on a specific network, as shown in Figure 1.4.

In another example, routers, which tie several networks together, need separate IP addresses to identify each of the interfaces they have to separate networks. IP routers may have a number of network interfaces—some have tens or hundreds, depending on their usage—each of which needs its own, unique IP address.

Note that the IP address is a *soft* address, which is different from the *hard* address embedded in the computer's network interface hardware, or in its network interface card (NIC). The NIC address is usually an Ethernet address, embedded in the NIC or the LAN interface hardware by its manufacturer. It is usually fixed and immutable, unless you change the hardware or the chip on which it resides.

A network could be a LAN, such as an Ethernet or a Token Ring network, or it could be a WAN such as the Internet. Devices that connect LANs and WANs, such as routers, have interfaces—and therefore IP addresses—for their LAN and WAN interfaces.

Summary

The unique identity that an IP address gives a networked computer doesn't fix its location. It only permits the computer to be found by a router so that traffic can be sent to it. IP addresses are transient identities, specifying an identity that lasts only as long as a computer is attached to a specific network.

Not even the classes of IP addresses impose any real significance on a networked computer. IP address classes were devised as an afterthought, to accommodate different sizes of networks. With the rapid depletion of address space brought on by the growth of the Internet, IP address classes have become more of an impediment to the growth of the Internet than an aid to network organization. To accommodate the growth of the Internet, address classifications are being replaced by newer classless addressing schemes. No matter what happens, the unique identity an IP address lends will be essential to Internet connectivity.

If IP addresses need only be unique, someone or something must assure uniqueness. In the next chapter, we will look at how IP addresses are assigned, and which organizations have been given the tasks of assuring IP address uniqueness.

CHAPTER

2

The Politics of IP Address Delegation

One of the primary rules of IP connectivity is that every IP address must be unique. It's not too difficult a concept to grasp, nor, from our own experiences with telephone numbers and Social Security numbers, to appreciate. IP addresses give identity; IP routers make devices with those identities reachable.

The IP addressing concepts and techniques we discussed in Chapter 1 identify Internet hosts, workstations, router ports, and servers uniquely. IP routing, as done by routers in the Internet, use IP network addresses to fix the locations of networks and objects within a collection of interconnected networks.

In this chapter, we'll examine where and how that uniqueness is achieved. The process is called IP address *delegation*, whereby authority to assign unique numbers is passed on from a top-level authority to a lower authority that needs addresses.

In the same way that phone companies that assign telephone numbers and the Social Security Administration that assigns Social Security numbers ensure uniqueness, there must be such an organization for the Internet and for IP numbers. Without an authoritative IP address assignment designee, no one could be assured of IP address uniqueness, and the Internet would not be possible.

What Is Delegation?

IP address delegation implies that someone or some organization was originally vested with the authority to assign IP addresses. It also implies that that entity has passed on the authority to make that assignment to another person or organization. Because IP addresses must be unique, it also means that the charter of address uniqueness, and some mechanism to assure that, has been passed along with the authority to do so.

The original authority to assign IP address numbers was established when the IP addressing scheme, described in RFC 791, was written. IP addressing was devised as a way to keep track of and to send IP datagrams to the computers in the original U.S. Department of Defense Advanced Research Projects Agency ([D]ARPA) network. This network was the ARPANET, which, though only an experiment, achieved legendary status as the precursor to the Internet. More accurately, the ARPANET is the network that evolved into the Internet.

As one of the creators of the IP addressing protocol, Jonathan Postel recognized that there was a need to track who would be assigned which network number, as well as which hosts were to be assigned on each network. This need was part of that uniqueness requirement, and it wasn't going to be met automatically.

In addition to the IP protocol, the IP creators also developed a numbering system to identify application-level protocols, such as Telnet and FTP, to the software on ARPANET systems. This set of numbers, for software sockets and ports, was much more limited, but it also required an authority to establish which numbers could be used as new protocols were invented and gained widespread use.

Postel saw the need for a numbering "czar," and he volunteered to be that person. At the time, in 1979, the task of the ARPANET numbering czar was relatively simple, as there were relatively few networks and hosts to track. There were a limited number of TCP ports and processes (255), but tracking IP addresses would be more challenging.

The growth of the network was inevitable, but in the beginning of the ARPANET, there was no need to have more than one person act as number assignment authority. The DARPA researchers could hardly have known that Postel himself would play such a key role in many other standards setting and establishment efforts.

Postel eventually took on the task of editing the documents that formally proposed changes or advancements in network technology, the

Requests for Comment (RFCs). In addition to being the numbering czar, Postel was also the RFC czar; he edited and reviewed the RFCs, and established the standards for their publication and distribution.

IANA

Although it took a good 10 years for the ARPANET to evolve into the Internet, the number of hosts and networks assigned by Postel continued to grow. To institutionalize the number-assigning authority, Postel created the Internet Assigned Numbers Authority (IANA), a federally funded organization established to manage the use of IP address space. The purpose of the IANA, which was headed by Postel, was to control the allocation of IP address space to universities, government agencies, and private corporations that used IP addressing.

In addition to handling IP address and autonomous system number assignments, Postel also managed the top-level domain naming operations, such as registering second-level domains under the .com, .org, and .net delineations. In addition to IP address assignment, Postel had also assumed responsibility for domain name assignments. Domain names are organized hierarchically under a limited number of *top-level* domain names like .com, .edu, and .net. Domains under these top-level domains, such as xyz.com, are called *second-level* domain names.

By 1985, it became apparent to Postel that the day-to-day tasks of handling address assignment requests and tracking the address change updates was too much for one person to handle. He requested that DARPA and the Federal Networking Council, which had sponsored and overseen much of the ARPANET work, fund a task to manage the day-to-day administrative tasks of IP address assignments.

The first contract for an Internet Registry (IR) was awarded to the Stanford Research Institute (SRI) in 1988. As Postel specified in RFC 1174, which described the delegation of authority to SRI, the IANA had always had the right to delegate the responsibility for address assignment to what it called an Internet Registry. SRI would become *the* IR; and the SRI would also create a Network Information Center (SRI-NIC), staffed by real people, to handle address assignment requests.

At the same time, Postel also argued that there might be a need for SRI to delegate its authority for numbering to other international organizations. A growing number of Internet-connected hosts were in Europe; and Japanese companies were also joining the nascent Internet. With the Internet taking on a distinctly international flavor, Postel believed, it would make sense for SRI to delegate some of its authority over IP address assignments to international organizations.

Meanwhile, as the Internet continued to grow, it became clear that whoever had the responsibility for IP address assignment should also have responsibility for other tasks needed to run the Internet. Take the Domain Name Service, the DNS, for example. Started as a utility that was part of the Berkeley distributions of the Unix operating system, DNS was a thoughtful convenience for end users. Instead of requiring the exact numeric IP address of the target of a transaction, DNS enabled users to enter a text name. Though the text name also had to be typed accurately, it was much easier for users to remember and proofread than an IP address. Today, few Internet users have any idea what the IP address is of the hundreds of Web sites they browse each week, thanks to DNS.

At the same time, the growth of the Internet and the dependence on Domain Name Services to translate text host names, such as ftp.isi.edu, to IP addresses, led to the idea that expanding the responsibility of the IR might be a good move. Postel thought it would be useful to the Internet at large if the IR task were expanded to include the maintenance of the master DNS files, as well as domain naming and IP address assignment.

In 1992, the Federal Networking Council, a government-sponsored organization with representatives from various civilian government and military agencies, decided to split the growing Internet into two parts: a military portion and a non-military portion. The group asked the National Science Foundation (NSF) to take responsibility for overseeing the non-military parts of the network. The Defense Communications Agency (DCA) took responsibility for the military part of the network.

Expanding the Task

In 1993, the NSF decided to expand the IR function to include IP address management and assignment, DNS *root file* maintenance, domain name registration, and the Network Information Center functions. The DNS root file is the master file that maps domain names to the DNS services that can resolve IP addresses for those names. The root zone file is copied by a dozen other DNS servers around the world so that the file is readily accessible to Internet users everywhere.

That year, the NSF entered into separate agreements with three companies to provide services for the InterNIC. Network Solutions, a small company located outside Washington, DC, was to register domain names; AT&T provided directory and database services; and a third,

General Atomics, provided help desk services. Together, these three services constituted the services of the InterNIC.

NSI had some experience in the NIC business. Starting in 1991, NSI had been one of the contractors running the U.S. Department of Defense NIC, providing address assignment and NIC services to U.S. military units. The U.S. military had been one of the original sponsors of the ARPANET, and most military units used the TCP/IP protocols on host systems and to communicate over a special X.25 packet-switching network, the Milnet.

The InterNIC agreement required NSI to manage the IP address space, assign and register domain names, and manage the Internet's master DNS server. The master DNS server is the Internet DNS server that maintains the master copies of the domain name-to-IP address translation table. Domain name registration, which has since become a big business for NSI, was, at the inception of the agreement, subsidized by the NSF. As the number of domain name registrations grew, the NSF agreed to permit NSI to assess an annual fee for each domain name in the .com, .org, and .net domains.

While still offering other InterNIC services free to Internet users (but paid for through the NSF contract), the new deal was for NSI to charge $50 per year for a domain name. Of that $50 fee, $15 was to be set aside in a special fund to be used by the federal government to improve the Internet's infrastructure. By the end of 1998, the NSF ended its involvement with Internet governance, and cut off the $15 fee for Internet improvement. Even so, the fund had grown to more than $60 million. NSI was allowed to use the remaining $35 fee to pay for the expenses of domain name registration and other InterNIC operations.

Meanwhile, on the international front, Postel wrote RFC 1466, which specified that IP address assignment should be handled by regional international authorities. It would be more practical, he said, if users in the Far East, for example, could work with an Asian registry that would speak their language and be located closer than the United States. A similar IR would be set up in Europe, to handle the growing number of European address assignment requests.

In 1993, address authority was delegated to two new international IRs. The first, the Asia-Pacific NIC (APNIC), was set up in Japan for the Pacific Rim region, including Australia and New Zealand. The second, RIPE (Reseaux IP Européean), was set up to serve users in Europe and Northern Africa. Meanwhile, IANA transferred its delegated authority for assigning IP addresses to the InterNIC, which was then being run by NSI. Now, instead of one IR, there were three.

Of the three IRs, the InterNIC had the most comprehensive charter. In addition to acting as the "IR of last resort" for IP address assignments, it also maintained the master DNS server, assigned Autonomous System numbers, registered second-level domain names, and ran a help desk function for the InterNIC. Autonomous Systems (covered in more detail in Chapters 10 and 13) are a group of routers that are administered by a single entity, such as a corporation or an ISP.

The Asian region IR, APNIC, is run by a consortium of organizations. Most of them are located in Japan, but APNIC also has representatives from Australia and Singapore, as it serves the entire Pacific Rim region. APNIC has since moved its headquarters to Australia. APNIC has been active in trying to keep the IP address space it has from being too fragmented, and in attempting to use its space as efficiently as possible. For example, APNIC has encouraged ISPs to consolidate network addresses in large CIDR blocks, by encouraging them to form addressing confederations and relationships. This simplifies routing within the Pacific Rim, as many network addresses can be represented in routing tables as one large block of addresses. APNIC also fostered the formation of national, rather than regional, NICs, and encouraged the use of country codes for domain naming within the region.

Because many of the hosts on the Internet were located in Europe, the RIPE organization, headquartered in Amsterdam, was further along the learning curve than APNIC. RIPE employed a more centralized approach to delegating addresses and assigning Autonomous System numbers. With a stronger tradition in software than APNIC, RIPE also developed a number of the programs that are still widely used to track and maintain addressing databases.

Winding It Down

As the Internet became more commercialized and more international in scope, the federal government sought to change its role in governing the Internet. The U.S. government wanted to turn over control of Internet governance to a private, nonprofit organization. The idea was that such an organization would assume responsibility for the functions that the NSF had performed, including managing IP address space, assigning domain names, and running the master DNS servers.

In 1996, the NSF, and later the White House and the U.S. Department of Commerce, undertook a number of initiatives to seek public consensus on how such an organization could be created, and what it would do. Among other things, in 1997 and 1998, the Department of Commerce published two proposals, called the Green Paper and the White Paper, which proposed the duties and operations of this new organization, and invited public comment.

The new organization, the Internet Corporation for Assigned Names and Numbers (ICANN), was formed in 1998. Headed by Esther Dyson, a widely respected technology consultant and author, ICANN assumed the Internet governance and administrative roles that IANA and the federal government had held.

ICANN also assumed responsibility for IP address assignment, which had once been a function performed by NSI as part of its InterNIC responsibilities. The commercialization of the Internet had also affected IP address assignment. In 1997, the NSF allowed NSI to spin off the IP address assignment function to a separate organization, the Assigned Registry of Internet Numbers (ARIN). IP address assignment duties were assigned to ARIN, which delegated address assignment authority to RIPE and APNIC for other parts of the world, and to the Department of Defense NIC for the U.S. military. Figure 2.1 depicts the past and present relationship of these organizations for IP address assignment.

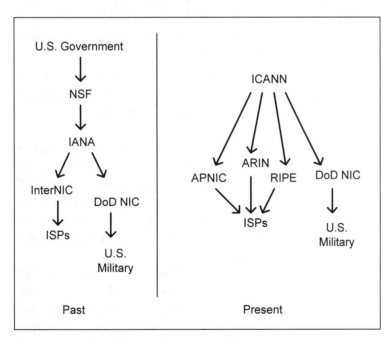

Figure 2.1   The address assignment family trees.

IRs and the ISPs

IP address assignment was permanently delegated to ARIN. In turn, ARIN invoked charges for IP address blocks it assigned to commercial Internet service providers (ISPs). The thinking was that since the ISPs benefited from IP addresses, they should have to pay for their use. Paying for the use of IP addresses would also encourage ISPs to use IP address space as efficiently as possible.

The guiding document that sets the policies the IRs and ARIN follow when assigning IP addresses to ISPs is, as one might expect, an RFC, specifically RFC 2050, issued in 1996. It establishes guidelines for issuing addresses and codifies policies that IRs should follow when assigning address space to requesting ISPs or other organizations. Those policies are:

Conservation. Addresses should be distributed fairly to organizations that request them according to their needs, and IRs and requesters should avoid stockpiling addresses that they really don't need.

Routability. IP addresses should be assigned to maintain a hierarchical relationship between smaller and larger address blocks, so that IP address assignments help, rather than hinder, routability and efficient operation of the Internet.

Registration. Addresses that have been assigned must be registered and documented in such a way that the information is publicly available, and can be used in network troubleshooting.

However, RFC 2050 acknowledges that, as admirable as these goals are, there are times when address conservation and routability can be conflicting goals. For example, it may be necessary to issue a new IP address block to an ISP that falls under a larger, national ISP, rather than keep the smaller ISP within the larger ISP's address space. The reason is that doing so frees the smaller ISP from being forever enslaved to the larger ISP's address block.

RFC 2050 also notes that, for a given individual, organization, or ISP that requests IP addresses, the application of any and all of these policies may conflict with their individual goals. Fairness is an admirable objective, but frequently the greater good becomes a more pressing requirement.

The ISPs are usually ARIN's biggest customers, but RFC 2050 specifies that ARIN or one of the other IRs must review any ISP's request for more address space, to determine if it is justified. For example, an ISP may request a block of 255 Class B addresses, but the IR must determine whether the request is reasonable. The IRs have the responsibility of examining how the ISP has documented its requests, what its experience has been with the ISP, how it has subnetworked or otherwise used efficiently other address space, and so forth.

Because IP address space is becoming a constrained commodity, IRs do examine requests for address space to determine justification. And they do consider the previous experience that they have had with an ISP when granting new address space. The IRs have to manage IP address allocations, and making informed judgments is part of the exercise of that responsibility.

The IRs do not, however, have the authority to impose any sanctions (except not granting more address space) on an ISP or organization that doesn't use addresses properly. It also can't control which routes an ISP announces to the world. Both of these are issues that the ISPs themselves deal with, because the IRs have no authority to enforce the good practices they are charged with using when assigning address space.

ARIN, on the other hand, does enforce good address usage practices with the address blocks that it assigns. For example, if an ISP uses a relatively small block of addresses efficiently, and documents the use of those addresses, then the ISP can qualify to get a larger block of addresses. The benefit of having a larger block of addresses is that those addresses will be announced to the Internet at large as a block of CIDR addresses (more on CIDR in Chapter 3). Having a sufficiently large block of CIDR addresses means that the ISP can avoid, for the present, the need to renumber all of its customers.

The ISP Viewpoint

ISPs are customers of the IRs, and they use the IRs' IP address product. The ISPs in turn distribute IP address space to their customers. While the IRs are concerned only with allocating IP address space efficiently and having the ISPs use it economically, the ISPs have a different view of their use of IP addresses.

The ISPs are in the business of connecting their customers to the Internet, so they are more focused on transmitting bits reliably and cheaply than they are on how address space is being used. A typical ISP is far more concerned with Internet routability than with how customers are using IP addresses. That is, an ISP is far more interested in how the addresses it "owns" have been announced to the Internet. And ISP also cares that its own internal routers and the routers in other ISPs know about those addresses, and route traffic to it quickly and efficiently.

At the same time, ISPs do have concerns about the addresses they have been assigned, and how customers are using the addresses. ISPs are under pressure from ARIN to make sure that the address space assigned to their customers has been used efficiently, and that its use has been sufficiently documented. It is much easier for an ISP to troubleshoot a customer's network connectivity problems if the ISP knows how the customer has used its address space. Frequently, customer complaints about poor Internet connectivity can be traced to problems with the ways the customer has used his or her address space or with his or her routers.

Furthermore, the ISPs must deal with the nuts-and-bolts routing issues that the IRs can conveniently ignore. The IRs delegate and assign address space; the ISPs have to make that address space work. So, in addition to making sure that their customers use their IP address space properly, ISPs have to work out all of the details of subnetworking address space; multihomed connections from customers to two or more different ISPs; internal and external routing protocols; alternate routing to upstream and downstream ISPs; the usage, performance, and reliability of their links to their customers and to their higher-level ISPs; route announcements; dial-up ports and port capacity; billing; and network management.

Acting as an IP address assignment authority for their customers is only one of a number of roles that the ISPs play. Customers often look to the ISP for advice and assistance in subnetworking. Frequently, customers aren't aware of the requirements that the ISPs (and the Internet community at large) must meet to use IP address space efficiently. The ISPs must carry the IP addressing usage message down to their users.

The Future of IRs

The transformation of the Internet from an informal research network backed by a benign, deep-pocketed government is now history. And we may be seeing only the beginning of the commercialization of the Internet and its use as a tool of commerce. The exotically high stock market valuations given to companies in the Internet "space" seem to indicate that there are lots of people willing to put lots of money to back the Internet's commercial potential.

The commercialization pattern that has been established by Internet governance organizations, such as ICANN, is likely to continue. Probably the most significant administrative change in the Internet that will come about in the next few years will be the change from U.S. federal government oversight and control of Internet governance to a more privatized form of governance.

As far as IP addressing is concerned, the IANA will most likely continue to exist as the "spiritual manifestation" of IP addressing, but its real control will pass through ICANN to ARIN, and ISPs will end up paying ARIN for IP address space.

We may also see the creation of new IRs to serve parts of the world that have either lagged behind in Internet connectivity or that have had relatively less need for specialized attention. For example, the IP addressing, domain name registration, and administrative needs of South America, Central America, the Middle East, and Africa are served by ARIN, the InterNIC, and RIPE. Growth in demand for Internet connectivity may make it feasible to establish separate IRs for those regions, if delegation authority and funding problems can be solved.

IP routing on the Internet may also undergo a change that could affect how IP address space is used. As we will discuss in Chapter 3, the explosive growth of the Internet has forced the top-level ISPs to take steps to reduce the size of the routing tables maintained by the routers at the Internet exchange points. CIDR addressing and strict address usage policies have helped slow the growth of those tables. In fact, they've become smaller than they were five years ago.

Still, there is nothing about an IP address that indicates anything about where it is or how to get to it. As the Internet continues to grow, it might be helpful to link IP addresses to a geographical or physical location, so that ISPs could base routing decisions on something other than a routing table lookup for each IP datagram.

The first proposals for the next version of IP, IP version 6 (referred to as IPv6, or as IPng, for IP Next Generation), had this concept built into it. IP addresses may be able to be grouped according to geographical area. Addresses in North America, for instance, could be consolidated into huge superblocks of space, as would addresses in Europe or those assigned to very large ISPs.

IPv6 also expands the IP address space from 32 bits to 128 bits. Presumably, ARIN will have learned from the problems caused by address assignment policies that predated its existence, and the far bigger address space of IPv6 will be used efficiently from the start. IPv6 clearly separates the routing part of an IPv6 address from the host part of the address.

For most systems that run IPv6, the host address will be derived from its Ethernet address, which is often referred to as its Media Access Control, or MAC, address. The benefit of this separation is that while the host address may never change, the part of the address used for network routing may become more dynamic. That is, what we think of now as the network part of an IP address will become fixed. Today, unless it is translated back and forth by an address translator, the IP addresses we use don't change (see Chapter 8 for further discussion of address translators).

Enabling software to change part of an IPv6 address to accommodate changes in the routing or the structure of the Internet would add a significant degree of flexibility to IP addressing. This would enable the whole scheme of identifying the expanding universe of Internet-connected devices to be far easier to adapt to changes in routing and the Internet's network infrastructure than it is today.

Summary

The organization and procedures of IP address assignment and delegation are undergoing the same kinds of changes as Internet governance as a whole. The U.S. government is stepping out of its long-standing role as chief arbiter of Internet policies and procedures, leaving those functions to private organizations like ARIN and ICANN.

Part of the challenge that both ARIN and ICANN face is how to carry out their roles and still sustain themselves without support from the federal government. ARIN charges fees to ISPs and others for using IP address space. ICANN, on the other hand, is charged with governing practically everything else about the Internet. In September, 1999, after extensive negotiations, ICANN reached an agreement with the Department of Commerce and the domain name registrars to establish a clear mechanism to fund its activities, and to recognize its role in Internet governance.

It is certainly in the best interests of the entire Internet community that some organization exercise authority and control over Internet governance. It was easy when the NSF and the Department of Commerce did it. No one challenged their authority, and they had funding from, and were part of, the U.S. federal government. Now the players have changed, with ICANN established in its new role in Internet governance.

Global
Internet Routing

While we most frequently associate IP addresses with computers, an IP address actually refers to a network interface, the connection of a computer to a network. That is, an IP address does not identify a computer itself, such as your PC or the host computer that maintains the BigCo Web site; rather, it identifies either of those computers' connections to their respective networks.

Anything with a network interface, or a connection to a network, can have an IP address. Computers with several network connections can have several IP addresses, each of which identifies a specific interface to a specific network. For example, a host computer or a server that runs a multiuser application, such as a billing or inventory control system, may be connected to more than one LAN, and it may have a separate, leased line connection to a WAN, through which it communicates with a central mainframe, a credit bureau, or some other system. If the computer uses the TCP/IP protocols, each of its network interfaces or connections will have a separate, different IP address. That may sound redundant, but it's necessary, in order to identify a specific interface on a specific network.

In another example, routers, which tie several networks together, need separate IP addresses to identify each of the interfaces they have

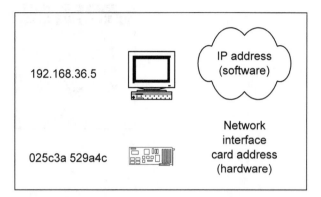

Figure 3.1   IP address in software; LAN address in hardware.

to separate networks. IP routers may have a number of network interfaces—some have tens or hundreds, depending on their usage—each of which needs its own, unique IP address.

Note that the IP address is a *soft address*, which is different from the *hard address* embedded in the computer's network interface hardware or in its network interface card (NIC). The NIC address is usually an Ethernet address, embedded by its manufacturer in the NIC or the LAN interface hardware. It is usually fixed and immutable, unless you change the hardware or the chip on which it resides, as shown in Figure 3.1.

A network could be a LAN, such as an Ethernet or a Token Ring network, or it could be a WAN such as the Internet. Devices that connect LANs and WANs, such as routers, have interfaces—and therefore IP addresses—for their LAN and WAN interfaces.

Routing

IP addresses are important in the Internet because they are the addresses to which Internet traffic is addressed and from which Internet traffic originates. A transaction between a PC and a Web server to download a Web server's home page may require hundreds or thousands of IP datagrams, each of which bears the IP source and destination addresses of the requesting PC and the Web server.

Each IP datagram carries part of the request for the Web page from the PC or part of the Web page file as a response to the PC's request.

Both sets of datagrams arrive at the Web server; the response arrives back at the PC after being forwarded, or routed, over the Internet.

Routing is the process of forwarding individually addressed IP packets, called *datagrams*, to specific hosts that are reachable over a TCP/IP network. Routing is done by special-purpose computers called routers, or by general-purpose computers that have been configured with special software for routing IP datagrams.

In most cases, there is no central controlling authority over how the routers operate or how they route IP datagrams through a network. There is no such controlling authority in the Internet, either. Routers function in a distributed fashion. That is, while they communicate with their neighboring routers to inform them about which networks they know how to reach, they operate autonomously, routing datagrams by whatever they perceive is the best way to get datagrams to their destination.

Although the processes are not exactly the same, a router makes routing decisions in much the same way that a mail handler sorts letters, to whom all that matters is the address on the envelope. At a central mail distribution facility, mail is sorted for forwarding to more local post offices, where it's sorted down to the postal worker who serves that route.

Internet and TCP/IP routing usually handles datagrams by making individual routing decisions on each datagram. To make routing decisions, routers go through these steps for each datagram they see:

1. Examine the destination address of each datagram.

2. Identify the network portion of the destination IP address.

3. Refer to a routing table that maps network addresses to network ports on the router, to determine the port through which the network is reachable.

4. Forward the datagram over the port indicated in the routing table to another network or another router.

Routers may also take other factors into consideration to determine where to send a datagram, such as how far away the destination network is located, the condition of the circuits, or other conditions set by the router administrator.

Note that a router doesn't really "care" whether an individual datagram ever gets delivered to its destination. Its only purpose is to forward each datagram as quickly as possible to a neighboring router.

Each router in the chain between the source and the destination nei-ther knows nor cares what happens to a datagram after it has been sent along the next router to get it to its destination. It's a completely decen-tralized process; and as much as it seems that routing leaves a great deal to chance, it works remarkably well.

Example of Internet Routing

To see precisely how this process works, let's look at what the routers on the Internet do when a user at a PC requests a Web page from an Inter-net Web site. Figure 3.2 illustrates a simplified version of the router configuration; the actual connections between a user's network across the Internet may be considerably more complicated than this.

As Figure 3.2 shows, the user's PC is connected to the Internet through a dial-up connection to an ISP. The ISP connects to another, larger, national ISP. The national ISP exchanges traffic with other, larger ISPs at an Internet Network Access Point (NAP). Another national ISP takes the user's Web site request, and forwards it across its network to the Web site, which is on a network operated by one of its customer.

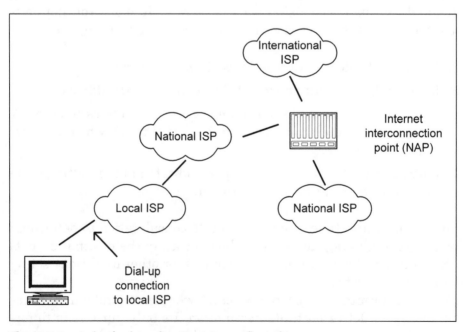

Figure 3.2   A simple view of an IP router configuration.

At each step along the way, routers read the IP address of each datagram, make a routing decision, and forward the datagram. Since the routers aren't centrally controlled or centrally managed, the network can expand or contract easily.

Everything in the Internet needs an IP address, which means the Web server has one and all of the network interfaces on the routers in the chain between the PC and the Web server have them. Only the PC doesn't have one. The IP addresses of the hosts and router ports are indicated on the diagram in Figure 3.3. The RAS in Figure 3.3 is a *Remote Access Server*, which allows users to dial into the network and assigns an IP address to remote users.

The PC will get an IP address when it dials into the local ISP's remote access server. The address will most likely change each time the PC dials into the network, but that's normal. Remember, all that matters about an IP address is that it's unique and that everything on the Internet can get to the host that has it.

The PC gets an IP address from the ISP when it dials into the network; the ISP holds a set of IP addresses that it hands out to dial-up users who connect to the network temporarily. But note, not just any IP address will do, because of the second requirement for IP addresses: reachability. The IP address must be one that everything else on the Internet knows how to reach.

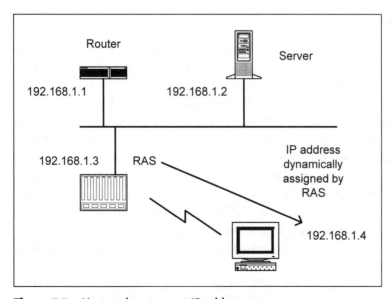

Figure 3.3 Host and router port IP addresses.

The ISP gives the PC one of the IP addresses from its assigned address space, probably one that the ISP has reserved for temporary use by its dial-up users. The PC will use it for the duration of its dial-up connection to the ISP. Once the user hangs up the phone, the ISP can reuse the address (and the remote access server port) for another dial-up user. When the PC user dials into the ISP again, his or her PC will probably get a different IP address. Again, it doesn't matter that the address is different each time, as long as it isn't held by any other network interface anywhere on the Internet, and as long as everything else on the Internet knows about its existence and can get to it through the Internet's routers.

The addresses that have been assigned to the local ISP are "known" to the Internet at large; that is, the routers on the Internet know where they are, which is somewhere in the network that is controlled and operated by the ISP. Precisely where they are on the local ISP's network isn't important to any other router on the Internet. Delivering datagrams to a specific destination IP address on the local ISP's network is the local ISP's concern, not that of any other network.

By the same token, the local ISP doesn't know or care precisely where the Web server is, nor which ISP controls its access to the Internet. As with the PC, all that matters is that the Web server has a unique IP address and that the routers between the local ISP and the Web server's network and its ISP know how to get to it.

It Takes a URL

The IP routing process begins when the PC user enters a URL in his or her Web browser. The Web browser is only an interface and a display interpreter for the HyperText Transfer Protocol (HTTP), which is the application protocol for the Web. HTTP "rides above" the TCP and IP protocols. It interfaces to the Web browser and is the intermediary between the Web browser and the lower-level TCP data transport and IP network addressing protocol.

The Web browser gets the IP address for the Web browser from the Domain Name Service (DNS). The browser takes the URL—for example, www.bigco.com—and asks the DNS for the IP address of the Web server of that name. Through a process of asking other DNS services on the Internet, the Web browser gets the IP address of the BigCo Web site, in this case, 192.112.36.5.

The HTTP module gives the URL and an HTTP header (see Figure 3.4) to the TCP module in the PC. TCP will control the flow of data

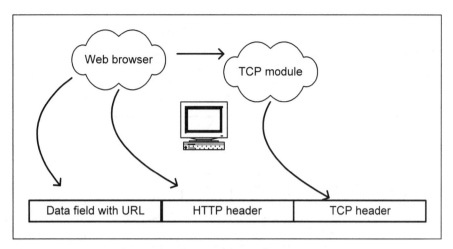

Figure 3.4 URL and HTTP header, as presented to TCP.

across the Internet between the PC and the Web site. The role of the TCP protocol will be to make sure that the Web site home page file, which will be packaged in hundreds or thousands of separately routed IP datagrams, is delivered reliably to the PC.

To Connect or Not to Connect

TCP, a *connection-oriented* protocol, will control this flow of data from both sides of the connection, by the TCP software in both the PC and the Web site. Each TCP module will examine each datagram when it arrives to make sure that it's the correct block of data in a whole sequence of data blocks that make up the Web home page file.

The routers in the Internet know nothing about TCP. When the transaction starts, the IP routers deal only with delivering the datagrams that contain the request for the Web page file to the Web server's IP address.

The IP module in the PC tacks the IP header, a 20-byte block that contains the PC's IP address and the Web site's IP address, after the TCP header and the URL for www.bigco.com, as shown in Figure 3.5. From the PC, the IP datagram goes back to the remote access server, which forwards it to the ISP's router behind its Internet connection. It's here that the routing journey begins.

The ISP's router receives the datagram on its Ethernet interface and presents it to the routing software. The routing software looks for the IP

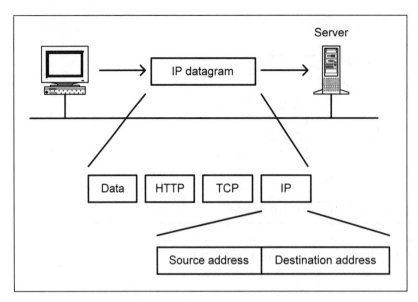

Figure 3.5 The IP header, attached to the TCP header.

header and locates the destination address, which is a 32-bit number. It's always in the same place, and it's virtually all the router is interested in examining. Unless the router has been configured to examine the source address, to determine if it has come from another host on the ISP's internal network, the router ignores the source address. It's not relevant to the task at hand, which is getting the datagram to its destination.

First, the router software dissects the destination address. In our example, the destination address, 192.112.36.5, is a Class C address, so it belongs to host 0.0.0.5 on network 192.112.36.0. The router asks: Where's network 192.112.36.0?, then consults its routing table to see if it has an entry for it. The router's routing table, depicted in Figure 3.6, is relatively simple. It knows about only a few networks, and it has no entry for 192.112.36.0.

Checking the Routing Tables

The basic parts of the routing table, by the way, were created in the router by the router administrator. The router administrator told the router the ports that were to be in use, and assigned host IDs, network IDs, and subnetwork masks, if applicable, to each router port. Also, the router administrator may have configured a number of other things, such as static routes to Internet gateways and routing parameters.

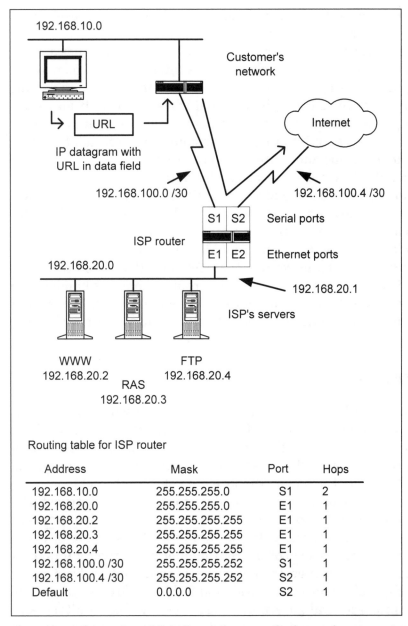

192.168.10.0

Customer's
network

Internet

IP datagram with
URL in data field

192.168.100.0 /30

192.168.100.4 /30

| S1 | S2 | Serial ports |

ISP router

| E1 | E2 | Ethernet ports |

192.168.20.0

192.168.20.1

ISP's servers

WWW
192.168.20.2

FTP
192.168.20.4

RAS
192.168.20.3

Routing table for ISP router

Address	Mask	Port	Hops
192.168.10.0	255.255.255.0	S1	2
192.168.20.0	255.255.255.0	E1	1
192.168.20.2	255.255.255.255	E1	1
192.168.20.3	255.255.255.255	E1	1
192.168.20.4	255.255.255.255	E1	1
192.168.100.0 /30	255.255.255.252	S1	1
192.168.100.4 /30	255.255.255.252	S2	1
Default	0.0.0.0	S2	1

Figure 3.6 The routing table indicates the networks that are known to
the router.

Once the router went into service, it may have used an interior or
exterior routing protocol (which will be discussed in more detail in
Chapter 12) to learn of other networks connected to adjacent routers.
The router adds these other network IDs to its routing table so that it

knows where to send traffic for IP network addresses it doesn't have attached directly to its own ports.

The router doesn't know where the network is, but that's not a problem. Another router, closer to the core of the Internet, may know. Without any warning, the ISP's router forwards the datagram to its default router, which is at the edge of the national ISP's network. It may have a more comprehensive view of the Internet's networks, so it may know where the network is. In less than a thousandth of a second, the ISP's router has done all this and routed the datagram.

The national ISP's router receives the datagram and repeats the process: find the destination address, identify the network number, and consult a routing table. Again, there's no match, so it forwards the datagram to its default router, at the top edge of the national ISP's network, which may know where in the Internet 192.112.36.0 is.

The possibility exists, of course, that network 192.112.36.0 or host 192.112.36.5 don't exist at all. None of the routers that has handled the datagram so far has been able to confirm that either exists. That's not a fatal problem, but somewhere in the Internet, some router does have to know.

Top-Level Routing

The moment of truth comes a millisecond or so later, when the national ISP's top-level router passes the datagram to its router at one of the major Internet interconnection points. Called Metropolitan Area Exchanges (MAE), Network Access Points (NAP), or other names, the MAEs and NAPs are the major transit points of the Internet.

Populated by some of the most bulked-up routers in the Internet, the MAEs are Internet traffic exchanges, where millions of IP datagrams in Internet traffic are passed between top-level ISPs' routers every minute. Here, at the top level of the routing hierarchy, the routers from the national ISPs exchange traffic, or *peer*, with routers from other national ISPs, such as Sprint, UUNet, and Cable & Wireless, as well as with routers from federal government agencies, the U.S. military, and academic networks such as CerfNet. But unlike the local and national ISPs' routers that have the luxury of a default router to which they can pass datagrams destined for networks they do not know, MAEs have no such luxury. They are the default routers of the Internet; simply put, if they can't determine where to send the PC's datagram holding its URL to get it to its destination, it won't get there.

The top-level router goes through the same process as each of the other routers: look for the destination IP address, determine the network number, check the routing table. The only difference is that its routing table has some 40,000 entries in it, comprising entries for every network in the Internet and for every network connected to it.

Fortunately, it has an entry for network 192.112.36.0 in its routing table. It's a network somewhere behind the NAP router of another one of the national ISPs. The datagram travels across the high-speed network between the two routers, and the destination router repeats the routing process.

This time, the national NAP router forwards the datagram to another router behind it. That router, inside the national ISP's network, knows about all of the networks within the ISP's network. One of them is 192.112.36.0. Its routing table says to forward the datagram to the ISP router that stands just outside the network that houses the BigCo Web site.

At last, maybe a second (on a good day) after it left the PC, the datagram is forwarded by the last router in the chain to the BigCo Web site. The same process will be repeated when the BigCo Web home page is subsequently sent back over the Internet to the PC.

Will the path the Web page takes back across the Internet to the PC be the same? Maybe, but then again, maybe not. Something might have changed in the few seconds it took for the Web site to respond. A link may have become congested with traffic, a router may have failed due to a power outage, or some other problem may have occurred. In any case, the routing tables in the routers handling the reverse path may know of some alternate route back to the routers of that local ISP that is faster, cheaper, or shorter than the path it just took. It's a distributed system, so the routers are really in control.

IP Routing Principles

Throughout their journey across the Internet, the traffic between the PC and the Web server has been controlled by several general principles of IP routing, including:

Connectionless routing. The routers that link the networks to clients and servers are connected to each packet independently among themselves as they go along, instead of creating a fixed path beforehand. The nature of packet switching leaves the delivery of data somewhat to chance, because the network does not know about nor plan an end-to-end path across the network before it happens.

Default routes. Many of the routers in the Internet know little about other networks on the Internet. Instead, many only know about the networks (and there may be relatively few of them, perhaps only a few hundred) that are in their own routing "domain." The routing domain usually comprises the networks served by a single ISP or a single organization. The routers in the routing domain pass routing information to each other about the networks in the domain and how to route traffic to them most efficiently.

Routing protocols. The routers use different types of routing protocols to pass information among themselves about which networks they can reach and what kinds of traffic they will accept. The information they pass among themselves, as routing table updates, help the routers maintain a dynamic picture of changes in the Internet. Routers use the routing updates they receive from other neighboring routers to learn about new networks in their own networks. They also use routing table updates to learn about changes in the conditions of the links between routers that affect traffic flow, such as congestion, line degradation, and delay characteristics.

Fixed IP addresses. Whereas many routers or routing hosts may handle datagrams as they progress through the Internet, the source and destination IP addresses don't change. Routers don't need to change the IP addresses to forward them to other routers, nor to switch datagrams to other internal router ports. However, some security measures, such as firewalls and proxy servers, may alter IP source or destination addresses to conceal the source of traffic.

Network Addresses. IP addresses have a network part and a host part, but only the network part matters to a router. Unless a host is on a network that is directly attached to a router, the host part of the address is unnecessary detail to the routers.

Routing Tables

A routing table is a relatively simple matrix that maps networks that are reachable through the router's ports, and the IP addresses of the adjacent router ports through which those networks can be reached. A routing table may also contain other information about the networks referenced in the table, such as some indication of how many routers there are between a router and the destination network.

The tables may also indicate something about the links between routers, such as cost, delay, or preference for using or avoiding that link.

For instance, the routing table may indicate that there are two or more ways traffic can be sent to get it to its destination. That is, there may be several adjacent routers, each of which is closer or farther away than the others from the destination network. The router will use the other information in the routing table about link status, cost, and preference to determine to which adjacent router it should send traffic.

Routing tables are either created by the person who is the router administrator or they are created through messages received from adjacent routers about the networks they know about. In most cases, the router administrator creates the initial base table, which is updated dynamically by the router when it communicates with its neighboring routers.

Routers refer to their routing tables to determine where they should forward IP datagrams they receive. Internet communications depend entirely on the capability of routers to make educated guesses about the fastest way to get a datagram to its destination. In many cases, routers don't know exactly where a network is, nor, for that matter, if it really exists at all. Their role is to keep pushing datagrams closer and closer to a router that eventually does know precisely where the destination network is located.

For example, Figure 3.6 shows a simplified version of the routing table that is maintained by the ISP's router that handles the PC's request for the Web page at the local ISP. It's a relatively simple routing table, in that it only lists a few networks, as well as a few hosts. This routing table doesn't appear exactly as it would in a specific vendor's routers, but it has been generalized to illustrate routing principles.

The router is a relatively simple one, in that it only has two Ethernet ports and two serial ports. One of the serial ports connects a leased line to the customer's router, and the other connects a leased line to routers elsewhere on the Internet. One of the Ethernet ports is on the ISP's LAN that houses its Web server, remote access server (RAS), FTP site, and other network services. The second Ethernet port is unused.

The routing table indicates which network is reachable via which router port. For example, the customer's network, 192.168.10.0, is reachable through the router's first serial port (S1). The network on which the ISP's three servers are located (192.168.20.0) is reachable through the router's first Ethernet port (E1). The table also lists specific hosts, such as the ISP's Web server (192.168.20.2), which are also reachable via the first Ethernet interface.

Note the last line, which indicates that the default network is reachable over serial port 2 (S2). This isn't a network address at all. The default network tells the router that this is the default gateway, where the router will send IP datagrams that are destined for networks not referenced in its routing tables. Obviously, a lot of networks aren't referenced in its routing tables, so a lot of traffic will be sent to the default route.

The other two entries on our highly simplified routing table are the *mask* and the number of hops. The mask is a number that looks like an IP address, because it is in the familiar dotted-decimal format. However, the numbers in the mask are a little too high for an IP address.

The mask isn't an IP address, but it tells the router something about the IP addresses being used by the networks attached to it; specifically, it tells the routers whether networks attached to it have been subdivided into smaller networks by using subnetwork addresses. Subnetworking will be discussed at length in Chapter 7, but for the purpose of this discussion, know that it is a method to subdivide a Class A, B, or C address into smaller size networks, without affecting global routing by the routers in the Internet.

The mask is the decimal representation of a binary number that indicates to the router which bits of an IP address are being used for the network part of the address. Subnetworking allows a network administrator to use some portion of the IP address that is reserved for the host part of the address for the network address instead. The mask indicates to the router if this is being done, as well as which of the host bits are being used to expand the network portion of the address.

As we will see in Chapter 7, this apparently flagrant violation of the rules of IP addressing is okay, as long as the routers know what's going on (and the network administrator or the router administrator has done his or her job correctly).

The Hop Count

The final entry in our simplified routing table is the Hop Count column, which indicates how many routers a datagram might have to pass through to get to the destination network. A *hop* is a traverse through a single router. In the example of the PC connecting across the Internet to the Web site, there are six routers, which makes six hops between the PC and the Web site.

Not all routing tables have a hop count entry. Some may have another entry, called a *delay count*, which does the same thing. Whether a routing table has a hop count depends on the routing protocol the router uses to get routing table updates from its neighbors. Some interior routing protocols (discussed shortly) use hop counts, while others use TTLs.

The purpose of the Hop Count entry is to give the router an idea of how far away a given network really is. If the router has a choice of two or more paths to a network, it will try to use the shorter of the two. In this context, shorter means having to go through fewer routers to get to the destination. Whether it's really shorter geographically is another matter that the router may not be able to determine. The router will use the hop count (or another measure that defines the same thing) and a *link weight* to determine where to send the traffic.

Link Weight

The link weight indicates the preference the router should make for routing traffic over a specific link. The preference weighting may be determined by the router administrator or it may be calculated by the router, based on routing updates it receives from neighboring routers. For example, the router administrator may have configured a router with a second link to another ISP. However, the backup link could be a satellite link, which might be more expensive than a terrestrial leased line, and because of signal propagation delays may take longer. So the router administrator could enter a higher value for the link weight than the terrestrial leased line, "prejudicing" the router from taking that link unless the preferred, main link is not working.

There may be a few other addresses in the routing table, such as the 127.0.0.0 address. This is a standard IP address that has been designated as the *loopback address*. That is, it is the address that systems implementing the TCP/IP protocols use to test whether they can send data between the IP and the network interface to the LAN, the leased line, or whatever is attached to a communications port. Anything sent to address 127.0.0.0 "loops back" to the IP software instead of being sent out on the network, so that IP knows that it has a live network interface.

Inside, Outside

IP router networks are like packet-switching networks, which have been designed to accommodate changes in the topology and connectivity of the network dynamically. This means that if a circuit or a router or even a whole part of a network goes out of service, other routers quickly learn about this change in the network. To adjust to this change, the routers modify their routing tables; they delete reference networks that are no longer reachable, add new ones that have come online, and adjust their views of the network.

They do this to be able to continue to route traffic even if the network changes. For example, if one of the local ISP's customers were to lose its leased line that connects it to the local ISP's router, the local ISP's router would quickly notice that its periodic "keep alive" messages between it and the customer's router were not being received. Assuming this is a line outage problem, within a few minutes, the local ISP's router would conclude that the customer's network, 192.168.10.0, was no longer reachable.

Dynamic changes in routing within the local ISP's internal network are propagated by interior routing protocols. Dynamic changes in routing between the local ISP and the national ISP, or between any larger routing domains, are propagated by external routing protocols. Generally speaking, exterior routing protocols are used between networks composed of routers that share the same router administration or the same interior routing protocol, as illustrated in Figure 3.7.

Networks that share a common router administration are grouped into Autonomous Systems, or ASes. The routers of the local ISP probably belong at their own AS, as do the routers of the national ISP. The system is considered autonomous because its routers are managed and operated as a group, or by themselves, by their respective ISPs.

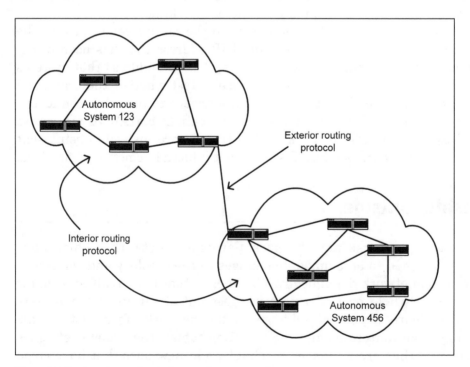

Figure 3.7   Interior and exterior routing protocols.

An AS is an administrative concept that was devised in the mid-1980s when the Internet started to get so big that not all of its routers could be administered and managed by DARPA or, for that matter, by any one entity. At the time, though most routers were Unix hosts, the first computers dedicated to routing were starting to appear.

It soon became apparent that coordinating upgrades in router capabilities and software among all of the different routers, not to mention simply keeping routing tables up to date, was about to become unmanageable. Nobody was in control of the whole network, and its parts were managed and operated cooperatively. Consequently, the concept of the AS, described in RFC 1930, was devised to allow for more distributed control of the network. Network operators could manage the networks under their control and give their routers a detailed picture of the internal connections and routing within their network. Instead of passing all of this detail to another network operator, they would relay to neighboring networks what amounted to a high-level summary of which networks are reachable within their networks.

Today, most ISPs operate their own Autonomous Systems, each of which has a unique ARIN-assigned AS number, or ASN. The ASN identifies the AS, and exterior routing protocols attach ASNs to network addresses to identify the AS in which a network is located. Therefore, the local ISP has its own ASN, because the local ISP controls and administers the routing within the ISP's network; and the national ISP has its own ASN, as do most of the other larger ISPs.

Interior and Exterior Routing Protocols

As far as Internet routing is concerned, the major differences between the interior and the exterior routing protocols are how much detail they reveal about the exact location of networks, and what they tell about how to reach a network. The exterior routing protocols, for instance, only need to reveal whether a network is located within or behind a larger group of networks, and whether the larger network will carry traffic bound for a network that may be reached behind it.

For example, take the customer network behind the local ISP. The local ISP reaches the Internet through the national ISP. The national ISP, in turn, passes traffic to other national ISPs through the NAPs or other Internet traffic exchange points. As far as Internet routing is concerned, the local ISP tells the national ISP which networks are located within it. The local ISP will use an exterior routing protocol, such as the Border Gateway Protocol (BGP; described in Chapter 13) to inform other ASes of the networks that the local ISP controls. The networks the local ISP announces to the national ISP will be its own internal networks (such as the one the remote access server to which the PC is dialed in is located), and any customer networks for which the local ISP provides Internet access.

It's not of much interest to the national ISP exactly where the networks controlled by the local ISP really are, nor does it care about the most economical or most efficient ways to get traffic through the local ISP's network to those individual networks. The national ISP is concerned with two things: accepting traffic bound for those networks from other ISPs, with which it is a peer at an Internet traffic exchange point or NAP, and passing that traffic as quickly as possible to the local ISPs it serves. The national ISP leaves the details of delivering that traffic to its destination networks to the other ISPs beneath it.

ISPs (and the exterior routing protocols) are also concerned with announcing to other ASes the networks to which they are willing to carry traffic. For example, the local ISP may have another connection to another local ISP or to a second national ISP, as illustrated in Figure 3.8. The former connection might be to pass traffic efficiently to another ISP in the same geographic area. The latter connection, to the national

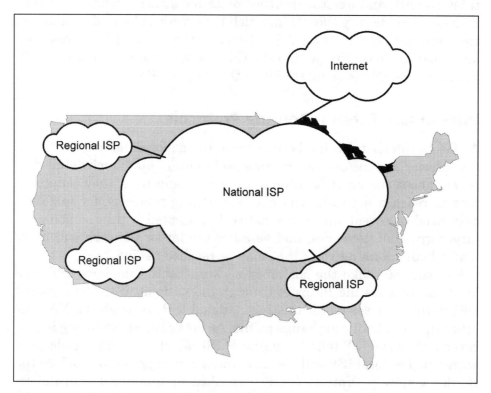

Figure 3.8   The hierarchy of ISPs, from customer networks to the Internet.

ISP, might be to give the local ISP a second access point to the Internet, perhaps to serve as a backup or an alternate route to the Internet, should the connection to the primary national ISP fail.

The other connections from the local ISP to a second local ISP and a second national ISP are both legitimate paths over which traffic to and from the Internet may flow. However, the local ISP only wants to receive traffic from the national ISP that is destined for networks within its AS, and not any other AS. Specifically, the local ISP doesn't want to be in the position of taking traffic from its primary national ISP, passing it through its own network, and delivering it to the other local ISP through its secondary connection to the local ISP. In other words, the local ISP probably doesn't want to be a conduit to and from the Internet for another local ISP. There may be a routing path from one local ISP through another local ISP to the national ISP, and then to the rest of the Internet, but the local ISPs with multiple connections like this don't want to be "transit ISPs" for other parts of the Internet.

Fortunately, exterior routing protocols like BGP allow ASes to announce the "reachability" of other networks, as well as the existence of those networks. In an exterior routing context, reachability means that an AS is willing to accept traffic that is destined for networks within another AS. That is, the AS will allow traffic destined for another AS to transit through it.

In most cases, transit rights, particularly for the commercial ISPs, are based on who is paying whom for Internet connectivity. Typically, part of the contractual relationship between a local ISP and a national ISP is that the national ISP will deliver traffic destined for the local ISP's networks. That said, unless it is specifically permitted, the local ISP can't act as a conduit for other ISPs to get to the Internet. Some national ISPs, for instance, prohibit local ISPs from reselling Internet access capacity. If they didn't have this right, and if it weren't supported by BGP, any higher-level provider, particularly one with high-speed Internet connections, top-level peering arrangements, or major international links, might find itself carrying huge amounts of traffic, from which it would derive no benefit, and worse, no revenue.

ASes and CIDR

To reduce the amount of detail the routers at the top-level national ISPs have to manage, exterior routing protocols like BGP allow ASes to announce groups of IP network addresses in routing table update messages. These *route aggregation* messages use CIDR notation, which are discussed next, to minimize the amount of detail needed to identify the networks within another AS and to reduce the size of the routing tables higher in the Internet routing hierarchy.

As we will see, the drive to aggregate as many network addresses as possible in CIDR blocks is one of the primary drivers for IP address renumbering. As the Internet has grown, the number of separate IP network addresses in use—each of which must be known at the top-level Internet access points—has grown dramatically.

CIDR

As resilient as the IP address scheme has proven to be, it hasn't been perfect. We are running out of IP address space, and what we have used we haven't done very efficiently. The Internet's top-level routers have routing tables that have become so big that they threaten to overwhelm their capability to keep track of all the networks in the Internet.

The response to these problems is the Classless Inter-Domain Routing, or CIDR. Described in RFCs 1517, 1518, 1519, and 1520, CIDR is a response by the IETF to rework the IP address allocation scheme until something better comes along and to prolong the connectivity of the Internet.

The objectives of CIDR are:

- Prolong the life of the IPv4 address space.
- Simplify the routing at the Internet's major traffic exchange points.
- Make more efficient use of the remaining IP address space.

The concepts of CIDR are relatively simple. Instead of filling routing tables—particularly those for the routers at the core of the Internet—with entries for individual network addresses, why not refer to a whole range of contiguous network addresses with one entry? CIDR does just that, by what is known as *supernetworking*. CIDR also eliminates the distinctions of Class A, B, and C addresses by subnetworking all IP address space into closely fitted "chunks" of address space. For example, let's say that all of the networks in the range from 190.100.1.0 through 190.100.255.0 have been assigned to a single ISP. That ISP is a customer of one of the top-level national ISPs, which advertises the existence of those networks. To other top-level ISPs, all those networks are reachable through the national ISP.

So instead of having the national ISP, as well as all the others at the Internet NAP, maintain routing table entries for 255 separate networks, why not just have one entry that represents them all? The CIDR entry for all 255 of those networks would be 190.100.0.0 /16. We will explain the /16 later, but, briefly here, it's a shorthand notation to indicate a block of 256 Class C networks, not just one network.

Using routers and routing protocols that can pass around network updates along with that /nn notation, network administrators can carve IP address space into appropriately sized chunks, instead of the large, medium, and tiny Class A, B, and C network sizes. ARIN can assign address space that way, too, instead of having to dole out huge chunks of classful address space.

Simplifying Routing

From the perspective of the operation of the whole Internet, the second objective in the preceding list—simplifying routing—has been the key benefit of CIDR. In fact, simplifying routing by forcing networks to use IP addresses that fall into "CIDR-ized" address space is one of the prime reasons for renumbering a network's IP addresses. Today, ISPs are required to use CIDR address blocks. Customers who move to a different ISP may find that they will be required to renumber their networks when they change ISPs, because their old IP addresses don't fall into their new ISP's CIDR blocks.

So while the IETF and ARIN and most sizable ISPs see implementing CIDR as a positive, even prudent, move, many customers think it is trouble. On the other hand, many of them never see it, unless they are required to renumber their networks to have their addresses fit into a CIDR block.

Despite this inconvenience to network administrators, CIDR's greater good for the Internet outweighs any drawback that CIDR may present. CIDR gives the Internet's top-level routers—the ones that don't have the luxury of a default route to another router with a more comprehensive routing table—a handy means to simplify their routing tables.

The result is that the routing tables in those already overstressed top-level routers can be smaller. CIDR gives those top-level routers a way to refer to a number of IP networks with a single router table entry, instead of tens of hundreds of entries. For the top-level NAP routers, CIDR works like a trash compactor: it puts the same stuff in a smaller, more manageable space.

An Imperfect World

In a perfect world, the designers of IP would probably have used CIDR from the start. The operation of the Internet certainly would have been simpler, and its organization would have been better, though the traditional IP address arrangement of Class A, B, and C addresses worked well while the Internet was a relatively small world.

Classful addresses, which divided IP address space into huge (Class A), medium (Class B), and tiny (Class C) address blocks, were given to network administrators for use in their networks. When Class B address space grew scarce, network administrators devised subnetworking (described in Chapter 7) to make more efficient use of the remaining Class B address space. With subnetworking and router software that supported dividing large blocks of IP address space into subnetworks, network administrators could tailor their address space blocks to meet specific needs.

Managing the Load

The growth of the Internet, and the subsequent explosion in the allocation and use of IP addresses, has placed tremendous strains on the central routers of the Internet. The routers at the Internet's central, top-level traffic exchange points, the Network Access Points (NAPs) have been straining to keep up with the loads placed on them.

When Internet growth really took off in the mid 1990s, the Internet's central routers were expected to track more and more IP addresses. The end game that seemed to be being played out was that, eventually, there would be more separate address assignments than the Internet's routers could handle. In self-defense, the NAP routers would begin to drop IP addresses from their routing tables, leaving networks with dropped addresses unreachable from the rest of the Internet.

In addition, address delegation authorities, like the InterNIC and the DoD NIC, were running out of IP address space. By 1995, it appeared that at the projected growth rate of the Internet, all available new IP address space would be assigned and exhausted by the turn of the century. New Class B address space, which had never been adequate to supply the demand for it anyway, would be completely assigned by the end of the 1990s, and Class Cs would all be assigned by early in the twenty-first century. For example, network administrators who had an entire Class B address block could split that block into hundreds of separate subnetworks. Holders of Class C address space, which could hold only 254 hosts, were not so fortunate, but they could subnetwork, too, to make maximum use of their available addresses.

The concept of subnetworking, first described in RFC 950, introduced the idea of the subnetwork mask, a binary number that indicates to a router which bits of an IP address are being used for the network part of an IP address. At the same time, more complex routing protocols, such as the BGP were introduced. One of the capabilities of BGP was that it understood subnetwork masks, and a subnetwork's masks could be passed with an IP network address to a neighboring router in router table updates.

CIDR Masks

CIDR removes many, but not all, of the network size constraints imposed by Class A, B, and C addresses. Instead of giving an ISP an entire Class A, B, or C address, ARIN now gives out a CIDR block of addresses, which amounts to a group of Class C addresses that can be sized to fit any network's needs.

A CIDR block is a range of contiguous (consecutively numbered) network addresses. CIDR notation indicates the first network address in the range; a trailing /nn notation indicates how many addresses there are in the range. For example, a single Class C address would be described as 192.150.0.0 in standard classful address notation, and 192.150.0.0 /24 in classless CIDR notation. The /24 notation, explained shortly, is called the *CIDR prefix*, even though it follows the IP address. The /24 indicates the length of the subnetwork mask, which is 24 bits long. The standard Class C mask, described in the illustration of subnetwork masks in Chapter 7, is 24 bits long.

However, CIDR breaks the dependencies of IP addressing on classful addresses, making IP addresses classless. It does this by treating all IP address space as units of Class C addresses. Class C networks may have as many as 254 hosts per network. CIDR notation, though, allows ARIN, ISPs, and other delegators of IP address space to give a company or organization as many network and host addresses as it needs, in 254 host blocks.

The benefit of this is that it eliminates the stranded address space problem of Class A and Class B networks. Instead of the huge leap between 254 hosts for a Class C network and 65,536 hosts for a Class B network, address delegators can assign a CIDR block that reflects an organization's true address needs.

The flip side of this customization is that Internet routers need to know that they're dealing with a CIDR block, and not a group of separate Class C networks. So Internet routers must use protocols like the BGP which understand CIDR masks. Otherwise, the Internet's routers would be choked on thousands of individual Class C addresses in their routing tables, which is one of the problems that CIDR is supposed to solve.

Groups of Cs

The CIDR prefix, referred to as the CIDR subnet mask, indicates how many former Class C addresses are in the CIDR block. The prefix is a subnet mask, but its interpretation, in CIDR terminology, is this: The CIDR prefix indicates the number of consecutive former Class C addresses blocks, starting at the IP address before the prefix.

The following list will help decipher the number of blocks of former Class Cs in a CIDR address:

CIDR	PREFIX	NUMBER OF FORMER CLASS Cs
/24	1	(One former Class C)
/23	2	
/22	4	
/21	8	
/20	16	
/19	32	
/18	64	
/17	128	
/16	256	(One former Class B)
/15	512	
/14	1024	
/13	2048	
/12	4096	
/11	8192	
/10	16,384	
/9	32,768	
/8	65,536	(One former Class A)

Let's look at the addresses in the 190.100.0.0 address range to illustrate what these prefixes mean. If we were to subnetwork a classful Class B address into Class C addresses by using a 24-bit mask, the Class C network addresses would be:

190.100.0.0

190.100.1.0

190.100.2.0

190.100.3.0

...

190.100.255.0

In this case, we have used the first and last available addresses, which are referred to as the *all-zeroes* and *all-ones* subnets.

The CIDR notation for each of these addresses would be:

190.100.0.0 /24

190.100.1.0 /24

190.100.2.0 /24

190.100.3.0 /24

...

190.100.255.0 /24

In this case, the CIDR notation doesn't look much different from the standard subnetworking. But if we were to subnetwork the address with a 23-bit mask, and compare that to how CIDR notation would describe the same thing, it would look different, as shown in the next list:

STANDARD SUBNETWORK	CIDR NOTATION	ADDRESS RANGE
190.100.0.0	190.100.0.0 /23	190.100.1.0
190.100.2.0	190.100.2.0 /23	190.100.3.0
190.100.4.0	190.100.4.0 /23	190.100.5.0

Note that the /23 CIDR mask means *the contiguous block of two network addresses starting at the base address before the prefix*. Thus, in CIDR notation, 190.100.0.0 /23 means *all of the addresses from*

190.100.0.0 through 190.100.1.0. By the same token, 190.100.128.0 /23 would mean *all of the addresses from 190.100.128.0 through 190.100.129.0.*

The network address before the prefix is called the *base address*, because it is the first address in the range of addresses starting at that address in the CIDR block. The prefix indicates the number of 255 host network addresses that are in the address range.

Still, we haven't seen huge differences with the /24 and /23 prefixes. The differences become more apparent as we use shorter prefixes. If we were to subnetwork the same address with a 22-bit mask and compare it to a /22 CIDR mask, the addresses would look like this:

STANDARD SUBNETWORK	CIDR NOTATION	ADDRESS RANGE
190.100.0.0	190.100.0.0 /22	190.100.1.0
190.100.2.0		
190.100.3.0		
190.100.4.0	190.100.4.0 /22	
190.100.5.0		
190.100.6.0		
190.100.7.0		

Now we can start to see how CIDR notation economizes on routing table entries. The CIDR address of 190.100.0.0 /22 now stands for the four addresses from 190.100.0.0 through 190.100.3.0.

If we were to shorten the prefix even further, we'd see even more addresses represented in a single CIDR address. Then, if we were to use an 18-bit subnet mask and a /18 prefix on the same range, we would have each of the following address ranges represented by a single CIDR number:

STANDARD SUBNETWORK	CIDR NOTATION	ADDRESS RANGE
190.100.0.0	190.100.0.0 /18	
190.100.1.0		
190.100.2.0		
...		
190.100.63.0		

STANDARD SUBNETWORK	CIDR NOTATION	ADDRESS RANGE
190.100.64.0		190.100.64.0 /18
190.100.65.0		
190.100.66.0		
...		
190.100.127.0		
190.100.128.0	190.100.128.0 /18	
190.100.129.0		
190.100.130.0		
...		
190.100.191.0		
190.100.192.0	190.100.192.0 /18	
190.100.193.0		
190.100.194.0		
...		
190.100.255.0		

The CIDR notation shown in the second column of this list shows that CIDR is a shorthand way of indicating an entire range of network addresses. Without CIDR, each of these addresses would have to be listed individually in Internet routers' routing tables. With CIDR, entire ranges of addresses can be carried in routing tables with a single entry, because the CIDR notation means all of the addresses in this range, starting with the base address before the prefix.

A good way to think of the prefix is as a subnetwork mask for Class B addresses. That is, the prefix indicates the number of Class Cs that could be created by applying a subnet mask of that many bits to a Class B address. So, a 24-bit subnet mask on a Class B address (255.255.255.0, or, in CIDR notation, /24) would create individual Class C addresses.

Note that in CIDR notation, a former Class A address, such as the 10.0.0.0 block, would be referred to as 10.0.0.0 /8. In this case, the 10.0.0.0 /8 notation means 65,536 networks, starting with network 10.0.0.0. Granting an organization a /8 is highly unusual, because it's a lot of address space. The last company to get one was the high-speed Internet access-over-cable provider @Home, which justified its request to ARIN on the basis of its proposed subscriber base.

But that doesn't mean that @Home or any other CIDR /8, for that matter, must break its networks into 65,536 separate Class Cs. @Home, or anyone with a CIDR block of any size, is free to subnet the space any way it sees fit. With Variable-Length Subnet Masking (VLSM), described in Chapter 7, the space can be carved up in whatever fashion suits the designee.

Enforcing the Rules

The practical effect of CIDR is that some ISPs have started to enforce its use, to protect Internet routing. The first of the biggest top-level ISPs to do so was Sprint, and other top-level, national ISPs have followed suit. In 1996, Sprint announced that it would configure its routers to filter out CIDR blocks that were longer than /19 in newly assigned address ranges. That is, Sprint's routers would drop any CIDR block that did not contain at least 32 Class C equivalents. Network addresses in those smaller block ranges that were dropped by Sprint would not be reachable from anyone behind Sprint.

The rule was applied only to address blocks in newly assigned IP address space; specifically, space assigned by the InterNIC (and subsequently by ARIN) after 1996. Therefore, it doesn't apply to IP address space that has been in use or to notoriously un-CIDR-ized address space in the infamous 192.0.0.0 block (see Chapter 4 for a discussion of the 192 block "Toxic Waste Dump").

As an accommodation to smaller users of IP address space, in early 1999, ARIN announced that it would allow organizations that had address blocks of /20 or fewer addresses (a /20 is 16 former Class C addresses) to announce their address blocks as /19s. The caveat was that they would have to demonstrate that they were using the address space efficiently.

The ruling means that an ISP or an organization that needs only a CIDR /20 block (the equivalent of 16 Class Cs) can request just that, instead of a larger /19 block that the ISP filtering rules might force it to get. Address designees now must pay ARIN for the addresses they get, so this also accommodates ISPs' cost sensitivities.

But keep in mind that CIDR notation is only a way to subdivide available address space to make it more flexible than classful addressing. Far more important is its benefit of address aggregation, which reduces the strains on routing in an already overburdened Internet routing core.

Summary

Given the complexity of the Internet, it's a wonder not just that routing works relatively quickly, but that it works at all. Like the telephone system, which is even more complicated, the Internet is composed of parts from different vendors and organizations that follow widely accepted engineering practices and use standard transmission techniques and protocols.

The key network component of the Internet is the IP router, a specialized computer that examines the destination addresses in IP datagrams, and decides where to forward these datagrams to get them to their destination. Unlike the telephone system, in which switches identify an end-to-end path for a call before sending the first sound, routers blithely accept traffic for destinations that may not exist. Datagrams may cross tens of routers, arranged in a hierarchical fashion by ISPs that may only communicate with their immediate neighbors, to complete Internet communications.

Changing the addresses in a network may mean that a network must be relocated by the Internet's routers. Network renumbering is frequently a consequence of the hierarchical structure of ISP routing. When ISPs can use IP addresses from only certain address ranges or CIDR blocks, moving to a different ISP may force a renumbering program. In the next chapter, we will examine some of the reasons why organizations may elect to renumber their networks, or why they might be forced to do so.

Why Renumber?

Changing all of the IP addresses in a network is not exactly the kind of thing that network administrators look forward to doing. There are as many reasons not to do it as there are to do it, as well as plenty of reasons to put off doing it until it can't be avoided any longer.

There are a number of sound reasons for renumbering, such as changing ISPs, acquiring a more or less permanent block of IP address space, and consolidating address space into a more manageable block of addresses. However, no organization undertakes a renumbering project unless it sees concrete benefits to doing so. Those benefits may be either maintaining connectivity to the global Internet or reducing the cost of maintaining routing or network administration.

At the same time, a number of techniques and technologies have been developed and implemented in recent years that may eliminate the renumbering problem. Network Address Translation (NAT), the Dynamic Host Configuration protocol (DHCP), and the use of private, reserved address space behind firewalls and screening routers have all reduced the need for renumbering IP space. These technologies, however, are not foolproof. Some may complicate network operations and add overhead to Internet transactions; others may prevent certain types of applications and protocols from working properly, specifically those that add security features to network transactions.

In a perfect world, which, of course, no network administrator could possibly inhabit, all networks would have completely routable, unique public IP addresses. In addition, there wouldn't be any problems routing IP datagrams to that space from anywhere else in the Internet. Such a perfect world does not exist, but unique IP address space does. Given the continued expansion of the Internet, and our desire to access it from ever more transient platforms, such as Personal Digital Assistants (PDAs) like the Palm Pilot and cellular phones, the need for more unique IP addresses will increase, not decrease. Network administrators can run, but they can't hide, and sooner or later they may have to grapple with the renumbering issue.

In this chapter, we'll look at the following issues:

- The reasons why a network administrator or router administrator would want to undertake the task of renumbering a network
- The benefits of renumbering
- The problems that a network renumbering project might bring

In Chapters 5 and 15, we'll examine a number of other issues related to renumbering, such as building a business case for renumbering, procedures for renumbering, and tools to manage IP addresses.

Reasons for Renumbering

There are a number of reasons for renumbering IP address space, some of which are influenced by internal network factors and some by external network factors. The internal network factors are those related to a routing or connectivity with a specific customer network or the network of an ISP. The external factors are those related to connectivity to and through the global Internet.

Of the two, external reasons are usually more critical than internal. Convoluted or inefficient routing within a network is one problem, but as long as the network still works, a network administrator may seek other solutions to the problem than renumbering.

External network factors usually affect the ability to see and be seen by other parts of the Internet. If Internet connectivity is the name of the game, then being part of the Internet implies universal access to every part of the Internet. If an external factor affects a network's Internet connectivity, such as having your network address blocked by a higher-level ISP, there may be no solution to the problem other than renumbering.

Internal Factors

Internal factors that may influence renumbering decisions are discussed in the following subsections.

Cleaning Up Legacy Routing

Many network administrators have seen the networks under their control undergo rapid and uncoordinated growth. Frequently, the growth has been haphazard, and subnetworks have been added without regard to how efficiently the routing among subnets works. If the network is large enough, the routing tables of the routers in the network can be quite large.

The problem may be exacerbated if the routers use an older interior routing protocol, such as the Routing Information Protocol (RIP) or the Interior Gateway Routing Protocol (IGRP). Both RIP and IGRP periodically broadcast their entire routing tables to their neighbors, giving them a complete routing table copy, whether or not they need it. This is one of the inefficiencies of these older, distance vector routing protocols, and it increases dramatically the amount of network traffic used for routing table updates.

There are two parts to the solution to this problem. First, the router administrator has to introduce a routing protocol that uses classless routing, such as the EGRP protocol. Second, to make use of classless routing (described in Chapter 3), the network may have to be renumbered so that the networks are arranged hierarchically.

The benefit of renumbering will be to make the operation of the network more efficient, and to allow for more orderly future growth. At the same time, the network administrator may want to increase the bandwidth of the links among the routers, as part of a networkwide modernization plan.

Documenting Incomplete Networks

The uncontrolled growth of subnetworks within an organization often has another side effect that may spur the need to renumber. A large, complex network may have grown so quickly that no one has bothered to document how its network addresses have been used. As a result, though such a network may have a structure that works, no one really knows which network addresses are in use or where.

In these cases, renumbering may be part of the solution, in that it will force the network administrators to redesign the network numbering plan. Renumbering will reorganize the network so that routing works more efficiently. An additional benefit is that the network's address blocks can be organized into hierarchical CIDR blocks, and advertised to upstream ISPs as full blocks.

Joining Networks with Business Partners

When one company wants to acquire another company, or wants to link its networks with those of a business partner to form an intranet, frequently, the two organizations will have conflicting methods for using IP address space. Either of these situations—linking to or acquiring another organization—may prompt renumbering on some scale, even if it is as simple as renumbering only the networks that conflict with each other.

For example, both companies could be using the same addresses from within the 10.0.0.0 private address space set aside by RFC 1918. They could both continue to use those same addresses, and use NAT to conceal the address reuse, but the more straightforward way to resolve the conflict is to renumber networks that use addresses that conflict with those already in use elsewhere.

Outgrowing Address Space

When a network has outgrown its existing address space, the network administrator may have to choose between getting another small address block or renumbering into a newer address block. While getting another smaller block will work, sometimes renumbering into a much larger address block is a more advantageous choice.

If a new block of address space is available from an ISP, or if it can be leased from ARIN, all of the company's hosts and networks can be put into the newer, single address block. A larger block of contiguous IP network addresses is easier to use more efficiently than an equivalent number of smaller, noncontiguous network addresses.

Companies that have a large number of small Class C network addresses may face the same choices. If the network needs more address space, the question is, is it better to get another Class C address or to get a larger CIDR block of addresses? The former will solve the problem temporarily; the latter will solve the problem for a longer period of time.

An additional benefit of renumbering into a CIDR block is that the organization can move to a more efficient routing protocol that uses CIDR prefixes and that improves routing and network utilization.

Moving to Private Address Space

Moving to private address space (specified in RFC 1918) from a discontiguous block of public address space is frequently used as a subterfuge to avoid future renumbering. However, unless the network administrator is building a network from the ground up, he or she will still have to go through a renumbering exercise to get into private address space. It is true that if the network uses the private Class A space 10.0.0.0, the network administrator may never have to renumber again (until IPv6 comes along), but he or she will have to get into that private address space somehow.

Private IP address space (covered in more detail in Chapter 10) does have a great deal to recommend it. It can be an entire Class A address (network 10.0.0.0) or some part of the reserved Class B or C address space. Some combination of all three of the private address blocks could be used, although most network administrators stick to using whichever block suits their needs.

The downside of private address apace is that its IP addresses must be translated to public address space, using network address translation, or NAT (covered in Chapter 8). NAT adds operational and management complexities, but it's an unavoidable consequence of using private address space.

Virtual LANs (VLANs)

Some large LANs have perpetuated legacy topologies composed of *bridged*, instead of routed, networks. Bridged LANs work, but they're anomalies in today's fully routed world. Bridged LANS were most likely designed and installed 10 or more years ago, when routers were expensive and switched LAN hubs were unavailable. They may have been designed as bridged networks years ago, when routers may have been too expensive, and switched LAN hubs unavailable. A large bridged network may have become so large as to be unwieldy, particularly as the network grew and interconnected to the Internet.

Today, routers and LAN switches are much less expensive and offer many more advantages than bridged networks. Network administrators of large bridged networks can see tremendous advantages in moving away from their old topologies and to routed or switched networks.

That said, a router-based network, and even a switched LAN network, must be subnetworked in order to take full advantage of routing and switching. Part of the deployment of a routed network or a switched LAN must include developing a subnetworking plan and renumbering network nodes to fit into it.

If the switched network will include Virtual LANs (VLANs), there should be a subnet for each VLAN. Routers will need one or more subnet defined on each interface, as well as a plan for aggregating subnets behind router interfaces.

External Factors

External factors may influence the decision to renumber a network, too. Some of the most common external influences are described in the following subsections.

Changing ISPs

Changing ISPs is one of the most common reasons for renumbering IP addresses on a network. In many cases, companies and organizations get their IP addresses from their ISP. The ISP "owns" the address space, having been assigned it by ARIN or, earlier, by InterNIC.

As a service to its customers, or because that's the way that ARIN works, the ISPs delegate IP address space to their customers. Everything works well, because the ISP announces the existence and reachability of these addresses to the rest of the Internet. The customer only has to use the address space properly, because the ISP handles most of the details of advertising the address space to the rest of the Internet.

Then one day, the company decides that it can get better, faster, or less expensive Internet access from another ISP. What appears to be a simple matter of moving the leased-line connection from one ISP's point of presence to another soon becomes an exercise in IP address renumbering.

The reason that changing ISPs may force renumbering is that, today, most IS address space is being forced into aggregated CIDR blocks. CIDR, as defined earlier (and covered in depth in Chapter 3), is a method of consolidating large numbers of separate IP network addresses so that IP addressing can be tailored more closely to the exact requirements of a specific IS or customer. CIDR also helps reduce the size of the routing tables of the Internet's top-level ISP routers.

The effect of CIDR on IP address assignments is that addresses in CIDR blocks can't be moved easily to other ISPs. There are ways around this by creating exceptions to CIDR address blocks, or "holes," in the CIDR address ranges. However, ISPs aren't required to create holes in CIDR blocks. In addition, if they're doing it for the benefit of customers who have since left them for other ISPs, they have no motivation for maintaining the CIDR block exceptions properly or to do so forever.

Frequently, an ISP who is losing a customer will agree to redirect traffic for the customer's address blocks to the new ISP for some period of time. This grace period may last only 90 days or so, which doesn't allow too much time for the customer to renumber all of his or her address space.

Provider-Independent Address Space

Renumbering caused by moving to another ISP is usually sufficient motivation for organizations to get what's known as Provider-Independent address space, or PI. From a renumbering perspective, getting PI space can be practically the same thing as changing ISPs.

PI is address space assigned to a corporation or an organization directly by ARIN, not by an ISP. It's provider independent because it doesn't belong within an upstream ISP's CIDR address blocks. It's announced independently as a separate CIDR block, so it's IP address space that is not dependent on being part of another, larger provider's address space.

The advantage of PI is that once it's assigned to an organization, that organization can change ISPs, create its own subnetworking scheme, or even connect to other ISPs directly, and not have to renumber its IP addresses.

The only catch to getting provider-independent address space today is that new IP address space is assigned by ARIN, and ARIN charges for the use of that space. Most organizations get their IP address space from ISPs, who "lease" it from ARIN. If a network administrator wants provider-independent address space for his or her corporate network, he or she is going to be in the same position as an ISP. ISP address space is also provider independent, meaning a corporation will have to pay the ARIN fees to get provider-independent space into which it can renumber its networks.

Aggregating Several Small Networks into Large CIDR Blocks

Even companies that have their own, assigned address space may find that they have to renumber if they want to get provider-independent address space. The reason is that address space assigned in the pre-ARIN days may be individual Class C network addresses. Though these are valid addresses, they may run afoul of the drive to consolidate address announcements into larger CIDR blocks. Renumbering into new, ARIN-assigned address space may be the only way to make that provider-independent space truly useful.

For example, let's say a company has five Class C addresses that it had been assigned years ago by the InterNIC. In CIDR notation, these five Class Cs are separate /24 addresses. Current ISP filtering and address announcement conventions allow for these five Class C addresses to be announced separately. They will also be carried separately in the Internet's top-level NAP routing tables. As the Internet continues to grow, however, the rules may change. Already, some top-level ISPs filter out addresses in new address space if they are in groups smaller than a block of 32 Class C addresses (a /19 CIDR block). There's nothing to say that they might not expand this filtering rule to other address space too.

The solution is to get new address space that is in a CIDR block; but new address space means renumbering current networks to put them in the new space. If, ask the holders of older Class C addresses, our Class C network addresses work, why should we give back our addresses and renumber? So, unless they do so voluntarily, holders of individual Class C networks have been allowed to keep their network addresses.

As long as the routers at the core of the Internet are able to juggle all of these smaller and individual address entries in their routing tables, it is likely that smaller network address blocks, down to and including individual Class Cs, will be allowed to exist. However, changing ISPs often forces renumbering, because ISPs are under pressure to announce whole CIDR blocks of addresses, not individual addresses.

Nonunique Addresses

It's hard to imagine that there could be TCP/IP networks in existence today that are not connected to the Internet, but they do exist. Some might be older networks that have never had officially assigned IP address space, but that are using IP addresses selected by previous network administrators. In this case, "selected" means "made up" by the network administrator. These addresses work internally, but they must be changed to unique address space if they are to be connected to the Internet.

The other option is to leave these unofficial IP addresses alone, and change addresses with network address translation. The only danger in doing so is that some of these internal, nonunique addresses may escape being changed by NAT, and thus escape into the Internet. Unlike RFC 1918-compliant private addresses, which Internet routers will discard, nonunique, unofficial IP addresses will be treated as real addresses. Traffic with unofficial, nonunique source addresses is less a problem than traffic bearing those addresses in the destination field. If the network does exist elsewhere in the Internet, that's where the return traffic will be delivered.

The best policy for handling unofficial IP addresses is to eliminate them by renumbering them into real, official IP address space or into private address space. The IP address shortage problem isn't so severe that network administrators should risk the integrity of the Internet just to avoid renumbering a network with a bogus address.

Networks without guaranteed unique address space are good candidates for deploying NAT, as long as the number of hosts that will have Internet connectivity is relatively small. For full Internet connectivity, the best solution is to renumber into unique address space. NAT isn't foolproof, and the safest way to handle nonunique address space is to renumber.

Swampland Reclamation

Routing in the Internet is either perpetually on the brink of collapse or a fabulously robust system that defies all attempts to make it collapse into chaos. Efforts to clean up Internet routing, through reclaiming certain parts of previously assigned IP address space from organizations that have been using it for some time, may also force IP address renumbering.

In the mid-1990s, a few of the top-level ISPs started to move toward CIDR address aggregation (see Chapter 3 for a complete explanation of CIDR). Their motivation was to reduce the size of the routing tables carried by the Internet's top-level routers. Without this step, they felt, the number of routing table entries at the Internet exchange points might become so large that the top-level routers couldn't keep all of the networks on the Internet in their routing tables. As a result, some networks would drop off the routing tables and become "forgotten." The result would be that the "forgotten networks" would be unreachable from many parts of the Internet.

The problem, however, is that in order to consolidate network addresses in CIDR blocks, networks to be put into a CIDR block must be contiguously numbered. That is, they must be numbered sequentially in series and they must be served by the same ISP. The reason for the second requirement is that if they are served by the same ISP, the routes to the CIDR block can be summarized in a single routing statement.

CIDR aggregation isn't a problem for recently or newly assigned address space, most of which is assigned in nice, neat CIDR blocks. It is a problem for any individual Class C address, and especially for a certain group of Class C network addresses.

The first block of Class C address space from which Class C addresses were assigned, the 192.0.0.0 block, is neither organized as neatly nor assigned in as orderly a fashion as it might be. In fact, it's a mess, so much so that it's referred to as the "swamp" or the "toxic waste dump," TWD for short. Why? Because when 192 space was first assigned in the early 1980s, it was done without regard to someday consolidating it into CIDR blocks.

As a result, the 192 space—also known as the *TWD*—is used by companies and organizations all over the map. Block 192 network addresses right next to each other are in use by universities, companies, and government agencies all over the world. Obviously, few are served by the same ISP, so the addresses can't be aggregated into CIDR blocks.

In fact, there are some 750 network addresses—all individual Class Cs—in the 192 block that are still in use and that still appear in the routing tables of the top-level Internet access point routers, for which ARIN doesn't even have current or correct network administrator or point-of-contact information. The only way to clean up the TWD and to aggregate those 192 addresses into CIDR blocks is to have the owners of those address blocks agree to give up those network addresses and renumber their networks into new CIDR address space.

Reclaiming the TWD address space, or "reclaiming the swamp," is one of the IETF's long-range Internet environmental projects. The Internet engineering community would like to take back a lot of the network addresses in the 192 block, in order to reclaim the address space.

This is all very sound from an Internet engineering perspective, but the companies and organizations that have 192 address space don't want to give it up, particularly if it's in use and it's working well. To give up the addresses would require them to renumber their networks or to use NAT to hide those addresses from the Internet. Consequently, the residents of the Swamp, ARIN, and the IETF are in a standoff. Few of the 192 holders want to give up their 192 block Class Cs, particularly since it would force them to renumber. ARIN and IETF policy has been to "grandfather" previously assigned address space, but to force new address space assignments into CIDR blocks.

Some of those 192 block assignees might find that their ISPs aren't willing to poke holes in their CIDR blocks to accommodate 192s out of their normal CIDR blocks. They might also find that the top-level ISPs tighten the restrictions on how small a block they will route. For now, though, the 192s have been left alone, but any that do decide to join a larger CIDR block will have to renumber to get there.

Network Expansion

Recently, companies and organizations that have had small networks for many years have seen demands for network space grow beyond the limits of a small Class C network address. A Class C address may have been suitable for a network of fewer than 250 hosts, but as networks grow, they need more address space.

For standard customer networks, the source of new address space is the customer's ISP. The ISP probably has new address space available, but it's in the ISP's interest to keep all of its customers' network addresses in the same CIDR blocks it has been allocated.

It is possible for an ISP to announce individual Class C addresses to other networks. Plenty of them do it, because older Class C addresses that have been in use for years have been grandfathered into Internet routing. However, an ISP may want a customer who asks for new address space to move all of that customer's addresses within the ISP's CIDR blocks, to maximize the benefits of summarizing routes to other networks.

Ipv6

While it is more of a future consideration than a current one, the next version of IP, IPv6, will require that current networks have a sound numbering plan already in place. It's not completely clear exactly how addressing will work in IPv6, except that the transition from IPv4 will require aggregated addresses.

IPv6 does include an autoconfiguration capability, so that the host part of the address will come from the device's media access (Ethernet) address. However, there will be a network part of each IPv6 address; it will be related to the topology of the network. The best plan for transitioning to IPv6 is to have a sound IPv4 addressing structure already in place.

Drawbacks of Renumbering

Renumbering can be a lot of work, and if it isn't done properly and carefully, it can have precisely the opposite effect its proponents intend; that is, it can render applications inoperative, cut off users from the Internet, and divide a network into uncommunicative factions.

The hardest part of a renumbering project is anticipating all the places where IP addresses have become embedded in the network infrastructure. In some cases, rooting out all of the code that might cause the Year 2000 problem is just like determining where and how renumbering a network might cause similar problems.

IP addresses are embedded in interfaces, and they're in applications, networks services, dial-up configurations, and access control lists. Rooting out and changing all of the references to the old IP address space and coordinating the transition to new IP address space is at the heart of the renumbering issue.

Certainly, there are numerous circumstances that may force a network administrator to consider a renumbering project, but it isn't necessarily the kind of thing a network administrator wants to do. It's a lot of work, and its benefits may not be clear to users nor to management, because it's a network efficiency and a network management thing, which neither end users nor executives may appreciate.

A network manager may, however, see renumbering as a network reengineering project, to change the network infrastructure to accommodate changing needs, changing technologies, and changing requirements for Internet connectivity and Internet routing.

Summary

Most network managers would probably rather fight renumbering than switch. If the IP addresses work, why change them? As we have seen in this chapter, there are some reasons why a network manager might voluntarily renumber a network, although most renumbering projects are undertaken only when keeping the old address scheme is an untenable choice.

Several circumstances, such as reorganizing a network, changing routing protocols, consolidating smaller networks, or even accommodating network growth, may justify renumbering. Other circumstances, such as changing ISPs, may require it whether the network manager likes it or not.

Hopefully, renumbering a network makes for a better-organized network, and one that is easier to manage. Renumbering to accommodate a new network routing plan, such as OSPF, or to replace an older routing protocol like RIP, makes future network growth easier to control, and easier to manage.

Renumbering a network, particularly a sizeable one, can be an expensive proposition. Sometimes the cost of the project can become large enough to consume a significant part of the IT department's budget. As we will see in the next chapter, the good reasons for renumbering we discussed in this chapter may have to be paired with an equally good business case justifying the cost of the project.

CHAPTER 5

Making the Business Case for Renumbering

Every network renumbering or IP reengineering effort assumes that there will be a number of technical challenges. Determining how to reengineer network addressing and how to reconfigure routing to accommodate a new, "future-proof" addressing scheme is enough of a technical challenge. A renumbering task, particularly one that involves many networks and several locations, requires a great deal of careful planning by technically astute people.

All that said, one of the more compelling challenges of any renumbering effort is selling corporate management on the need for a renumbering task to begin with. Depending on the level of technical expertise of management, as well as their appreciation for the needs for network improvements, this may be an easy or a hard sale. Selling a technical plan to management is not the kind of task that network administrators or systems designers like to do, but it's a necessary evil. It justifies and legitimizes the task, and subjects it to a crucial review, answering, what is its business justification?

Don't expect it to be an easy sale. Management's opinion may be that if the network isn't broken, why fix it. If the company or the organization already has IP addresses that work, managers might reason, why change them? Thus, the first part of the management of renumbering or network reengineering will be making a business case for it.

The Business Case

Making a business case means giving management sound business reasons for conducting a network renumbering task. Sound business reasons don't necessarily mean profit-making reasons. They may be operating reasons, to make the network or the infrastructure work more effectively, or to work more efficiently. They may be cost-reduction or cost-avoidance reasons. They may also be network connectivity reasons, to make the network fit into Internet and ISP routing schemes.

For an ISP, the justification for a renumbering task may be business growth reasons as well as an operational necessity. An ISP exists by providing its customers with Internet connectivity; and new address space, or renumbering into a larger block of address space, may give it the address space room it needs to grow. Without enough IP addresses to delegate to its customer base, an ISP's chances of growing and competing can be strangled.

What's in a Business Case?

A business case is a justification of a technical change, such as a renumbering project, that relates the costs of the task to its benefits. The business case also justifies the costs of the project and clarifies its benefits.

The business case will also help the network administrator, the CIO, or the director of the information technology department understand the steps required to complete the renumbering task. The business case doesn't have to detail all of the steps of the plan, but it will be necessary to indicate that someone has thought through what it will take to get from the current numbering scheme to the new addressing plan.

Many people who will pass judgment on the business case won't get past the executive summary (defined shortly). Either they don't have to or they don't want to. The executive summary isn't the most important part of the business plan, but it is the part that most people will read. Consequently, the executive summary must be direct, to the point, and convincing.

Some organizations will take the word of their IS people and network engineers that if network renumbering is necessary, extensive written justification of the project isn't. Just do it, they say. On the other hand, if an outside consulting company has been brought in to reengineer a customer's network, part of its job may be to provide extensive justification for any proposal to reengineer or renumber a customer's network. ISPs, who are wary of moves that may impact customers' networks, will proceed cautiously with renumbering, and only after understanding all of the technical implications of such a move.

If a written business case of a renumbering project is necessary, the parts of the business case justification may include:

Executive summary. Summarize simply, with as little detail as possible, the renumbering project's objectives, risks, and recommendations. The purpose of the executive summary is to make executives aware of what is going on and why, and to gain their blessing for the project. Though detail isn't necessary, candor is.

Project overview. Describe what you are going to do, such as: change the IP address plan, renumber the network, or reorganize parts of the addressing plan. The audience is those people who are more concerned with the mechanics of the implementation of the project, so the project overview should contain the detail necessary to enable a technical manager to understand the steps necessary to complete the project.

Benefits. Specify the benefits of the project, both technical, operational, and, if relevant, financial, to include cost savings or cost avoidance. Emphasize the most positive parts of the project's benefits, because this is the part of the document that will sell the project to an otherwise skeptical user or technical or customer community.

Technical justification. Include all of the detail the overview and executive summary sections left out. This is the part of the document in which technicians and network engineers will be most interested; therefore, it must be most convincing to them. Renumbering is a technical project, and the technical justification must both justify the project and describe exactly how it will be done, including the sequence of events, renumbering phases, and other project details.

Diagrams. Use diagrams of current and proposed network addressing, route summarization, internal and external routing, and route announcements to help explain the technical justification. Diagrams serve a more worthwhile purpose for whomever does the renumbering project, because they are the blueprints that will guide the project. If the project is extensive and complex, it may be necessary to create a simplified set of diagrams for the business case document, as well as a more detailed set for network managers and systems administrators to use during the renumbering project.

Costs and resources required. To the extent possible, estimate the cost of the project and the number, skill level, and time required of the people who will be assigned to the project. A large network renumbering project may take months and involve dozens of people in many locations. The largest cost of renumbering is for people, although there may be extra expenses for new or upgraded routers or changes in applications code. Once these costs have been estimated as accurately as possible, they should be matched against the corresponding benefits of the project.

Risks. Renumbering carries with it a number of risks, not the least of which is that a network that functions perfectly well today may no longer operate quite so well once renumbering begins. Assess the risks of the renumbering project realistically, including problems that might occur with internal and external routing. At the same time, contrast the risks against the alternatives—that is, not taking the risks—such as losing Internet connectivity or inefficient routing.

Recommendation. Recommend that the network renumbering project be done according to the plan specified. If you've specified a complete plan that is justified on a technical and a business basis, recommend that it be completed. Finally, include a time table, and propose a start date.

The business case for a renumbering project is really its technical justification, but it must also indicate the business benefit of the project. Network connectivity is no longer an operational luxury, and few would argue that a modern business can afford poor Internet connectivity. The business case documents and justifies the project, and specifies its positive operational benefits.

Composing the Business Case

Many networking and technical people approach a business plan document as if it were a Ph.D. thesis. It's not a scientific justification, although the technical reasons for undertaking the task should be cited. It's a selling document, to convince management—and maybe even yourself—that there is sound justification for reengineering the network or its IP addressing plan.

These are some of the principles that you should use in writing this document:

Keep it simple. Describe as simply as possible what the project is all about, leaving out most of the technical detail. Although you are discussing a subject that is rooted in arcane technical jargon, as much as possible, describe the project in simple language. Your audience probably isn't interested in the technical detail, and frankly, it probably would take too long to describe it to them. If you think that you must get into a technical explanation of IP addressing, routing, or route aggregation, try to take out more detail than you leave in. Someone who understands the subject will be able to fill in the details; to most others, excessive detail will be wasted.

Get to the point. If the point of a network renumbering project is that the network is going to operate more efficiently, say that. It's a very simplistic explanation, and you may be able to amplify that statement by saying that you'll also be able to make the network bigger in the future. Determine the point of what you are trying to express, then say what you have to say.

Use bulleted lists. Readers love bulleted lists, because they highlight the key points. In fact, if you can make bulleted lists of what you are doing, why you are doing it, and how it will benefit the organization, you can use them as the basis for the entire business case document.

Stop when you're done. If you've described what you want to do, specified the benefits, laid out a plan, and made a recommendation, there's not much more to say, so stop. Mystery novels often need surprise endings; a business case does not. If you've covered the subject and you're done, stop writing.

Justifying an Address Space Request

Selling the renumbering task to your company's or organization's management is one thing. If you are requesting new or different address space, either from an ISP or from ARIN or one of the other address delegation authorities, you must also justify why you are making an address allocation request and how you plan to use that address space.

The reason for this second justification is that IP address space, which was once handed out both freely and for free, is now considered a valuable commodity. Internet connectivity is no longer an altruistic scheme to connect researchers and academics, but a fully commercialized, international network. Today, IP address space is regarded as valuable territory with commercial value.

Furthermore, the U.S. federal government has elected to relinquish its responsibilities to operate, adjudicate, and finance operations on the Internet. With no federal agency taking up this responsibility, the National Science Foundation (NSF), the departing Internet "sponsor," is in the process of handing off its responsibilities for running the Internet (as best it can be "run" by anyone) to the private sector.

Network Solutions (NSI) had been given, at one time, exclusive responsibility for handling domain name registration operations in the .com, .org, and .net domains, and for making domain name registration a fee-based, self-supporting business. The original idea had been to reimburse NSI for the expense of running the domain name registration business, which has become a huge administrative operation in the past few years.

When domain name registration was done by the InterNIC, it was a free, federally subsidized service. But federal government sponsorship of the domain name registration business, as well as managing and supervising other parts of the Internet infrastructure, is ending, leaving the operation of what has become big business, to commercial entities. As we noted in Chapter 2, other companies have been allowed by the U.S. Department of Commerce to enter the domain name registration business, and to compete with NSI.

Few people would contest that domain names, as the signposts on "real estate" in the Internet, are without intrinsic value. They have value, and people are willing to pay for their use.

IP Address Space Value

IP address space has gone through the same transformation. Until 1998, assigning IP address space had been done by the InterNIC (which is also run by NSI as part of its agreement with the NSF). However, even when it decided to drop its Internet administration responsibilities, the NSF recognized the need to make administration of the Internet infrastructure a commercial and, in some cases, a profit-making venture.

So, in a modification of its agreement with NSI, the NSF allowed NSI to spin off the address assignment business to a separate entity, which is ARIN. Instead of giving out address space for free, ARIN has established a fee schedule for the use of new IP address space. Like Internet domain names, IP address space now has a perceived intrinsic value, and ARIN charges its customer annual fees for the use of new IP address space.

Since IP addresses are a technical necessity for operation on the Internet, ARIN is a not-for-profit agency, with a fee structure designed to cover its expenses. Even though IP addresses can be thought of as having an intrinsic value, address allocation was never seen as a business, nor an operation that should be competitive. Thus, ARIN provides a necessary service, in return for fees that recover its costs.

ARIN is also charged with the responsibility to see that its customers use IP address space efficiently. So, ARIN evaluates each request from ISPs or from any other organization that requests IP address space according to address allocation and usage guidelines.

Apply Yourself

Justifying an address allocation request to ARIN or to one of the other regional registries in the rest of the world means several things:

- Justifying the amount of address space you are requesting.
- Specifying how that address space will be used.
- Describing the topology and routing in the networks that are being readdressed.
- Identifying the criteria by which you plan to assign the address space.

Each of these points is addressed in a different part of the address space request. The actual application templates categorize an address space request according to current usage, planned usage, and routing.

RFC 2050 is the document that provides guidance for ARIN and other registries for allocating address space. The regional registries may establish their own administrative procedures, but RFC 2050 specifies the criteria the registries must use to evaluate address requests.

Current Address Usage

The first part of a justification for requesting new address space from an address registry will be a description of how you are using the address space that you are currently assigned. ARIN and the other registries are charged with the responsibility for encouraging (although some would say enforcing) efficient address utilization. Obviously, they want to see evidence that an ISP or an organization requesting global address space has made efficient use of its current space before they agree to give it more.

Registries have similar guidelines for how much address space must have been used before they will grant new address space. An application from ISP or a company or organization requesting new address space will be considered if it has used 75 to 80 percent of its address space.

The other consideration will be whether that address space has been used efficiently and allocated carefully. In addition, you may have to show evidence of a reasonable growth projection, to illustrate how whatever address space remains will be used.

Applicants may also be expected to show evidence that they have taken certain address space conservation measures, such as using carefully designed subnetworking schemes, using all-zeroes and all-ones subnets (to make complete use of subnetworked address space), and implementing CIDR address aggregation. Wherever practical, applicants will be expected to have made use of private address ranges, although private network addressing (discussed in Chapter 6) may not be suitable for all network environments. Applicants should make note of any special circumstances that may bolster their claim to having used address space efficiently, including whether they have turned back unused address space.

Current address usage also affects network routing, so the applicant should also include a description of how interior and exterior routing protocols have been used. The goal is not only to make efficient use of address space, but also to foster efficient Internet routing. The objective of the routing plan description is to enable the address registry to determine how well address aggregation has been implemented within the networks covered by the current address assignment.

The responsibility chain for efficient use of address space extends down from the registrar to the ISPs who assign address space to their customers. In some cases, ISPs who apply for address space may be required to present addressing plans used by their customers, particularly if they have large blocks of space in use.

Future Address Usage

Once an applicant has passed the test—that is, proving they have utilized the addresses they have efficiently—they must justify how they plan to use the new space for which they are applying. The applicant must first specify the total number of host addresses that are being requested (not networks) and the rate at which the applicant expects those addresses to be used.

Applicants specify the number of hosts, not networks, because they will be expected to subnetwork whatever CIDR space they are allocated into smaller subnetworks to suit their needs. Registries assume that subnetworking will be used. With CIDR block allocations, there's no practical way around subnetworking; and besides, it's the only way to subdivide CIDR blocks.

The time frame during which the addresses are expected to be used is a key factor in evaluating the addressing request. To that end, the registry may ask the applicant to specify how many addresses are expected to be used in the first 12 months and then through a full 24 months. Some registries may ask for a five-year projection or require a shorter schedule of address usage.

The purpose of inquiring about address usage projections is to prevent address stockpiling. It could be argued that the larger a block an applicant gets, the more it might be able to aggregate its address space into larger and larger CIDR blocks. For example, an ISP that can only justify a /19 CIDR block for use in the next two years may be able to justify a /18 over three years. If the ISP were granted the /18, it would be able to announce a more highly consolidated address block to its next higher provider. However, the standard time horizon is two or three years.

The future usage plan will include a description of the network topology and routing plan with the new address space. It will be similar to the topology and routing plan in the current address usage section, but it will reflect the addition of the new address space.

Next, the registry may want a description of how the ISP or organization plans to allocate addresses to its users or within its networks. The plan should also include the network topology; how routing will be configured and managed; and a plan for subnetworking and subnetwork masking, including how the applicant thinks the addresses will be subnetworked over time.

Of course, it may be impossible for an ISP to predict exactly how much demand its customers will place on the address space or how large its address block allocations will be. The key is to present a reasonable plan that is grounded either in past business operations or in expected future growth.

A certain number of addresses in an assigned address space will most likely not be permanently assigned to hosts. Instead, they may be assigned dynamically by an ISP or by the corporation to dial-up users or to a pool of host addresses that connect through a Network Address Translation (NAT) gateway.

In the interest of address space conservation, addresses for dial-up users should not be assigned to them permanently. Instead, dial-up users, such as those who connect to an ISP's dial-up ports, should get a temporary address assigned at connect time. The address would be one of a pool of however many addresses are necessary to permit the maximum peak number of dial-up users. The dynamic addresses could be taken from private address space, but that would force NAT on each of the addresses. As a practical matter, most ISPs assign "real" assigned addresses to their dial-up pools, and assign them back to dial-up users when they connect. When the dial-up user disconnects, the address is returned to the pool and reused on another dial-up user who calls into the network later.

NAT devices may use the same address pool concept to tag connections to external networks with an externally visible address. Since the external addresses are required only for the duration of a Web site session or an FTP transaction, the NAT device can reuse addresses from an address pool repeatedly.

Summary

Selling the renumbering plan is a management issue as well as an address registrar issue. Management must be sold on the merits and business benefits of the readdressing plan. Likewise, if a new block of address space is needed, the address registry will have to be sold on the technical merits of the plan before it will allocate more IP address space.

Bothersome though both may be, these tasks serve a useful purpose. Convincing management ensures that there is a business benefit to renumbering, and establishes some bounds on anticipated costs and benefits. Convincing the IP address registry that address space has been and will continue to be used efficiently helps certify the technological justification for the plan. More important, it also ensures that the addressing plan will fit into the Internet address aggregation plan and help preserve the IP address space that remains.

Diagrams and Documentation

Renumbering is a lot like painting (and, some might say, just as much fun). House painters will tell you that they spend more time preparing the surface than they actually do painting. Similarly, renumbering a network is the easy part. The hard part is all the preparatory work of determining which addresses are in use, where they have to be changed, and how to reengineer a numbering plan that can survive until it's time to convert to IPv6 or to renumber again.

Most network managers want to do it right the first time, and so are willing to make the effort necessary to ensure that result. The success of a renumbering effort, as well as how smoothly the work progresses, not to mention how transparent it is to end users, is directly proportional to how well the work has been planned.

Anyone who undertakes a renumbering project needs to understand the network's current environment, as well as the shortcomings and limitations of its current numbering plan. In networks that have been planned properly and "grown" with some forethought about where network expansion and change are headed, the current numbering plan may be satisfactory, and only the IP addresses will have to be changed.

Dependencies

Even though it would make the work a lot simpler, a network number-ing plan doesn't exist in isolation from other network elements and ser-vices. IP addresses may be embedded throughout the network, in host and PC configurations, in host name files, and in the DNS records and in DHCP server address pools. Routers use IP addresses, and the iden-tities of the network addresses in use are updated periodically in rout-ing table updates from other routers.

The better part of the planning stage will be spent on these four tasks:

- Identifying the current addressing plan.
- Specifying which network elements use which addresses in the current addressing plan.
- Determining how address numbering should be changed to foster more efficient routing.
- Assessing how to best allow for future growth.

We'll look at these tasks from the perspective of a renumbering plan for a small organization of fewer than 1,000 hosts, in three locations. Obviously, other renumbering projects may be larger or smaller in scope, but a project of this size helps direct the exercise toward good design principles that can be applied to renumbering projects of almost any size.

Preparing the Surface

The following subsections will address the networking issues a network designer must investigate in order to plan a network renumbering task.

Site Plans

A network topology, or the layout of the physical space it occupies, can be more difficult to determine than it would seem. A network adminis-trator needs to know the physical layout of the networks to be able to design a workable network addressing plan.

At first sight, it might seem that the physical layout of the space the networks occupy is irrelevant to the addressing plan. In fact, an under-standing of the physical layout can help a network administrator map addresses to networks. At the least, having a diagram of the network's physical layout will make it easier for the administrator to visualize where the networks will be located and what will be connected to each.

In addition, network cabling is often installed to fit a specific physical space, and network administrators are fond of mapping address ranges to physical sites, floors, or other physical layouts. That is not to say that either the old or the new addressing plan will necessarily follow a specific physical layout. A relationship between the physical layout of a network and its logical addressing topology does not necessarily exist. Nevertheless, site diagrams of the buildings or the locations the addressing plan will cover make it easier to visualize how the networks will be connected and arranged.

Existing Networks (LANs and WANs)

Since this will be a network renumbering project, the next issue to address is to determine which networks exist. Renumbering is not necessarily a network redesign task; that is, renumbering may be done as part of a more comprehensive network redesign project, such as rewiring a building, moving from standard to switched Ethernet, creating VLANs, or consolidating networks.

One of the assumptions that we will make is that if network redesign is part of the task, it has already been done, as those tasks are beyond the scope of this book. We will also assume that we're not going to be making radical changes to the physical or logical layout of the network to do the renumbering. However, some minor corrections may be necessary along the way, such as consolidating or moving LANs to different router ports.

If you're lucky, detailed diagrams already exist that specify the physical layout of the networks in each of the buildings or offices involved, as well as the network addresses that are in use. What we're looking for is something like the network diagram illustrated in Figure 6.1. By "something like" that, we mean they should show enough detail of routers, router port usage, workstation networks, servers, and network services to help you understand exactly what's out there.

The diagrams must also show the IP addresses that are in use on each port, network, host, and server. Obviously, the network addresses now in use, any subnetworking plan, and the range of network addresses in use are critical to analyzing the current numbering plan and to designing a new one. Whether you are reorganizing the address numbering using the current address space or renumbering into new address space, you

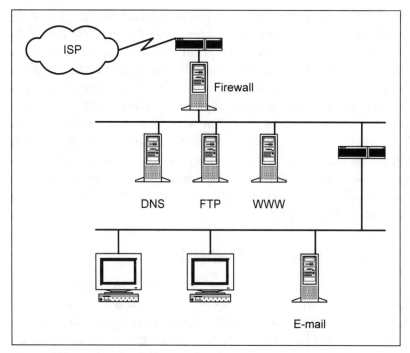

Figure 6.1   A sample of a network diagram for use in documenting network configurations.

must start with a solid understanding of how the address space is currently being used.

Routing

One of the first uses of the network diagrams will be to help you analyze how network routing is currently being done. You'll have to examine the router configuration files to determine which interior and exterior routing protocols are being utilized by the routers and exactly how the network has been divided into subnetworks.

The routing protocols in use are important because you will want to be able to configure networks so that they make best use of the internal and external routing protocols. For example, a network that uses the original version of the Routing Information Protocol (RIP-I) doesn't understand subnetwork prefix masks. Consequently, a network, or a part of a network, that uses RIP-I can't use subnetwork prefixes to aggregate routes.

ADDRESS DISCOVERY TOOLS

A number of programs are available that can survey a network to determine the current addressing plan. The diagrams and reports that these programs create can be of tremendous assistance in assessing the current plan and in planning a new addressing plan.

For example, Optimal Surveyor, a program from Optimal Networks, Inc., can create detailed network maps, showing network servers, routers, workstations, and hosts, as well as IP address ranges in use, addresses of router and server ports, and a number of other network characteristics. All of this information is invaluable to an addressing redesign task, and programs like Surveyor can do it automatically in a matter of hours.

Surveyor, like other network inventory programs, uses SNMP requests to locate network devices and to discover their network addresses. Like other programs of its ilk, it's not perfect. Devices that are set to deny SNMP requests, such as firewalls, shield anything behind them from the program. In addition, it sees only SNMP-monitorable devices, so everything in the network that is to be "discovered" must understand SNMP queries. Since SNMP works by passing a *community string*, similar to a password, to queried devices, they must also be set to use the same community string as the network survey tool.

Even though they may not be entirely complete, the network maps and IP address information that a network survey tool can provide can be of tremendous assistance in a network design project.

Other interior protocols, such as IGRP, understand these route aggregation prefixes and can be configured to consolidate or aggregate routes to an exterior gateway. Designing a network reengineering plan implies creating a flexible and adaptable addressing plan. It also implies developing an addressing plan that meshes with an internal and external routing plan. In the interests of simplifying routing on the Internet at large, a network addressing plan should be designed so that the network gateway or gateways announce as few networks as possible to other ISPs or to the Internet.

External WAN Links

A network's wide area network (WAN) links to other networks may also affect the network reengineering plan. The router interfaces to most WAN links must be assigned IP addresses that are part of the company or organization's network address space. In most cases, router interfaces to WAN links are numbered from a small subnet, just big enough for the two interfaces required.

Interfaces to other types of WAN links can be numbered from a larger pool of addresses, or even left without any IP addresses at all. For example, a frame relay network that connects several router WAN interfaces into a multipoint network can be numbered on the same subnet, so that the router interfaces see each other across the frame relay "cloud," as if they were part of a small, private subnet.

The point is that the type of WAN links and the number and hierarchy of WAN interconnections must also be understood to develop a sound readdressing plan.

Current Addressing Plan

Network routing, WAN link types and configurations, and existing network configurations are the background information for the current addressing plan. You'll need all of the items we've discussed so far, including the site plans, routing protocols, WAN links, and LAN configurations and types, to assess the current network addressing plan.

At the least, you'll want to draw a network addressing map that illustrates the IP addresses that are in use today on the LANs, WANs, and routers. The first problem that you will have is to determine which network addresses are in use.

Types of Addresses in Use

While CIDR address ranges break down the traditional boundaries between Class A, B, and C addresses, the network designer can use the address map to identify the types of addresses in use. Are all of the organization's IP network addresses derived from the same Class B address block? If so, the organization probably holds a class B allocation, which it may subnetwork throughout all of the company's locations.

Class B addresses are difficult to get today, so holding a Class B address may also mean that the organization has held the address space for quite a while. Holding address space for several years may mean one of two things, or both. First, it probably means that host addresses from the Class B range have had years to become embedded in applications, host address tables, configuration files, and access control lists. Consequently, they're going to be harder to root out of the network. The second thing is that a Class B address usually means that the organization has had enough address space to subnetwork it to a fare-thee-well, drawing out smaller and smaller pieces of it to meet its addressing needs. On the other hand, a Class B address space is large enough that an organization can do less subnetworking, and assign addresses more liberally. The upside of this is that the organization probably may not have had to get additional address space outside the Class B space.

Previously, any IP address would work as well as any other, so keeping all IP addresses within the same address block hasn't been a huge concern of network managers. But CIDR address aggregation has changed all of that. And an organization that has numbered from a single Class B may have also acquired other Class C addresses that it was assigned by an ISP for a branch office or a special Internet service. Since Class C addresses have been, and still are, relatively easy to get, there may be a number of Class Cs in use in the organization's networks. The problem may be that they've been assigned over a period of time by a number of address delegators. As a result, they may not be contiguous, so the Class Cs may be difficult or impossible to consolidate into any kind of CIDR block. That's not a fatal problem, but the network designer who is trying to aggregate addresses may well have to renumber the networks to do so.

Unaggregated or Unaggregatable Addresses

A network readdressing plan should be designed to aggregate as many addresses as possible, so that other networks see as large a block of addresses as possible from your network. This helps simplify routing on the Internet, and it makes it possible for your own network to use routing protocols like OSPF.

The address space that is in use now may be composed of a completely random selection of Class Cs. If they were acquired over time, and requested as they were needed from an ISP or another address delegating authority, the addresses may be neither contiguous nor, for that matter, anywhere near each other.

If address space from the same CIDR block has been assigned to the organization, but not used so that address space can be aggregated, it may be possible to renumber the networks so that the addresses can be aggregated. Of course, if the renumbering project is to be done in completely new address space, such as from a different ISP, the old address block is irrelevant.

Private Address Space

Private addresses are easy to identify, because they always fall in the same address ranges, as specified by RFC 1918, which sets aside network addresses 10.0.0.0, 172.16–32.0.0, and 192.168.1–255.0. These addresses are unroutable on the Internet. IP routers know that traffic from these private network addresses is not intended to be on the Internet, so IP routers anywhere in the Internet will discard traffic addressed to or from private addresses.

The private addresses were originally set aside for use on networks that were operated for experimental purposes. However, as the address space crunch has made it more and more difficult to get more IP address space, some organizations have used private addresses for their own internal networks. The private network addresses must be translated to unique, public network addresses for the traffic to reach Internet addresses.

First, use of private network addresses implies that network address translation (NAT) is being done somewhere on the network, probably at the firewall. It also means that the organization has some real, routable "public" address space, most likely configured on the firewall, NAT device, or proxy server. That public address space, which may be available only by examining the configuration files of the proxy server, NAT device, or firewall, is an indication of how many public addresses the organization really needs, assuming that everyone in the organization has Internet connectivity.

Keep in mind that since private address space is free of the constraints that are imposed on public address space, the organization may not have been careful to use that space in the most efficient manner. In addition, there's little reason to summarize routes with private address space, because there's no benefit to be gained by announcing a complete block of private address space to an outside network. As a result, the addressing plan of a network that uses private address space may be a good candidate for reorganizing the use of addresses in an address reengineering project.

Private addresses aren't bad, nor do they imply an inefficient internal routing architecture. A network designer may elect to continue to use private addresses, assuming there is a justification for doing so. Some of the reasons to continue using private address space, even in a renumbering project, are:

Security. Internal network hosts that use private addresses are fairly secure from outside attacks, because an external attacker can't address them directly.

NAT. A firewall or proxy server that does network address translation may be in place, requiring translation of all internal addresses anyway.

Address space conservation. Private addresses conserve public address space, although address space conservation is a benefit of using private address space, not a reason to use it.

ISP portability. ISPs assign externally visible IP addresses for their customers, so the use of private address space on an internal network is not affected by changes in the external addresses assigned by ISPs.

Private address space adds the complication of network address translation, but organizations that don't mind that complication, or that have experience with NAT, may want to continue to use private address space.

Subnetworks

The subnetworking plan that has already been implemented is a clue to how efficiently the current address space has been used, whether the current interior routing protocols can use it, and how aggressively the address space can be subdivided in the future. Subnetworking is essential to address aggregation, so its use in the current addressing plan may be an indication of how it can be used in a future plan.

While the address ranges will most likely change in a readdressing project, the subnetworking plan may not. A good subnetworking plan, evidenced by efficient address aggregation or efficient interior routing in the current network, can be carried forward into a new addressing plan.

Business Partner Address Ranges

If you're going to the trouble to change the addresses in your networks, you must also consider the address ranges that business partners or other organizations to which you have permanent connections use. That is, if your organization and a business partner are both planning to use private address space, you should avoid using the same private address space.

And because business partners often turn into merger and acquisition targets, private address space can be an issue because two firms involved in an acquisition may have chosen to use the same private addresses. Of course, it's not feasible to predict how potential acquisitions will affect addressing.

Renumbering does become an issue in a merger or an acquisition if the acquired company's networks are merged into the new parent company's networks. If all Internet connectivity is to go through the parent company's Internet connections, it may be necessary or desirable to renumber the acquired networks to get them into the parent company's CIDR blocks.

Network Expansion Plans

Renumbering is a forward-looking process, in that it is an opportunity to redesign the network to meet future needs. Therefore, a network designer and the numbering plan redesign must anticipate those future needs, but they can only do so to the extent that the organization's network expansion plans are known.

We can't foretell the future, but we can anticipate growth and we can plan for it. Even the process of justifying a request for new or additional address space from an address delegator or from an ISP includes some provision for future growth. An addressing plan must allow for future network growth, and even for unanticipated changes in network size and configuration.

One way to allow for controlled, orderly growth is to design a hierarchical addressing structure, such as one required for Variable Length Subnet Masking, or VLSM, which is discussed in Chapter 7. Some of the branches of this structure can be left empty, to be filled later when the network grows into the additional space.

The drive to conserve address space and to force address aggregation make it difficult for network designers to plan too far into the future of their networks. Unless you have an entire Class B address or a sufficiently large CIDR block of Class C equivalents to work with, accommodating both future growth and address aggregation are competing, and not necessarily compatible, goals.

Available Address Ranges

One of the things that a network survey will reveal is the address ranges that are currently in use in the network. Presumably, someone in the organization will have records of which addresses have been used and where they have been used, but that's not always the case. Obviously, if the network redesign doesn't call for obtaining any new address space, it will have to use the address space already available.

If the objective of network readdressing is to reorganize the network to make routing more efficient, it's likely that the current address ranges can be reused. It may, however, be necessary to do some aggressive subnetworking to design an efficient routing architecture, but that's a desirable outcome, too.

It is also possible that a network survey will *not* reveal address ranges that are assigned to the organization but that aren't in use. Before designing an addressing plan that will reuse current address ranges, the network administrator should check with his or her ISP or with his or her address delegation authority to determine the exact address ranges that have been assigned to the organization.

The InterNIC's WHOIS database should also be searched to verify that the addresses that are in use really do belong to the organization. Probably they wouldn't have worked had they not been assigned properly, but it's worth checking.

ISP Connections

Maintaining the network's connections to the Internet may be one of the prime motivations for readdressing the network, so the nature, number, and configuration of those connections is one of the key elements of a numbering plan redesign.

One of the goals of readdressing may be to improve IP address routability. If it is, the new routing and addressing plans must be designed from the ISP connections down through the network. The goal will be to build a hierarchy of addresses, starting at the ISP connection, in order to aggregate the network's addresses to as few external routing announcements as possible.

A secondary, compatible goal will be to design a hierarchy of subnetworks that will subdivide the network into smaller address ranges to accommodate the network's hosts. The subnetworking design will also permit VLSM, which will help shape the subnetworks more closely to the size of subnetworks needed.

Router Layout and Connectivity

The numbers, locations, and capabilities of the routers in the networks behind the ISP connections will influence the subnetworking plan.

Some routers may have to be moved or repositioned to support the subnetworking plan.

Say, for example, a company currently has two Class Cs in use in its Los Angeles and San Diego offices. If the company plans to establish a new office in the San Bernardino area, the network designer will have to decide whether to take the addresses to support the new hosts from the Los Angeles or the San Diego address ranges. In either case, a new router may have to be positioned in the San Bernardino office, and configured to support the appropriate subnet of Los Angeles or San Diego. If both the Los Angeles and San Diego offices and the new office will be numbered from a single CIDR block, all three routers will each have to be assigned a CIDR subnet of the new address range.

Renumbering may also be a good opportunity to upgrade routers, add more router ports, or upgrade router operating systems. The countervailing argument to that, however, says that renumbering can introduce its own errors and confusion, and that changing the routing infrastructure at the same time as renumbering networks may compound any problems that occur.

To simplify troubleshooting, it's probably best not to attempt to upgrade routers and renumber networks at the same time. One of the goals of a renumbering project is to make users largely unaware that it has happened, and interrupting network operations with a lengthy outage won't accomplish that goal.

Interior and Exterior Routing Protocols

The interior and exterior routing protocols in use can only be confirmed by examining the configuration of the network's routers. The routing protocols fall into two categories: interior and exterior routing protocols. The interior routing protocols are used by the network's routers to describe the network to each other. The exterior routing protocols pass routing information to ISPs or to other business partners.

The routing protocols may not be affected at all by renumbering. But if the network uses a simple interior protocol such as RIP-I, and the renumbering plan uses subnetworking (which it probably will), it will be necessary to upgrade the interior routing protocol. RIP-I does not include subnetwork mask information in routing table updates, so it cannot support VLSM or other route aggregation strategies.

If the network is using static routes to an ISP, and therefore is not using an exterior protocol such as BGP4, it's probably best to try to continue doing so. If the networks are renumbered, the static routes your network is announcing will change. However, if static routing works, and the network has nothing to gain from using an exterior protocol such as BGP, it's probably best not to add the complication of BGP if you don't have to do so.

Firewalls and NAT

Firewalls, screening routers, and other security devices play a double role in a network. They may act as security devices and they may also function as network address translation (NAT) devices. The issue in a network redesign will be to identify the location and precise function of the firewalls and screening routers, and the address ranges they translate, if they are configured to do address translation. Many firewalls merely screen traffic, but NAT may be configured to conceal internal host addresses, or to translate private IP addresses to public addresses.

Firewalls have traditionally been placed at the entrance points to networks, such as where the ISP connection enters the network. However, it may be more practical to place them deeper within the network, as close as possible to applications and hosts, in addition to at the Internet access point.

An internal network may be so large that it's not sound security practice to assume that all intruder attacks will come only through the Internet connection. Systems and applications must be protected from internal attacks and probes, too, and the most practical way to do that is to position firewalls and intrusion detection systems inside the network, adjacent to systems with sensitive or confidential data. Internal security systems may not address translation, but they do have rule sets describing access rights.

The network designer can't expect to understand fully what a firewall has been configured to do unless he or she can examine the firewall's rule sets. The rule sets describe the actions that are permitted and denied by a firewall. Actions may be permitted or denied by application type (based on the TCP port numbers in the TCP header) or on specific host or network addresses that are allowed or denied access.

A network readdressing plan must accommodate the address screening rules on a firewall or screening router. The addresses that the firewall screens must be mapped back to the addresses of the users who are allowed access, so that the rule sets can be changed after renumbering. If DHCP is used to assign users dynamic addresses, the addresses of permitted users may fall in a range of addresses assigned by DHCP, instead of identifying specific host IDs.

In addition, if the firewall does network address translation—as many firewalls do—either its internal and external address range, or both, may change in a readdressing plan. If the reason for the read-dressing program is a change of ISPs, the externally visible addresses will change, assuming that they had been assigned by the previous ISP and they aren't provider-independent addresses. The firewall may have to be configured with the new internal address ranges, particularly if the firewall does static address translation.

Authentication of externally connected devices, such as remote users who connect over VPN services through the Internet, probably won't be affected by readdressing. Their addresses are usually assigned dynamically by an ISP's dial-up service, so the firewall may not care what the external address is.

Intrusion Detection Systems (IDS)

An IDS monitors external traffic that comes into the network to detect attacks from intruders or to screen internal users' access to prohibited Web sites or applications. In an address redesign, the address ranges for internal systems that are screened by the IDS will change. External address range screens won't change, except when the addresses of border routers with other networks also change.

An internal IDS system, used to detect browsing or intrusion from internal network users, must also be changed in a readdressing plan. An internal IDS is usually configured to know about all of the internal network address ranges, so that it can distinguish between traffic that originates from hosts inside the network and hosts that have passed through the firewall that screens external connections.

Proxy Servers

Proxy servers often do network address translation when they set up a proxy connection to an external host, in that the connection originates from the proxy server's address, not the address of the real source. If the proxy server is positioned behind the firewall, as it usually is, then the address range that the proxy server uses for its proxied connections will also change in a readdressing program.

The firewall will also have to be configured to accept the new address ranges from the proxy server. The firewall will most likely have a rule set that permits external connections only from specific addresses, which are the ones the proxy server uses for its external connections. If the internal addressing plan changes, the addresses to which the proxy server translates proxied connections will also change.

The network designer may also have to check the firewall rule sets to see if there is some special way the firewall handles proxied connection requests and connection requests from privileged users whose connections are not proxied. That means the firewall's rules may call for hosts in different address ranges to be handled differently, and the rule sets must be modified appropriately in an addressing redesign.

Dial-Up Access or Remote Access Service (RAS)

Dial-up users won't be affected by a network readdressing program, except to the extent that the address pool from which they receive dynamically assigned addresses will change. However, those addresses are usually assigned at connection time, and as long as they work, remote users aren't particularly concerned about what their temporary IP address is.

But if the RAS is outside the firewall, its new address range will have to be configured on the firewall, so that the addresses are permitted to pass inside the network. If the firewall does NAT, the new inside address range will already have been configured on the firewall, and won't affect the RAS server's addresses. If the addresses do change, as they might when the organization is changing ISPs, the firewall will have to know about the new RAS address pool range.

Domain Name Service (DNS)

Changes in network addressing will affect the Domain Name Service (DNS) records, particularly those that refer to internal network hosts. The DNS may be configured as a single service for the network, with all records for internal and external hosts. Networks with firewalls or NAT devices usually have two DNSes, one listing internal hosts and some external hosts, and a second DNS outside the firewall with only a few externally visible hosts.

If the network addresses change, the DNS addresses will have to change, too. Coordinating the address changes in the DNS services with the changes in the addresses on the network will be one of the challenges of the readdressing project. It may be necessary to keep both sets of addresses in the DNS until the readdressing project has been completed.

The extent to which the DNS records will be affected by readdressing also depends on how many hosts there are in a DNS. For example, many DNS services only list resource records, or RRs, for hosts that provide network services, such as e-mail and the DNS service itself. In networks with PCs that host personal Web pages, there may be DNS records for many of the PCs on the network. DNS records for individual PCs may be updated dynamically by the DHCP service, if both the DNS and the DHCP know about each other, and both the DNS and DHCP have been configured to update the DNS files when an address has been assigned to a host. Windows NT DNS and DHCP, for example, can be configured to do this.

The addresses of externally visible hosts, such as a public Web site, an anonymous FTP site, a mail exchange host, or the externally visible DNS name service itself on an outside DNS will have to be changed only if the network's external address range changes. That means if the organization is renumbering the network to make internal routing more efficient, or to consolidate addresses into more easily summarized routes, external DNS addresses won't change. But if the organization is changing ISPs, and therefore changing its external address range, too, all the externally visible DNS addresses will also change.

The network designer may have to coordinate DNS address changes with whomever administers the DNS. It may be done by the organization's DNS administrator or by someone in the IS department. If the DNS is maintained by an ISP, address changes will have to be coordinated with the ISP.

Applications

Applications sometimes have IP addresses embedded in them. The addresses may indicate the server or host on which the application runs, or the clients that are permitted to access the application. In some networks, IP addresses are embedded in application clients or servers for security reasons, to restrict access from specific hosts or to specific servers.

For example, an application may be designed to be accessible only by specific users. As a security measure, the application may require that data updates or inquiries only be permitted from specific IP addresses. These IP addresses may be the host addresses or the network address range of the authorized users of the application or of other hosts or applications with which the application must work.

Similarly, the addresses of the servers or hosts running the applications may be embedded in the client-side code, to direct all data or transaction updates to the correct host. Often, this is both a security and a transaction assurance measure, so that application transactions that originate at specific network clients are bound to specific hosts running the application.

Embedded IP addresses are usually static, meaning they are not changed dynamically, as DHCP addresses are. Consequently, servers or hosts that run applications or that run network services are usually assigned static network addresses. Their addresses can't be dynamic, because client-side applications or clients that need dependable access to network services have to know a fixed address to reference each time. It is possible to assign dynamic addresses to servers and application hosts, and resolve them through DNS lookups, but it's usually not efficient to do so. The implication is that just as specific blocks of addresses in an address range will be assigned dynamically by DHCP, another block of addresses will be assigned permanently to some hosts, servers, and even client-side PCs and workstations.

Application-embedded addresses are often the most difficult to find. Because they are embedded either in the client or the server side of an application, and not necessarily in DNS files, they frequently escape notice until after readdressing has been completed. Only then do users find that some applications don't work or that certain applications don't get data updates, because clients and servers with embedded addresses can't find each other any more.

The network designer must coordinate the addressing redesign plan with whomever controls network applications. Otherwise, embedded addresses may not be discovered until midway through the process or after the address conversion is completed, when applications stop working. Rendering applications dysfunctional isn't one of the desired consequences of a readdressing project.

Hosts and Printers

Like the addresses embedded in applications, some hosts, printers, and other legacy systems may also have IP addresses embedded in them. It is not uncommon for the IP addresses to be configured in the host or printer's configuration files. These addresses must also be changed if the network is renumbered.

Sometimes examining applications for embedded IP addresses will help the network administrator compile a list of hosts, printers, and other systems that have hard-coded IP addresses. Frequently host applications specify a list of printers to which print jobs can be sent. A host application may only list the name or alias for printers, leaving the

IP address resolution to DNS. The application may also maintain a table linking printer names to addresses.

Summary

This chapter does not include everything to consider before doing a network redesign, but it does point out to the network designer most of the network elements that will affect or be affected by a network redesign or a network renumbering project.

Like those house painters who spend most of their time preparing the surface, not actually painting, the network designer will also spend most of his or her time planning and designing; the actual adding of address ranges will take a relatively short amount of time.

Subnetworking

There comes a time in most network administrators' lives when they realize that either they aren't going to write the great American novel or that their network address space isn't quite as big as they thought when it was first assigned. Admittedly, few network administrators see themselves as the next Hemingway, so the latter is a more likely conclusion than the former. In fact, running short of usable IP address space, and then devising ways to tailor whatever address space is available, is a common problem for the network administration set.

To the casual or IP address-challenged observer, the three types of IP addresses—Classes A, B, and C—appear to be immutable, unyielding to any attempt to modify their rigid structure to accommodate changing or new network conditions. In fact, this structure can be made to bend, thanks to the way that IP routers work. IP routers allow a network administrator to subdivide IP address space in ways that were not originally intended by Postel, Cerf, & Company back in the late 1970s.

This technique, known as subnetworking, allows network administrators to tailor IP address space to their specific needs, and is an important tool for network administrators for three reasons:

Flexibility. Network administrators may want to or need to tailor the IP address space they have been assigned, to accommodate changes in network structure and topology.

Efficiency. IP address classes impose limits on how efficiently a network administrator can employ the address assigned to his or her networks.

Simplicity. Subnetworking simplifies the external appearance of a network, which simplifies network routers' jobs to get traffic to it quickly and efficiently.

Subnetworking allows network administrators to carve up Class A, B, or C network addresses into many smaller networks. More important, this network tailoring can be made invisible to anything outside of the network on which it is done. Most important, subnetworking can work its magic without disturbing the operation of the Internet. The flexibility and transparency of subnetworking are key to making the sometimes arbitrary boundaries of Class A, B, and C addressing fit more closely to an organization's specific networking needs and circumstances.

Less Wasted Space

Another benefit of subnetworking is that it helps make complete use of the available IP address space. Without subnetworking, a great deal of the IP address space that has been assigned or that is available would be wasted, stranded in assigned, but unused, address blocks.

The problem of stranded IP address space is an unfortunate consequence of the IP address numbering system that creates Class A, B, and C network addresses. More sophisticated address management and assignment techniques, such as Classless Inter-Domain Routing (CIDR), alleviate this problem. We discussed CIDR more fully in Chapter 3.

While the story did not turn out so happily for her, at least Goldilocks was able to find one of the Three Bears' porridge bowls, rocking chairs, and beds to be exactly right and just her size. Less fortunate are many network administrators who find that both Class A and Class B network addresses are too large for their needs and Class C network addresses are too small. Without a happy medium—smaller than a Class B, yet bigger than a Class C address (a Class B$\frac{1}{2}$, maybe?)—many network administrators ask for Class Bs but end up with a number of Class Cs.

The problem is most evident in the disparity between the number of host addresses available in a Class B network address and the number available in a Class C network address. A Class B address uses the first 2 bytes of the 4-byte, 32-bit IP address space for the network ID, and the last 2 bytes for host IDs on that network. That means that each Class B network can have more than 65,000 hosts on it. This is all well and good; and from the 1980's perspective of Jonathan Postel, Vinton Cerf, Leonard Kleinrock, and others who created the IP addressing scheme, it was not unreasonable. After all, at that time, it was possible that the number of computers would grow, and they might be connected as endpoints over a single large national or global wide area network.

A Class C address, on the other hand, uses the first 3 bytes for the network number, and only the last byte for hosts on that network, meaning there can be only 255 (2^8) hosts on a Class C network. Again, from that 1970's perspective, it was thought that this small network size might be useful for very small closed community networks or experimental systems. Postel and his colleagues might have foreseen the development of local area networks like Ethernet; it had been described in an ACM article in 1978 and introduced as a commercial product in 1980. A Class C address was suitable for an Ethernet, even if it was a little small for the 1,024 device limit per Ethernet segment.

So, a Class B can house more than 65,000 hosts, and a Class C can do the same for 255 hosts. However, the problem is that there's no standard IP address block anywhere between 65,000 and 255. For most organizations, one is too big and the other is too small. This is why, in days gone by, many organizations asked for and got Class B network addresses, even if they had only a few hundred hosts on their networks. The alternative for an organization with a few hundred or even a few thousand hosts was to get a set of Class C addresses. From a management standpoint, it was thought easier to keep things in a single address block, so most organizations asked for a Class B address block.

Let's say that BigCo had 5,000 hosts on 20 LANs. Through the miracle of subnetworking, the Class B address, BigCo's network administrator could separate the Class B address space into as many as 255 subnets. This all works, but there's one catch: Though it doesn't affect the network administrator, it exacerbates the problem of IP address supply. That is, the growth of the Internet has sent demand for IP addresses skyrocketing. The 32-bit IP address space can provide 4.3 billion separate host addresses. However, 65,000 of these IP addresses are in BigCo's 190.150.0.0 address block, and BigCo is only using 5,000 of those addresses. No other company can use the 190.150.0.0 address block, because the Internet's routers wouldn't have a single destination for all traffic in the block.

As a result, more than 90 percent of the usable address space in the 190.150.0.0 address block will be unintentionally stranded. It will be unused by BigCo (although it might be used in the future) and unavailable for use elsewhere in the Internet.

The Basics of Subnetworking

The purpose of IP addresses, and in a larger sense, IP itself, is to identify a specific host on a specific network somewhere on the Internet. The IP address may be hard-coded into the host's software, assigned by DHCP or bootP, the Unix version of DHCP, or configured into the system's network interface configuration by the system administrator. The IP address identifies the host or the interface as the endpoint on a network somewhere on the Internet.

The IP address is divided into two parts, defined here and depicted in Figure 7.1:

Network identifier. Identifies a specific network.

Host identifier. Identifies a specific host, which is located on a specific network.

The combination of the network ID and the host ID constitute the IP address of a specific device somewhere on the Internet or network. We say somewhere, because today there is no correlation whatsoever between a host or a network's IP addresses, and where it is physically located on the Internet or where it is in the world.

To use the phone number analogy again, the physical location of phone numbers can be targeted by deciphering the area code and the local exchange number. There is no such correlation between IP addresses and physical location. Routing on large, complex networks like the Internet might be less complicated if there were, but IP addresses are assigned today without regard to physical location, even though there is a proposal to "regionalize" IP address assignments with the proposed next version of the IP protocol, IPv6.

A host is part of a network, and the combination of the host ID and the network ID constitutes the host's IP address. However, the networks to which those hosts belong have IP address identities, too. Net-

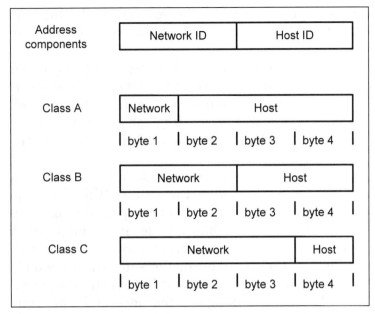

Figure 7.1   Network and host identifiers in an IP address.

works are identified by the network portion of the IP address alone, not the host portion of the IP address.

So, a host with an IP address of:

26.5.0.2

is host number 0.5.0.2 on network 26.0.0.0. If we interpret the IP address as a regular IP address, the first number falls in the range between 1 and 127. Therefore, it's a Class A address, which means the first number identifies the network and the last three numbers identify a host on that network.

IP Addresses and IP Routers

Although that full IP address is essential for identifying a specific destination computer, IP routers don't care about all that. They're interested in getting IP packets as quickly as possible to a router or a computer that serves as the gateway for the network on which a specific host is located. Eventually, the router or computer that is a gateway to the network will have to worry about the host ID as well, to deliver the packet to the destination computer, but the routers on the Internet aren't concerned with that. All they care about is the network portion of the IP address.

The Internet's routers see the full, 4-byte IP address, but they're not interested in the host ID portion. They need to identify only the network portion of the address. Once a router has identified the network portion of the IP address, it checks its routing tables for a route by which to get the packet to that network; thereafter, it forwards the packet.

Because routers only care about network IDs, and as long as a network administrator understands what the routers "think" is happening, he or she can play around with the address space through subnetworking, to make better use of it than IP's designers intended. A network administrator can subdivide, or subnetwork, a Class B network into tens, hundreds, or thousands of smaller subnetworks, simply by making routers think that they are sending IP packets to a single, unified Class B network. Subnetworking is a charade—and a perfectly legal one, if it's done right—that gives network administrators a wide measure of IP addressing flexibility that was never designed into the IP addressing scheme.

Subnetworks and Addresses

Consider this example of subdividing a single Class B network address with IP address subnetworking. Let's say that BigCo requested and, by some miracle, received a Class B network address of 190.150.0.0. It's a Class B, and by definition, a classful address, so the first 2 bytes (190.150) of the address identify the network and the last 2 bytes (0.0) are to be used for hosts on that network.

Remember, ARIN, BigCo's ISP, or, before that, the InterNIC, assigns network IDs, not host IDs. Assigning a network ID gives the network administrator the responsibility and the flexibility to assign host IDs within that IP address space in any way that is suitable.

BigCo's network administrator wants to use the 190.150.0.0 address space for all of the hosts on the company network, which is located behind a router connecting it to its ISP. The network administrator can use the last 2 bytes of the 190.150 network address to assign 65,536 separate host IDs. That's more than enough for BigCo's computer systems and servers. But the network administrator doesn't want everything to be on the same network; he'd like to have a number of smaller

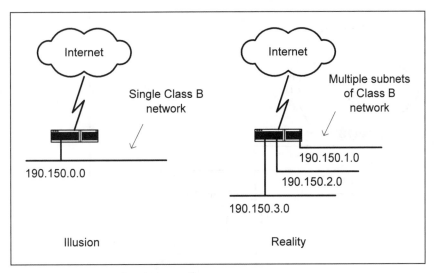

Figure 7.2 Route advertisement by an IP router.

networks connected behind the main router, and he doesn't want to have to ask for another Class B network address or deal with a number of smaller Class C network addresses.

BigCo's network administrator decides to get creative with the 190.150.0.0 IP address space. After all, he thinks, BigCo's router (depicted in Figure 7.2) would only advertise to other Internet routers a route to network 190.150.0.0. Since Internet routers only care about the network ID part of an IP address, all Internet routers will send anything with a destination IP address starting with 190.150. to his router.

Once it gets to his router, he thinks, he can tell his router how to direct traffic to the networks behind it. External routers won't see anything that he has done behind the router, as long as the subdivided networks behind his router appear to the outside world to be the single network 190.150.0.0.

To create the subnetworks behind his router (something his router and all other routers support), BigCo's network administrator decides to number all of the hosts on the router's backside Port 2 with host IDs that start with 190.150.1. The first host is 190.150.1.1, the second 190.150.1.2, and so forth, up to 190.150.1.254. On Port 3, he numbers all hosts with IDs that start with 190.150.2. The first host is 190.150.2.1, the second 190.150.2.2, and so forth, up to 190.150.2.254. Figure 7.3 illustrates this configuration.

What the network administrator has done is to subdivide the Class B network address space into a number of smaller networks, while main-

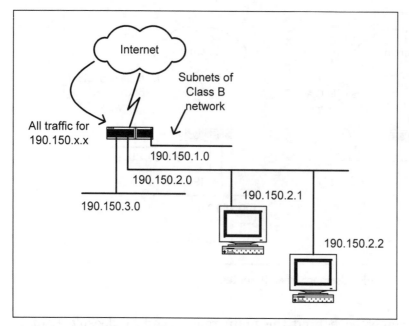

Figure 7.3 Subnetworked addresses from a single Class B network address.

taining the integrity of the Class B network address space; that is, his router still advertises a route to network 190.150.0.0. As far as Internet routers are concerned, an entire Class B network lays behind his router. In fact, it does, but the network administrator has made different use of the address space.

The key point here is that as long as the router understands what is happening, specifically that the Class B address space has been divided into subnetworks, and that the router knows how to get to the subnetworks behind it, none of the details of subnetworking make any difference to Internet routers. In fact, all of the details of subnetworking, not to mention that it has been done it at all, are completely hidden from anything outside the router.

By using the third byte of the IP address space as part of the network address, the network administrator created subnetworks 190.150.1.0 and 190.150.2.0. The value of the third byte can go up to 254, so the network administrator could create as many as 254 separate subnetworks, through 190.150.254.0, behind the router. Since only the value of the third byte would change, each of the subnetworks could be referred to as 190.150.1.0, 190.150.2.0, 190.150.3.0, and so forth, up to 190.150.256.0.

Of course, these numbers for the subnetworks would actually be the decimal equivalent of binary numbers in the "real" IP address. The first of these, 190.150.1.0, would be this decimal translation of the binary number:

10111110.10010110.00000001.00000000

The next network address, 190.150.2.0, would be this decimal translation of its binary equivalent:

10111110.10010110.00000010.00000000

The last subnet, 190.150.254.0, would be the following decimal translation of the last binary number:

10111110.10010110.11111110.00000000

Again, what really counts is the binary number, not its decimal equivalent. Although it's easier for us to understand the decimal equivalent, it's important to keep in mind the binary math behind the decimal numbers. When we discuss more advanced subnetworking, picturing the binary numbers will be essential to understanding the concepts.

Stockpiling Subnets

Another benefit of subnetworking is that BigCo's network administrator wouldn't have to use any of the subnetworks until he had a requirement for a new one, or an available router port. Until then, the subnetworks would simply sit idle, in reserve for the organization's use.

In our example, the network administrator subnetworked the Class B address space by using the third byte as an additional part of the network number. This is known as *subnetworking on a byte boundary*. Class A addresses use the last 3 bytes for host addresses, so the same thing can be done with a Class A address. A Class A network can be subdivided by using the second byte, or the second and third bytes, for the subnetwork identifier.

A network administrator who really wanted to get fancy could even create subnetworks of subnetworks with a Class A address, by using the second byte as a primary subnetwork ID and the third byte as a secondary subnetwork beneath the primary subnetwork. On the other hand, this might get too confusing to be worth the trouble.

Masking

The router is the key to making subnetworking work; it hides the sub-networks from external routers, and it has to keep track of which sub-networks have been created behind it, and how to find them.

The tool the router uses to determine how to interpret IP addresses, and to discover if it is doing subnetworking at all, is a concept known as a *mask*. A mask is a binary number that identifies to the router which bits of an IP address are being used for the network ID number. A binary 1 in the mask indicates a bit of the IP address that is being used as the network number, and a binary 0 indicates a bit that is being used for the host number.

Subnetworking depends on using part of the IP address space that is supposed to be used for something else (the host address) for another purpose, which is to create more network addresses. The trade-off is that using part of the host address space for network IDs reduces the number of host addresses available. However, that's a worthwhile compromise, because subnetworking is usually done where the host address space is too large anyway, such as in Class B address space.

The mask, or *netmask*, is a tool to indicate to the router whether sub-networking is being used. The router applies the mask against IP addresses to determine which bits it should use to identify the network number, in order to make a routing decision to get data to a specific network. In the absence of a mask, or the use of a default mask, IP routers conclude that subnetworking is not being done, and that Class A, B, and C addresses should be interpreted according to the original RFC 790 definitions.

For example, a standard Class B IP address uses the bits of the first 2 bytes for the network ID, and the bits of the last 2 bytes for the host ID. A binary 1 in the mask indicates which of the bits of the binary IP address are to be interpreted as the network address. The mask for a standard Class B address would look like this:

11111111.11111111.00000000.00000000

This mask tells the router, "The bits in the first and second bytes are to be interpreted as the network number."

If the network administrator decides to subnetwork the Class B address by using the first, second, and third bytes of the Class B address as the network ID, the mask would look like this:

11111111.11111111.11111111.00000000

This mask tells the router, "All of the bits in the first, second, and third bytes are to be interpreted as the network number."

Misleading Masks

Masks aren't difficult to understand, but they can be misleading. The first misleading aspect of a mask is that, like an IP address, the binary digits of the mask are usually translated back to a decimal number for our use. When, for binary-challenged humans, the mask is expressed in decimal form, it looks like an IP address: It has the same dotted decimal format—but the numbers are unusually high for "real" IP addresses. For example, the binary version of the standard Class B network mask is:

11111111.11111111.00000000.00000000

This mask's binary numbers translate to this decimal value:

255.255.0.0

The second misleading aspect of masks is that for two different networking schemes the masks might be identical. For example, the mask for a subnetworked Class B address that uses the first, second, and third bytes of the IP address as a network address would be:

11111111.11111111.11111111.00000000

However, the mask for a standard Class C network address also uses the first, second, and third bytes of the IP address for the network address. Consequently, the standard Class C netmask is also:

11111111.11111111.11111111.00000000

Even though these two netmasks are identical, and both translate into decimal as 255.255.255.0, the router knows that one is a subnetwork to a Class B and the other is a standard Class C netmask. How does the router know this? In the same way that we can distinguish between a subnetworked Class B address and a standard Class C address. Like us, the router can tell if the address is a real Class A, B, or C address by looking at the first bits of the first byte. If the first bit of the first byte is a 0, it's a Class A. We do the same thing when we look at the decimal value of the first byte of the address. If the decimal value of the first byte is between 1 and 127, it's a Class A, for instance.

All that said, it doesn't really matter to the router if the address is a subnetworked Class B or a standard Class C address. All the router cares about is identifying whichever part of the IP address is being used as the network number, so that it can do a routing table lookup and forward the packet. Remember, address classes are immaterial to routers; all they care about is identifying a route to a network.

Beneath the Byte Boundary

Subnetworking on even byte boundaries is the simplest form of subnetworking, but it doesn't meet the needs of every circumstance. Sometimes, network administrators need to tailor their IP network address space even more carefully, by subnetworking on part of a byte, rather than on an even byte boundary.

For example, subnetworking a Class B address by using the third byte as part of the network address, in addition to the standard first and seconds bytes, will permit the network administrator to create up to 256 subnetworks. With only the 8 bits of the last full byte for numbering hosts on each subnetwork, each of the subnetworks can have 256 hosts (2^8).

But the network administrator may want to use that Class B network address to create more subnetworks with fewer hosts or fewer subnetworks with more hosts on each subnetwork. The network administrator could use half of that third byte of a Class B network address, instead of all of the byte, as part of the network address. Doing so would create 16 subnets, and each of the subnets could have as many as 4,096 hosts on it.

Similarly, the administrator could use more or fewer bits in the third byte, or even use some of the bits of the fourth byte, to tailor the number of subnetworks and hosts on each subnet. The only compromise would be fewer hosts per subnetwork. The converse would also be true: more hosts per subnet would result in fewer subnets. Just as designing a sailboat implies a compromise between speed and stability, subnetworking implies a compromise between subnetworks and host addresses. When you give up one, you gain the other.

Here's how this more precise kind of subnetworking—that is subnetworking on bit boundaries—works: Let's say that our network administrator in this example has determined that he wants to create 50 sub-networks. He's made this determination based on the number of networks he has to support today and the expected growth of his networks in the next few years. While it will probably be replaced in a few years, the router connecting his network to the ISP can be expanded to more than 50 ports.

Having made this estimate of what the requirements for networks and host addresses will be, the administrator can calculate exactly how to tailor that Class B IP network address to get 50 subnetworks. The same principles of subnetworking and netmasks apply, but the number of subnetworks that can be created is a power of 2. Therefore, the network administrator has to pay closer attention to exactly where to break the IP address between the network and host parts, and be able to do some minor calculations in binary arithmetic.

The principles of subnetworking on bit boundaries are:

- Use as many bits of the host address space as necessary to create a sufficient number of subnetworks.

- Use however many bits remain in the host address space to number hosts in each subnetwork.

While the network administrator needs 50 subnetworks, the closest power-of-two binary value to 50 is 64, which is 2^6. The next lower value, 32 (2^5), is too small, so he has to create 64 subnets. To create 64 subnetworks, he has to use the first 6 bits of the third byte of the Class B address space (in addition to the first and second bytes). As for the subnets he created earlier by using the entire third byte, numbering those 190.150.1.0, 190.150.2.0 and so forth, he numbers the subnets starting with the rightmost bit of the 6-bit field. The binary representation of the first subnetwork looks like this (a space has been inserted after the sixth bit to separate it from the two remaining bits of the byte):

10111110.10010110.00000100.00000000

What the administrator has done is to use only part of the third byte of the Class B address, instead of all of it, as he did earlier, to create subnetworks. This now leaves 10 bits (the remaining 2 from the third byte, and all 8 bits of the fourth byte) from which to number hosts on this first subnetwork. Note that in the previous example of "standard" byte boundary subnetworking, the administrator numbered hosts with the bits in only the fourth byte. In this case, he has all 8 bits of the last byte, plus 2 more left over at the end of the third byte. He can use all 10 to number hosts, giving him room to number 1,024 (2^{10}) hosts on each of the 64 subnets.

Thus, the binary version of the IP address of the first host on this first subnet would be:

10111110.10010110.00000100.00000001

The binary address of the last host on this first subnet would be:

10111110.10010110.00000111.11111110

The last step is to translate these binary numbers back into decimal, to get the "human-readable" version of each host address. Note that the same rules for translating from binary to decimal apply here, too. Even though the subnetworking boundaries no longer fall on even byte boundaries, the administrator still translates binary to decimal in the same 8-bit bytes. So the decimal value of the IP address of the first host on the first subnet would be:

190.150.4.0

The value of the last host on this first subnet would be:

190.150.7.254

Note that, unlike the even-byte boundary subnetworking example, the decimal value of the third byte changes, instead of staying the same. Subnetworks are defined on *bit*, rather than *byte*, and boundaries are defined by a *range* of host addresses, instead of a *constant* value in a specific byte. To illustrate this, let's look at the binary version of the IP address of the first host on the second subnet. It would be:

10111110.10010110.00001000.00000001

The binary address of the last host on the second subnet would be:

10111110.10010110.00001011.11111110

The decimal value of the IP address of the first host on the second subnet would be:

190.150.8.1

The value of the last host on the second subnet would be:

190.150.11.254

As with the first subnet, this subnet is defined not by a specific subnetwork number, but by a *range of host addresses*.

Subnetwork Masks

Getting the mask right is even more critical for bit-boundary subnetworks. As you may recall, the mask identifies the bits used for the network part of the address. In the previous example, our administrator used all of the bits of the first 2 bytes, plus the first 6 bits of the third byte, as the network address. So, the netmask would be:

11111111.11111111.11111100.00000000

This netmask (255.255.252.0) tells the router that the network portion of the IP address is composed of all of the bits of the first 2 bytes, plus the first 6 bits of the third byte. Any host addresses that fall into that range will belong to that subnetwork, and the router will forward packets to the interface to which that subnetwork is attached.

Class C Subnetworks

We've used the example of subnetworking a Class B network address because Class B network addresses are most commonly broken into subnetworks. However, there's nothing to prevent our subnetworking Class C addresses, too.

The same principles apply to creating Class C address subnetworks on bit boundaries that were used in creating Class B subnetworks. Let's say that we want to subdivide a Class C address, which can hold 255 hosts, into five subnets, each of which would hold about 25 hosts.

Just as we did in the Class B subnetworking example, we start with the number of subnets we want to create. The closest power of 2 greater than 5 (for the five subnets we'll need) is 8, which would use 4 bits. However, we only need five subnets, which we can number with the first 3 bits of that fourth byte of the Class C address range.

As we did with subnetworking the Class B address, we will subnetwork the Class C address 192.168.1.0 by using part of the last byte of the Class C address—the part that's normally used for the host address—for the network address. The network address for our subnetworked Class C will consist of all of the first, second, and third bytes, as well as (in this case), the first 3 bits of the last byte.

Since we will use part of the fourth byte for a network address, hosts on each subnetwork will be numbered from the remaining 5 bits of the fourth byte. Figure 7.4 illustrates this division of the Class C address space.

We will need to create a mask, too, to tell the router how we are subnetworking the address. The binary version of mask would be:

11111111.11111111.11111111.11100000

which would be represented in its decimal format as:

255.255.255.224

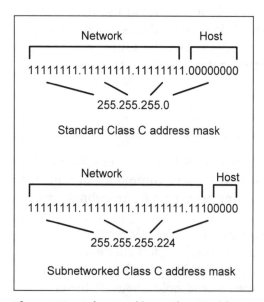

Figure 7.4 Subnetworking a Class C address.

If we use the first 3 bits of the last byte for the network address, the binary address of the first host on the first subnet 192.168.1.0 would be:

11000000.10101000.00000001.00100001

which would be represented in decimal as:

192.168.1.

The binary address of the last host on the first subnet would be:

11000000.10101000.00000001.00111111

which would be represented in decimal as:

192.168.1.63

Continuing to the next subnetwork, the binary address of the first host on the second subnet would be:

11000000.10101000.00000001.01000001

which would be represented in decimal as:

192.168.1.65

The binary address of the last host on the second subnet would be:

11000000.10101000.00000001.01011111

which would be represented in decimal as:

192.168.1.95

Finally, the binary address of the first host on the last subnet would be:

11000000.10101000.00000001.11100001

which would be represented in decimal as:

192.168.1.225

The binary address of the last host on the last subnet would be:

11000000.10101000.00000001.11111111

which would be represented in decimal as:

192.168.1.255

As we noted earlier with the Class B subnetworking example, sub-networks on bit boundaries are represented by ranges of IP addresses, not by specific whole numbers in a specific byte position.

And though we don't include an example of it, Class B addresses can also be subnetworked down into the fourth byte. That is, with a single Class B address, we could create several thousand subnetworks, each of which could have a hundred or fewer hosts on it, by using the entire third byte and part of the fourth byte for subnetwork numbers. One of the conveniences of standard subnetworking is that it offers network and router administrators a wide degree of latitude to tailor IP address space for a variety of networking needs.

Admittedly, the math of subnetworking can be drudgery, and network and router administrators need to understand its binary numbering foundation to make sure they are doing it correctly. To help with that, the following lists itemize the netmasks, subnetworks, and host addresses that can be created for various types of Class B and C networks.

Class B
(Subnetworking within the Third Byte)

BITS	MASK	SUBNETS	HOSTS
2	255.255.192.0	4	16384
3	255.255.224.0	8	8192
4	255.255.240.0	16	4096
5	255.255.248.0	32	2048
6	255.255.252.0	64	1024
7	255.255.254.0	128	512
8	255.255.255.0	256	256

Class C
(Subnetworking within the Fourth Byte)

BITS	MASK	SUBNETS	HOSTS
2	255.255.255.192	4	64
3	255.255.255.224	8	32
4	255.255.255.240	16	16
5	255.255.255.248	32	8
6	255.255.255.252	64	4
7	255.255.255.254	128	2

All-Zeroes, All-Ones

Another complication to subnetworking is determining whether the first and last subnets in a range of subnetworks can really be used. The answer is that sometimes they can be used, but not always.

Subnetworking a Class B network address by using the entire third byte as part of the subnetwork address *seems* to allow for the creation of 256 subnetworks ($2^8 = 256$), but most examples of subnetworking illustrate only 254 subnets, discarding the first and last possible subnets.

For example, if we subnetwork the Class B address 190.150.0.0 by using all of the bits of the third byte, it would seem that we would have subnets numbered 190.150.0.0, 190.150.1.0, 190.150.2.0, and so forth, through 190.150.255.0. However, most examples (including the one in the previous discussion on subnetworking) don't use 190.150.0.0 and 190.150.255.0. Excluding these two subnetworks—referred to as the *all-zeroes* (190.150.0.0) and the *all-ones* (190.150.255.0) subnetworks—reduces the number of subnetworks from 256 to 254.

What's wrong with using the first and last subnets? RFC 950, which describes subnetworking, doesn't specifically prohibit them, but it does "strongly discourage" their use. The reason is that the all-zeroes subnet might cause confusion for a router that uses an older routing protocol, such as the Routing Information Protocol (RIP). The all-ones subnet, on the other hand, might be confused with a broadcast to all subnets.

Today, the all-zeroes and all-ones subnets can be used, depending on the routing protocols implemented by routers, and whether the router software allows it. Usually, both can be used, but they must be specifically configured in the router software.

SUBNET ZERO

Establishing subnetworks on a router interface allows the network administrator to use any legal subnet address. If the router software permits it, the router administrator may also use the first and last subnets in a subnet range, which are known as the all-zeroes and all-ones subnets.

For example, the 172.168.0.0 Class B address may be subnetworked into separate Class C-sized subnetworks, such as 172.168.1.0, 172.168.2.0, and 172.168.3.0, and thence up to 172.168.254.0. Two of the possible subnetwork numbers, however, are not normally configured. They are subnetworks 172.168.0.0 and 172.168.255.0, which are known respectively as the all-zeroes and all-ones subnetworks. Unless otherwise configured, the all-ones subnetwork is a broadcast address, while the all-zeroes address could be considered a legal subnetwork address.

RFC 791 governs all-zeroes and all-ones subnetworks. It prohibits the use of the all-zeroes subnet, and strongly discourages the use of the all-ones subnet. The problem with the all-zeroes subnet (172.168.0.0) is that it can easily be confused with the base network address, which is also 172.168.0.0. The all-ones subnet (172.168.255.0) is a broadcast address for subnet 172.168.0.0, and that subnet address is prohibited by RFC 791, as well.

However, some vendor router software may allow the use of the all-ones and all-zeroes subnets, but unless address space is extremely tight, the all-zeroes and all-ones subnets should not be used.

To be safe, router and network administrators can sidestep the whole issue by skipping the all-zeroes and all-ones subnets, unless they must wring all available subnetworked address space from an address block.

Variable Length Subnetwork Masking (VLSM)

As much flexibility as subnetworking gives network administrators, it does have certain drawbacks. While subnetworking is largely hidden from the outside world, routers must understand precisely what is going on in the subnetworks behind them. In addition, a subnetworked address space must be interconnected so that every part of the subnetworked address space is directly connected together. However, for many network environments, these are limitations that most network administrators can live with.

As we have described it so far, normal subnetworking on bit or byte-level boundaries gives network administrators the capability to tailor IP address space to their needs, but it must be done on a one-size-fits-all basis. That is, normal subnetworking allows network administrators to use only one subnetwork mask for each separate block of IP address space. You can't switch subnetwork masks in the middle of an address redesign project to cut the address space more closely to meet different network needs.

But there is a way out, called *Variable Length Subnetwork Masking* (VLSM), and fortunately, modern routing protocols support it. VLSM gives network administrators the ability to shape a large block of IP address space to create subnetworks of various sizes, even within the same block of IP address space.

Standard subnetworking, as described in this chapter, lets a network administrator create subnetworks of variable sizes. The problem is that sometimes routers and routing protocols don't understand that all subnetworks within a certain network address don't necessarily use the same subnetwork mask.

For example, if a network administrator were to subnetwork a single Class B block with standard byte-boundary subnetworking, he could create as many as 255 separate subnetworks within that Class B block. Using a standard 255.255.255.0 subnetwork mask, the 190.150.0.0 Class B block could be subdivided into subnetworks 190.150.1.0, 190.150.2.0, and so forth, up to subnetwork 190.150.255.0.

Those 255 Class B subnets give the network administrator the ability to put as many as 255 hosts on each subnet. But what if he really needed three or four big networks with about a thousand hosts on each network, about a hundred networks with 255 or fewer hosts, and another 10 networks with fewer than 20 hosts, as server farms, remote access server LANs, and the like?

The answer is VLSM, which, as its name implies, permits subnetwork masks of different sizes—and therefore subnetworks of different sizes—within a single, subdivided block of address space. For example, part of the 190.150.0.0 Class B address block could be broken into several large address blocks containing a thousand host addresses or more, as well as a few very small networks for the servers. The rest of the address space could be subnetworked with "standard" class B subnetworks, each of which would be equivalent to a Class C network.

The keys to making VLSM work are:

- Designing the network properly
- Using interior routing protocols that support VLSM

First, the network that uses VLSM must be designed carefully, so that no subnetworks are hidden from each other. The general rule is that subnetworks should be arranged hierarchically, with smaller subnetworks grouped under larger subnetworks.

Second, the internal routing protocol used by the routers that connect the subnetworks together into an internal network must be capable of understanding VLSM. The original interior routing protocol, version 1 of the Routing Information Protocol, or RIP-I, made the assumption that there was only a single subnet mask in use within a subnetwork. So, RIP-I routing table updates won't include any information about a subnetwork mask.

However, more modern interior routing protocols do understand VLSM. For example, the newer version of RIP, RIP-II, can understand VLSM, as can the Interior Gateway Routing Protocol, or IGRP. Other routing protocols that are VLSM capable are Open Shortest Path First (OSPF) and Interior System-to-Interior System (IS-IS). Network administrators must be sure their routing protocols can support VLSM before they decide to try to use it.

Another important benefit of VLSM is that if it is done properly, it can reduce the size of the routing tables that are maintained by other, external networks, including those carried by the routers at the core of the Internet. Simplifying routing tables through route aggregation is one of the long-term goals of the top-level ISPs. While CIDR addressing is the primary tool for aggregating address blocks, VLSM can also help achieve that goal.

Summary

Subnetworking was one of the first tools employed by network managers and administrators to make more efficient use of IP address space. Without subnetworking, the Internet would have run out of IP address space a while ago. So, subnetworking has permitted the Internet to continue to grow, and it has allowed network managers to make more efficient use of the IP address space they have.

The nice thing about subnetworking is that it may be entirely invisible and, for that matter, irrelevant, to ISPs and other networks on the Internet. It is also an important tool in managing the internal routing of networks, in segregating smaller parts of networks to manage traffic, and to establish network security zones.

The downside of subnetworking is that its use isn't apparent from looking at an IP address. In fact, without the subnetwork mask, or worse, without detailed network documentation, it may be difficult for someone to divine the subnetworking scheme in a network. It may work, but it may also be difficult to explain to someone who isn't thoroughly familiar with subnetworking techniques and concepts.

The subject of the next chapter, network address translation, may obscure IP addressing schemes even more. NAT translates network addresses to different addresses, for security or network management purposes.

CHAPTER 8

Network Address Translation

The growth of the Internet has been so phenomenal that, in the last decade, many times more IP address space has been used than in all the years before that combined. As more and more users continue to jump onto the Internet, IP address space is indeed a rapidly dwindling resource in the Internet GNP.

As anyone who has used the Internet can testify, IP address space has not been the only part of the Internet that has experienced excessive strain in the past few years. For users with slow local access or a tendency to frequent popular Web sites, Internet performance has become an oxymoron, like jumbo shrimp. But degrading Internet performance is also the reason for the success of high-speed Internet access technologies. Some of these, such as ISDN, have suffered near-death experiences, only to be brought back from the brink by Internet access.

Part of the problem has been that Internet routing—reading and making routing decisions on those IP addresses—has not been able to keep pace with the growth of Internet traffic. Were it not for the development of new ways of handling IP routing and address designations, such as CIDR, the Internet's routers long ago would have started to shed routes, losing parts of the Internet along the way.

It is thanks to address space conservation tactics, CIDR, and Network Address Translation, or NAT, that the Internet did not run into serious connectivity problems by the mid-1990s. The tremendous growth in the use and adoption of TCP/IP, as evidenced by the growth of the Internet, has certainly been the primary reason for the consumption of more and more IP address space.

As explained in the beginning of the book, part of the problem has been that IP addresses must be unique throughout the Internet—except for the shrinking number of TCP/IP networks that are not connected to the Internet, whose IP addresses need only be unique within those networks. As long as networks that don't have unique addresses don't come in contact with other networks, their address space doesn't affect routing in the global Internet. But, as just mentioned, the number of TCP/IP networks not connected to the Internet, or at least to some other network, is shrinking rapidly. Networks by nature are built to be connected, and isolated networks are becoming living fossils.

The Need for NAT

Referring to an address as "unique" means that the address has been assigned by ARIN, RIPE, APNIC, or another organization that manages the use of the stockpile of IP addresses, and ensures that the same IP addresses aren't assigned to two or more organizations. IP addresses must be unique, or routing to deliver traffic to those addresses won't work reliably.

Network Address Translation is a method to ensure the uniqueness of IP addresses on the Internet, even if the IP addresses that specific devices or networks are using aren't unique. NAT replaces nonunique IP addresses with unique ones when traffic enters the unique address world, such as the Internet. When the traffic comes back to the network that doesn't use unique IP addresses, NAT changes the addresses back again.

NAT is achieved via software by a computer, a router, or a firewall that is positioned at the point where the network with nonunique addresses meets the Internet or another network that uses unique addresses.

NAT Basics

The concept of NAT is simple: read the source or destination address (or both) of an IP datagram, replace the address with some other IP address, and forward the datagram to its next destination. Though it's called address translation, strictly speaking, it's address substitution or replacement; one address is replaced by another one. NAT is not like language translation, because there's nothing inherent in the IP address that indicates anything about the address to which it should be translated.

The usual objective of NAT is to replace the IP address of traffic from a specific host, server, or application with one that the system administrator wants the outside world to see or must make the outside world see, usually for security purposes or to make Internet routing work properly.

NAT sounds simple, and to a certain degree, it is. But it's also tricky. The first trick is to do the address translation quickly and correctly. The second, and far more important trick, is to translate addresses correctly for traffic that comes back from the Internet as a response to an inquiry or a transaction from whichever host or server created the original query or transaction. Clearly, NAT isn't just address substitution; it's also a traffic monitor, ensuring that the NAT box can substitute the correct address.

Let's say that for traffic management and Internet access control reasons, a proxy server creates a proxy inquiry to a Web server on the Internet. It does this because a workstation on the internal network points all Internet HTTP transactions to the proxy server. The proxy server, acting as an intermediary, creates its own separate connection to the Internet server. In doing so, it may also translate the source address to another address (maybe its own) before forwarding the traffic to the destination Web server.

Changing a destination IP address on incoming responses from the Internet to the correct internal IP address is the most important NAT trick. As we will see, NAT tracks the transactions between internal and external systems, in order to direct incoming traffic to the correct source address. NAT uses TCP port numbers on outgoing and incoming traffic to determine where to send responses to transactions for which it has translated addresses.

Why NAT?

Here are the most common reasons for using NAT:

Security. To hide the existence or identity of systems on an internal network.

Proxy services. Proxy services may use a different address when they set up the external service connection for an internal user.

Private addressing. IP traffic that bears an IP address from private network address space must be changed before it can be routed to an external or Internet destination.

Routability. Organizations that change ISPs, or that have addresses that aren't known to the Internet, can use NAT to get routable address space.

Business partners. The networks and systems of business partners, acquired companies, or subsidiaries can be kept at an arm's length.

NAT for Security

One of the first principles of security is concealment. If an intruder doesn't know that something exists, or doesn't know where to find it, he or she probably won't take it. Those small jewelry safes that look like soft drink cans can be left out on a countertop or in the refrigerator, and still not be touched by a burglar. They conceal the existence of valuables quite well—unless you have the misfortune to be victimized by a thirsty burglar.

Concealing the existence of computer systems, servers, and workstations on a company network can be just as effective a computer security tool. If a hacker or an intruder doesn't know about the existence of servers and hosts on your network, he or she might not attempt to break into them. If they're located behind a firewall or a proxy server, the IP addresses of those hosts or servers can be concealed from the outside world by NAT.

A firewall that protects an internal network from attacks from the Internet may be configured to do NAT for all of the systems behind it. If the system administrator does not need to conceal the addresses of internal hosts and servers, the firewall may be configured not to do NAT. It's an optional capability for firewalls, but most firewall administrators turn it on.

A firewall is usually the gateway between the internal network and the Internet, through which all traffic from internal hosts to the Internet (or any other external network) passes. When the firewall sees traffic destined for an external IP address, the firewall replaces the source address of the IP datagram with a different source IP address. The new source address is taken from a pool of IP addresses maintained by the firewall, which it uses for NAT. If the internal network addresses are from private address space, NAT adds a second layer of security. Private addresses aren't reachable from outside the protected network, so the original addresses can't be attacked anyway.

NAT, however, is not that strong a security measure. Hidden addresses aren't regarded as difficult obstacles to overcome by a knowledgeable hacker; there are other holes he or she can exploit to discover what's on the network. NAT is, though, a first step. Why not conceal what you want to secure?

NAT for Proxy Services

Network proxy services don't necessarily need NAT. However, as a practical matter, proxy services usually translate addresses, so that it appears that all proxied traffic originates on the proxy server. A proxy service intercepts a request for an external connection, such as from a client machine that wants to reach a URL on a Web server on the Internet. The proxy service responds to the client to make it believe that the client is connecting to the Web server. At the same time, the proxy service establishes a second, completely separate, connection to the Internet Web server on behalf of the client.

As far as the Web server is concerned, the real requester, and the originator of the HTTP session, is the proxy server. To make this charade credible, the proxy server uses an HTTP client, and behaves just like any real Web client.

Obviously (or maybe not so obviously), the proxy server changes the IP source address of its HTTP transaction to its own address or to another address it wanted outside servers to see. But there's a catch: If the proxy server changes the original client's source IP address to its own IP address, and it does this for a number of clients (perhaps thousands of clients for a heavily used proxy server), how does the proxy server know what to do with the response that comes back from the Internet Web server? If the proxy server substituted its own IP address as the source address on the transaction to the Internet Web server, the destination address on return traffic would be that of the proxy server, not the originator of the request.

The key for the proxy server—and, for that matter, a number of devices or services that do NAT—is to track the TCP port numbers that have been used by clients. The proxy server manipulates TCP port numbers, and it uses those port numbers to figure out the correct IP address to which it must translate traffic that comes back from the Internet.

If the transaction were a simple, UDP-based request-response transaction, the proxy server could leave the source address alone, and let the Internet service respond directly.

NAT for Private Address Space

Networks that use private address space, or public address space that a network administrator really doesn't want to renumber, are the top candidates for NAT. In those cases, NAT isn't an option; it's a necessity for Internet connectivity, as well as for communications to other networks.

Take a company that has elected to use the private address space 10.0.0.0 for its internal network at company headquarters. Network 10.0.0.0 addresses won't be routed on the Internet, but they can be routed internally. That is, routers on both internal networks and on the Internet are configured by default to discard datagrams addressed to private address space.

However, if a network administrator uses private address space in an internal network, he or she must also configure the internal network routers to allow them to route private addresses. Private addresses are valid IP addresses; it's just that they are addresses well known to be unroutable.

Because those private addresses are unroutable on the Internet, they must be translated into routable addresses before they can be sent out onto the Internet. The usual solution to this problem is to install NAT at the boundary between the internal network and the Internet.

Of course, the addresses that NAT uses as its external addresses must be "real" IP addresses: unique, assigned IP addresses. Thus, using NAT when translating from private address space to public address space still requires at least some routable, unique, and public IP addresses.

NAT for Routability

There's not much point in being connected to the Internet if other hosts on the Internet can't reach you. Your networks and the address space they use must be routable, or able to be found by Internet routers. If you change ISPs, or if you must change the address space that you are using, NAT may reduce or eliminate the need to renumber network addresses.

In fact, changing ISPs is one of the most common reasons for renumbering. Many networks use IP address space that has been delegated to them by their ISPs. In many cases, if an organization changes ISPs, the organization may have to get IP address space from the new ISP, rather than keeping the old address space.

The reason for this inconvenience is that ISPs announce to higher-level ISPs the networks under them. Route announcements from lower-level ISPs tell the higher-level ISPs where to send traffic for customer networks behind them. When a company's network moves behind an ISP, the ISP that is losing the customer will drop the network from its list of announced routes. Because of route aggregation at the Internet NAPs, the gaining ISP won't announce a network that isn't in its assigned address range. And address space that is unannounced is also unreachable. The Internet's routers don't know that it exists, so they can't tell how to get traffic to it. The result? It falls into a black hole, and for all intents, disappears from the Internet.

Therefore, the customer may either renumber into the new ISP's address space or use NAT to hide the old address space. That is, the customer may try to keep the old address space, to avoid renumbering, but use NAT to translate internal addresses to the new address space received from the new ISP.

In summary, NAT is a potential solution to the problem of Internet reachability, but it really isn't the best solution when changing ISPs. NAT is not foolproof; some applications, such as FTP, may embed IP source addresses within the data fields of IP datagrams. The effects of a NAT slip-up, such as missing an embedded source IP address, may affect the reachability of whoever uses that old address space. The losing ISP may eventually reassign that address space to a new customer, and continuing to use that address space, even behind NAT, may render the new customer's networks unreachable.

NAT for Business Partners

Sometimes a company gets the same brilliant idea as another company at the same time. In some cases, it leads to patent litigation. But if the brilliant idea is to use the same private address space to number internal networks, and at some time in the future those two companies' networks need to communicate with each other, that coincidental, shared brilliant idea may lead to NAT.

Numbering networks in private address space is an attractive option for companies that have large networks with large numbers of hosts. As we have already noted, private address space gives companies the option to create a complex addressing structure, without regard to the restrictions on obtaining or keeping public address space.

But if two companies that use the same private address space decide to become business partners, this capability may require NAT. Let's say that BigOne company and BigTwo company both use the 10.0.0.0 private address space. Then BigTwo becomes a business partner of BigOne, and they want to link their networks to share information, applications, or databases. Since neither uses unique public address space, their internal subnetwork structure may overlap. Assuming that they want to continue using private address space (which probably they will), they have two choices, both of which involve NAT. First, they could use NAT to translate the subnets of 10.0.0.0 that "see" each other over a private line link into public address space. Second, they could translate their internal 10.0.0.0 addresses into private Class B (172.1–32.0.0) or Class C (192.168.1–255.0) space.

In either case, both organizations would probably also want to firewall the connection to the other, so that traffic between BigOne and BigTwo could only go to specific hosts, instead of to potentially any host on either company's network.

How NAT Works

As we noted earlier, NAT is address replacement, not address translation, despite its name. It's usually done by a firewall, a proxy server, or a router, although any computer that understands IP can be configured to do NAT. It's not uncommon, for instance, for a Unix host to act as a router between two networks. Unix systems usually do IP, and they can be programmed to do NAT. In fact, many routers use a variant of Unix as their operating system, so a router that does NAT could be considered to be a stripped-down, special-purpose Unix host.

The difficulty of NAT is not in substituting one IP address for another; that's a relatively easy task. The hard part is reversing the process, and doing it quickly and accurately. If a router or a firewall changes the source address of an IP datagram when it goes out to the Internet, how does it know what to change it back to when the response returns from the Internet? Figuring out how to do that is one of the challenges of NAT, which we'll illustrate with an example.

Let's say that BigCo has an internal TCP/IP network at its headquarters in Los Angeles. To keep our example simple, let's also say that all of the internal LANs at the company's offices in Los Angeles are connected to one another through a set of internal routers. Any user on those networks can connect to the Internet through a single, high-speed connection to a local ISP.

BigCo believes in practicing safe Internet access, so it has a firewall positioned as the final device on its connection to the ISP. The firewall's primary task is to protect the systems on the BigCo internal network from the Legion of Doom, the Merry Pranksters, and all of the other casual and committed hackers on the Internet. It's also there to protect the BigCo network from BigCo's competitors, such as HugeCo and MegaCo who otherwise might have a marvelous conduit via the Internet to conduct industrial espionage.

BigCo's security director believes that an ounce of concealment is worth a pound of interdiction (prosecution), so he's mandated that the outside world should know as little as possible about what's on the BigCo internal network. To that end, BigCo's IS department has decided that NAT is one of the tools that will do that. Since it's the last stop between the internal BigCo network and the Internet, the firewall is the logical place to do NAT.

The first question the IS team has to deal with is not how to do NAT on the firewall, but which addresses to translate to and from. Getting the firewall to do NAT isn't usually a problem, as it's a standard capability of most firewalls. All of the major firewall vendors, including Checkpoint, Raptor, ANS, CyberGuard, Firewall-1, and others, support NAT. It's simply a question of enabling and configuring NAT, and determining whether it's to be done with the firewall's proxy services.

Again, the more problematic issue is determining which addresses to translate to and from, as well as how many addresses BigCo will need for the addresses to which its internal addresses will be translated. Let's say that BigCo has 10 internal LANs, each of which has been assigned a different Class C network. The Class Cs were assigned by BigCo's ISP. An eleventh Class C network address has been assigned to BigCo by the ISP for use on the DMZ network where the firewall and its external DNS, Web server, and email relay machines are located. The DMZ is a small LAN reachable through the firewall on which Web servers, email relays, and other externally-visible hosts are positioned. It's called a DMZ not because it's demilitarized, but because everything on the LAN is controlled by the firewall. Traffic can't move to or from the DMZ without passing through the firewall.

NAT can translate on a one-for-one basis, using a static or dynamically assigned address for each internal address. A more conservative, exhaustion-friendly approach is to use only as many external addresses as are needed to support the number of peak or average external connections. If, for example, there are 1,000 hosts on internal networks, and, Internet usage ranges between 10 and 50 percent of the network users, two Class C network addresses would suffice for NAT.

The network administrator would probably add a number of other addresses to that total, such as for mail relays, DNS lookups, and network servers that communicate with the Internet. Using as little public address space as is necessary, such as two Class C addresses, constitutes "doing the right thing." Furthermore, "as little as necessary" may be all the address space an ISP will be willing to grant. Remember that ISPs are under pressure to demonstrate that they, too, are using the address space they are delegated efficiently.

Only by Proxy

The network administrator may also believe in controlling and managing Internet usage and access by its employees, so all employees' Web browsers point to a proxy server. The proxy server, which is located behind the firewall, shortstops all HTTP transactions. The proxy server logs all HTTP transactions, and screens them against the company's list of "no-no" sites (as set forth in the company's Internet Acceptable Use Policy). It also resolves the source IP address of each HTTP transaction back to the machine name of the workstation that created the HTTP transaction, and writes that in the log of HTTP activity.

The proxy server does this in addition to its real job, which is to create a second, separate HTTP transaction to the Web server on the Internet. Creating and managing these "proxied" connections are the raison d'etre of the proxy server, as all HTTP traffic goes through and is monitored by the proxy server.

The proxy server, incidentally, may also act as a proxy for other services, such as FTP, Telnet, and other TCP/IP application protocols. Just as the proxy server can allow certain types of proxied connections, it can also disallow them. For example, a company that wants to control employee usage of the Web through HTTP proxies may also want to restrict their use of other Web services, such as AOL. Like a firewall, a proxy server can be set up to prohibit access to some services or to restrict access to specific addresses.

Since all external connections go through the proxy server, it also does network address translation on all of the connections it manages. External (in other words, Internet) services see the IP address assigned to the proxy server as the source address of all connections, not the IP addresses of the workstations that are the "real" sources of the traffic.

Positioning NAT

A network address translator will usually be positioned at the border, or gateway, of a network. If the purpose of NAT is to translate internal addresses into externally visible or externally routable addresses, it makes sense to do NAT only when and if it's necessary. As noted, NAT isn't foolproof, so it should be used only when it's really necessary.

Most firewalls have NAT capabilities, and address translation is usually done there. Screening routers on the periphery of a DMZ may also be configured to do NAT. However, because they are on the outside of the network's DMZ perimeter, and may therefore be the target of hackers, it's preferable to do NAT on the firewall or further inside the network.

A proxy server would be located inside the network's security perimeter. One of the advantages of doing NAT on the proxy server is that it relieves the firewall of the NAT burden, and moves the address translation function back to a device that does it as part of its basic network service. But if the network uses private address space, using a proxy server behind the firewall still throws the NAT burden on the firewall to translate private addresses to public addresses.

NAT's Dark Side

We pointed out repeatedly that although network address translation is relatively simple in concept, its actual implementation may be more complicated. Even though only the IP address is being translated, some applications and protocols aren't particularly NAT friendly. They may rely on specific IP addresses to validate users, or they may not realize that NAT is being done.

For example, when NAT changes the IP address in the IP datagram header, it must also recalculate the header checksum and substitute it for the original checksum, because the original checksum isn't correct any longer. It must do the same thing on returning traffic. Furthermore, applications that encrypt datagram headers, or that use the source address, the destination address, or the checksum itself as part of an encryption algorithm, may also foil NAT.

Some applications, such as FTP, embed source or destination IP addresses in the data fields of IP datagrams. Worse, certain applications protocols, such as SMTP, may include the clear text version of the host name of the system that created or forwarded the mail message, or its IP address. Unless a NAT device is sufficiently "application aware" to know where these address references are in the data field, addresses that are intended to be concealed may "escape" into the Internet. Some may interfere with routing, while others may pose security risks.

Network management protocols like the *Simple Network Management Protocol* (SNMP) depend on seeing the "real" IP addresses of managed devices. If the source address has been changed by NAT, SNMP-based network management systems may not be able to see the devices they're supposed to manage. NAT-modified addresses can also complicate the process of obtaining DNS services from an external DNS host; and NAT can cause problems getting ICMP-based programs, such as Traceroute and Ping, to work properly.

NAT may also complicate the lives of DNS administrators. For either security reasons or because the network uses private address space, the DNS administrator may have to split the DNS database between an inside and an outside DNS. If the DNS has in-addr records for reverse name lookups (to translate IP addresses back to host names, instead of the usual name-to-IP address translation), the in-addr records may be incorrect, or they may point to addresses the NAT box can't resolve back to the correct address.

NAT and TCP

On the surface, NAT is simply IP address replacement. However, to make applications work with NAT, we must have a method to track applications and processes running on clients or servers that are using those translated IP addresses. That's the role of the TCP protocol and TCP ports, which link applications to the IP addresses of network interfaces.

That TCP Port Thing

IP is really only concerned with addressing datagrams to specific destinations on an IP network, such as the Internet, not with how the data gets there, or even with making sure that all of the data gets to its destination in the correct order, or without errors.

Addressing is a complex issue (obviously, one could write a book about it), and it's one that other protocols don't have to worry about. Similarly, IP doesn't concern itself with the other mundane details of data transmission, such as how data gets delivered reliably to its destination. In the complicated world of TCP/IP, that's the role of the Transmission Control Protocol, the other half of the TCP/IP duo. Other protocols, such as X.25, ATM, or LAN protocols such as Ethernet, are focused on how to encode data to transmit it across a physical path, such as a phone line or 10BaseT cabling.

TCP is the protocol "above" IP in the hierarchy of the TCP/IP protocol "stack." It is above IP because it's closer to the application protocols, such as HTTP, FTP, SMTP, and Telnet. In fact, those application-level protocols interface directly with TCP. It's TCP's responsibility to hand data to IP, which is below it in the protocol stack, to figure out where to deliver it.

TCP Ports

The main purpose of the TCP protocol is to establish a logical connection with the TCP protocol module in another TCP/IP system somewhere across the Internet, and to pass data reliably across that connection. The sending TCP module addresses its data to a TCP "port" on the destination system. The TCP module on the receiving system "listens" for data addressed to that port, and acknowledges receiving the data from the source "port" on the sending system.

Internet Web servers have to answer requests from a number of Web browsers simultaneously. Web servers, like other Internet hosts, use TCP port numbers to identify the different clients that contact them and to maintain the "thread" of transactions with different hosts. You'd think that they could use IP addresses, but a Web client might be a program running on a multiuser or a multitasking system, too. If the Web server sent the Web page back to your PC using only its IP address, how would your PC know whether to deliver the data to the Netscape Web browser, to Microsoft Word, or to Adobe Photoshop? The TCP port number identifies the source and destination of data uniquely, for delivery to specific applications.

In a sense, TCP port numbers are like IP addresses, but they serve a different purpose, and they aren't universally unique, as are IP addresses. In addition, TCP port numbers are temporary and transient, valid only for the length of a TCP "session," and are used, say, to FTP a file from one host to another. The IP address, even if it is only temporarily assigned by DHCP, identifies the system interface on a network, not applications within that system.

While there is a good deal of standardization of the numbers used for familiar services such as FTP, HTTP, and other protocols, the numbers chosen for the sending and receiving ports really don't matter as long as both TCP components agree on the port numbers that are being used. For example, if I wanted to contact a Web site on the Internet, I'd probably use the HTTP protocol. If http:// didn't precede the URL on a Web browser's To line, most people would probably be completely unaware of the existence of the HTTP protocol. I could use FTP or Telnet, because Web hosts can do those too, but HTTP is by far the most common protocol for Web browsing.

It may seem obvious to you, the user, what you're trying to do when you type a URL into your Web browser, but it's not so obvious to the Web server; and, like most everything in the computer environment, you have to tell the distant system exactly what you want to do. Fortunately, most of the details of the transaction, as well as setting it up and taking it down, are hidden from you by the Web browser and by your computer's TCP/IP software, but in practice, there's a complicated division of labor among the pieces of the protocols to bring the Web page back to your computer. Your browser, for instance, only gives you the Web browser interface, interprets your mouse clicks, and translates the HTML tags on a Web page to display the Web page. It also passes your requests for Web pages (either by typing in a URL or by clicking on a link) to the TCP software. The Web browser understands the HTTP protocol as a means to request a specific file (a Web page), but it has no idea where the server that has that page is located, nor how to get the Web page from it.

That's part of the role played by TCP. When you type in the URL and press the Return key, the Web browser's HTTP software calls on the TCP software. TCP's role is to contact the remote server across the Internet, tell it what you want to do, and set up a mechanism for transferring the Web page reliably across the Internet. TCP will use IP to add the IP address of the distant system to the data.

Establishing the Connection

TCP has to establish the connection to the remote TCP process first, before you ever see the first part of the Web page. Using the IP address, which was resolved from the text URL by a call from the HTTP application protocol to the DNS, TCP creates a simple hello message that it sends across the Internet to the destination system. This message, called a *synchronization message* (SYN), tells the destination system's TCP software that it wants to open a connection to it. The data will follow a short time later; but first, the two TCP processes have to identify themselves, agree on what they're going to communicate, and how they're going to do it. Only then can the two systems exchange data over the reliable connection that has been established by the two TCP processes (see Figure 8.1).

The SYN message also identifies the port number both systems will use to pipeline that data to and from a specific higher-level application protocol. In this case, it's HTTP, which is TCP Port 80. Other application-level protocols, such as FTP and Telnet, have their own well-known TCP port numbers.

Let's say that the sender (the client) is a computer named Fred and that the receiver (the server) is named Wilma. The SYN message from Fred's TCP process to Wilma's TCP process tells Wilma's TCP process to give the data (when it comes along later) to the HTTP application. At the same time, Fred's TCP process uses a TCP port number to identify the application from which the data originated. Even though the origi-

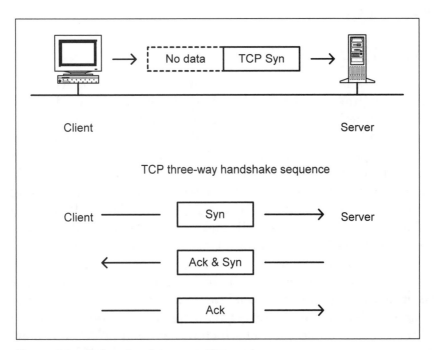

Figure 8.1 Exchanging data over a TCP session.

nating protocol is HTTP, Fred's TCP process chooses a different number, taking one from a pool of general-purpose TCP port numbers.

The reason the source port number is different (and not the HTTP port, 80) is because it's from an HTTP client, not a server. The system Fred is using is probably a PC, and not a Web server; but there's no guarantee it isn't a host that is running other client processes. To prevent confusion in a server or a host that operates both client and server processes (many Unix systems do this), the destination port on Wilma's system is the standard HTTP TCP port (Port 80). The source port is a number selected by Fred's TCP process from the available, unassigned and unreserved port range (256 through 65,536).

The SYN message that Fred's TCP software sends to Wilma's TCP process to open the connection also includes two other numbers, both of which are key to the reliable delivery of data, which is what TCP is all about. They are the Sequence number and the Acknowledgment number. Both Fred and Wilma will use these numbers to keep track of how much data they've sent to each other and to control the flow of data between them.

The details of the process are not worth going into here, but, in short, by incrementing the Sequence and Acknowledgment numbers, Fred and Wilma's TCP processes will be able to tell if what one sends has been received by the other.

Back to the Ports

Let's get back to the TCP port number. The port number is what the firewall, router, proxy server, or host that does NAT will use to keep track of the transaction from the real source to the destination. When it does its outbound NAT address substitution, the NAT device will build a table that maps the original source TCP port to both the original address and the new substituted address. The source port may already be in use by another internal system for which the NAT box is doing address substitution. If that is the case, the NAT box will have to change the source TCP port as well, and note in its translation table that for any response from the Internet, it must translate not only the destination address, but the destination TCP port as well.

But what if there are devices on the internal network for which the NAT box is not doing address translation? For instance, an internal DNS name resolver may make direct inquiries to an external DNS to resolve Internet host names, few of which it may know. NAT may slow down this process; and because allowed and disallowed DNS inquiries can be effectively filtered by a firewall or a router, it may not be necessary to do NAT on DNS.

To Connect or Not to Connect

The concept of communications without a connection may sound nonsensical, but IP is a "connectionless" protocol. TCP, on the other hand, is connection oriented. That means that before TCP sends any data from System A to System B, it holds a brief dialog, called a *handshake*, with the other system. This dialog allows the two systems, which may never have communicated with each other before, to identify each other, to agree on how much data they will send at one time, and to set up markers that will control the flow of data between them.

The TCP processes on each side of a TCP/IP transaction go through this type of negotiation before they ever send any data. Once the two TCP processes agree that they can transfer data, as well as how much data they will transfer at one time, and establish markers (the Sequence and Acknowledgment numbers) to track the data transfer, they have set up a connection between them.

IP, on the other hand, wouldn't know a connection if one walked up to it with a resume complete with an 8 × 10 glossy photo. IP makes no prior arrangements with anything to establish an IP connection or session. When IP creates the IP header for an IP datagram, it hands the addressed IP datagrams to a network for delivery. This is why IP is called a connectionless protocol; again, it has no concept of prior arrangements or logical connections over which it communicates. It leaves all those details to other protocols, such as TCP. And, if TCP has created a logical session or connection with the destination system, why should IP duplicate that effort? IP doesn't need a connection, because TCP makes one for it.

That IP is a connectionless protocol is one of the Internet's greatest strengths, but it has also exposed one of its greatest weaknesses. The upside is that IP has no requirement to establish an end-to-end path from source host to destination host through a number of the Internet's routers, so IP can blast out datagrams to routers whenever they're ready. IP routers, in turn, are freed from the overhead that connection-oriented sessions imply. The downside is that IP routing as we know it today can neither predict nor guarantee IP network performance, and, by implication, data delivery. Bandwidth-intensive and delay-sensitive applications, such as voice, streaming video, Webcasting, and the like, never know beforehand how they will be routed through the Internet, because routing decisions aren't made by routers until they see the datagrams.

Furthermore, a connectionless protocol like IP neither knows nor cares if a number of IP datagrams are part of a transaction, all of the parts of which logically belong together, and should be delivered together. First, each IP router makes a routing decision that is independent of the routing decisions made by any other IP router. Second, there is nothing in the IP protocol to tell IP that a sequence of datagrams are related to each other and are part of a stream of data. Third, nothing in IP alerts an IP router that it should give priority to one datagram over another.

IP routers treat each IP datagram as if it has no relationship to any other datagram, in the same way a mailperson, who only reads addresses and delivers mail, makes no judgments about the order in which envelopes should be delivered or cares whether any envelope contains something that is related to any other envelope.

Several companies and organizations have proposed solutions to the Internet's quality of service (QoS) problem, which is really an IP QoS problem. Remember that, as far as IP is concerned, there is no QoS problem. Some of the solutions are:

Reservation Protocol (RSVP). An IETF-designed protocol to allow applications to request or reserve bandwidth on an IP network, and for RSVP-aware IP routers to assign priority to IP traffic between those devices.

IP switching. A technique devised by Ipsilon Networks (now part of Nokia) to examine IP traffic to identify lengthy TCP transactions, then switch them over reserved paths across a network of Ipsilon IP switches.

Tag switching. A technique devised by Cisco to add a "tag" of several bytes to the IP header of traffic that needs QoS. The tag would identify the datagrams of a transaction or datastream that should be pipelined across a router network. The router network (composed of Cisco routers that understand tag switching, of course) would also set up a predefined path over which the tagged datagrams would flow.

Bandwidth managers. Special routers, positioned at a network's entrance to the Internet (for example, behind a firewall), to monitor traffic going to and from the Internet. The bandwidth manager is configured to give priority to traffic to and from certain devices or to and from certain internal (or external) IP addresses. While the operation of a bandwidth manager has no influence on how IP traffic is handled on the external network, such as the Internet, a network administrator can throttle traffic from lower-priority sources, hence giving more Internet access bandwidth to those with a higher priority.

Dedicated QoS VPNs. Some ISPs are provisioning dedicated bandwidth across their networks for use by their customers' applications that require dedicated bandwidth. The dedicated paths are virtual private networks (VPNs), but for now, they must run on the ISPs' own networks.

IPv6. IPv6 is aware of QoS requirements, so it can understand a QoS request (if TCP can pass it down from a higher, application-level protocol) and interface to a physical transport system that can honor a QoS request, such as ATM.

It does not matter that connection-oriented TCP is "watching the store" to make sure that all of the data gets delivered. Though it creates a logical end-to-end connection, TCP has no sense of urgency about data delivery. Its designers included a priority transmission mechanism as one of the TCP optional features (the Priority flag bit in the TCP header Options field), but transmission priority is rarely implemented. As a TCP option, it only influences how a data transfer is handled inside the source and destination, not in the network's routers.

Summary

NAT was originally proposed as a way to connect networks with unroutable, private network addresses to public, routable networks, without forcing renumbering. This convenient way of connecting the unroutable to the routable has since been employed in a number of ingenious ways, most particularly as a security measure.

Today, NAT is commonly used on firewalls to conceal the addresses of devices on internal networks, presenting a small number of addresses of publicly-accessible hosts. NAT has also helped reduce the growth of top-level Internet routing tables, by making what are often huge networks composed of many different IP network addresses, reachable through only a few addresses.

Of course, the benefits of NAT come at a price. NAT increases the complexity of network management, and it can make certain applications that must see the real source address of IP traffic not work at all. In addition, the load of address translation can slow the operation of a firewall to a crawl.

NAT can also cause the Internet's version of Directory assistance, the *Domain Name Service* (DNS), to give misleading or incorrect information. As we will see in the next chapter, DNS is a key part of the operation of the Internet, and renumbering affects DNS services as well.

CHAPTER 9

DNS Considerations

The Domain Name Service (DNS) is one of the network components that is affected most significantly by network renumbering or IP address plan modifications. Most users of a network, and, for that matter, users on the Internet, depend on the DNS for fast, reliable, and accurate translation of text names of hosts to IP addresses. If the IP addresses of hosts change, many of the changes must be reflected in the DNS or the hosts with the new addresses won't be found.

Renumbering affects the DNS in other, more subtle ways. Most DNS services aren't dynamically updated whenever the IP address of a host or a server changes. Therefore, if an IP address of a host or server changes in a renumbering project, the IP addresses listed in the DNS won't necessarily be updated to reflect the new addresses.

DNS services are essential to the operation of most networks, so they are backed up in primary and secondary DNSes. The latter may act as secondaries for more than one primary DNS. This means that updating the DNS files in a primary DNS doesn't necessarily update it immediately in any one or in all of the secondary DNSes.

Managing the complexity of a network's DNS services can be a daunting challenge for a network manager charged with renumbering an address plan. Creating and implementing a network renumbering plan is one of the issues the manager must handle; updating and maintaining the DNS services is another, completely different, issue. The network manager or network administrator who undertakes a network renumbering program must be aware of the effects of IP address renumbering on the DNS.

Ideally, the network administrator is also the DNS administrator, but frequently the two responsibilities are separated. In any case, the network administrator should understand the structure and operation of the DNS, so that IP address changes can be propagated back into the DNS during renumbering or network reengineering.

The DNS Database

The Domain Name Service is one of those network services that operates almost transparently on a network. It performs a vital service that makes the use of the Internet—or any other network—more convenient for users.

The primary function of the DNS is to translate text host or Web site names into the IP addresses for those hosts. A text host name is far simpler for a network user to remember, and is less likely to be mistyped than a numeric IP address. All communications on the Internet or on a TCP/IP network depend on accurate IP source and, particularly, destination addresses. So the DNS automates one of the essential parts of IP communications. It allows most users and systems to refer to hosts and services by text names rather than IP addresses, even though IP addresses are really used for Internet communications.

At its simplest level, the DNS is a database, arranged as a table, that matches or maps host names, Web server names, or even the names of router interfaces to their corresponding IP addresses. Obviously, if the IP addresses of hosts change in a network renumbering program, the corresponding DNS tables that refer to those host names and their IP addresses must also be changed.

From a network renumbering perspective, the problem is that there isn't necessarily a link between giving a host a new IP address and updating the DNS entries to reflect that new address. In many cases, the DNS files are maintained manually, and IP addresses must be made in the DNS tables by the DNS administrator. Newer versions of the DNS, such as 8.4.1 of the Unix DNS, and the Windows NT DNS Service, can be configured as Dynamic DNS services (DDNS). A DDNS is often linked to a DHCP service that assigns IP addresses dynamically, so that DHCP address changes are automatically sent to the DNS and added to the DNS tables.

DNS as a Network Service

The DNS is an application that provides a network service; it is a client-server program that runs on a host, but its functions are rarely requested specifically by a user. The DNS program operates in a host or a server on the network, responding to the DNS name-to-IP address requests from users' application programs and from other network services.

In most cases, users of the network or the Internet are not even aware that the DNS service exists or that it is operational. For example, a user who runs the Netscape Navigator Web browser simply types in a URL in the Location: window on the Web browser screen. Unbeknownst to the user, the Web browser calls on the DNS client program in the user's PC to translate the URL to an IP address. The DNS client then finds a DNS server and asks it for the IP address of the host that has been referenced in the URL, as illustrated in Figure 9.1.

To make what could be a very complicated and long story short, a DNS somewhere on the network or on the Internet responds with the IP address. The IP address is used by the IP client software in the PC to create the destination address for the Web site in the IP datagram,

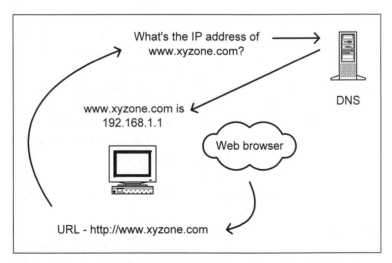

Figure 9.1   Resolving a URL to an IP address through a DNS inquiry.

which allows the IP routers in the network to route the datagram to its destination.

As just mentioned, in most cases, users are unaware of the existence and operation of the DNS. The only clue they may get is when the DNS can't be reached or when the network link to the DNS is down. When that happens, URLs that ordinarily are resolved quickly to IP addresses can't be translated at all. The user may receive a message indicating that the DNS doesn't contain an entry for that host or that the DNS is unreachable. Whatever the text of the message, the import is not that the DNS doesn't have an entry for a host name, but that the client couldn't reach a DNS that does have the entry, because it couldn't reach it before the client timed out the request.

DNS Services and Domains

The DNS isn't a single service, even though it is commonly perceived as a single entity that can resolve all text name-to-IP address requests. The DNS is a distributed service, running in several different hosts. Each instance of the DNS service may know about only the host names and IP addresses of a relatively small number of hosts. DNS services can refer IP address resolution inquiries for host names and domains that they don't know about to other DNS servers.

The distributed nature of the DNS service has implications for network renumbering, too. If the person drawing up the network renumbering plan doesn't have a sound understanding of how the DNS service works, it is likely that all of the DNSes that contain IP address references for the domain may not be updated. This may render some renumbered networks and hosts unreachable until the DNS records are corrected.

Most DNS services map host names to IP addresses for a specific part of the Internet host-naming hierarchy known as a *domain*. A domain is an administrative subdivision of the Internet host name space. For example, if the hosts that are run by the BigCo Company are named www.bigco.com, ftp.bigco.com, mailrelay.bigco.com, and so forth, they are said to be part of the bigco.com domain. The bigco.com domain name has been registered with Network Solutions, which acts as the primary Internet domain name registry.

The bigco.com domain is also part of another domain, which is the .com domain. Besides the .com domain—which is intended to be for commercial organizations—the other top-level domains are the .org, .net, .edu, and .mil domains. They are intended to be for organizations, Internet resources, colleges and universities, and the U.S. military, respectively.

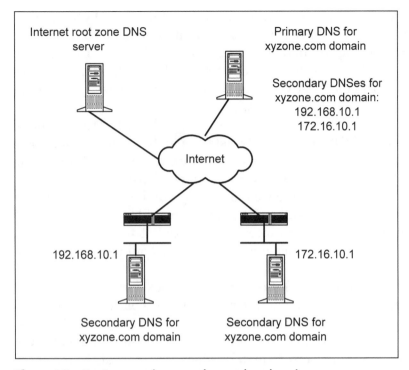

Figure 9.2   Root zone, primary, and secondary domain name servers.

The bigco.com domain is a second-level domain, because it is one of millions of domain names that have been registered under the .com domain.

DNS services provide name-to-IP address resolution for specific domains. For example, BigCo or its ISP maintains a DNS that translates host names in the bigco.com domain, such as www.bigco.com, ftp.bigco.com, and mailrelay.bigco.com, to their corresponding IP addresses. The DNS server that does this is known as the *name server* for the bigco.com domain. Higher-level DNS services, such as the ones that maintain the domain names in the .com domain, list the host names and IP addresses of the DNS services in the secondary domains in the top-level domain name server, as illustrated in Figure 9.2.

Name Resolution at Work

When a DNS client somewhere on the Internet asks its local DNS to resolve a host name, such as the URL for www.bigco.com, to an IP address, that simple action can set off a complex series of DNS inquiries. For this example, let's assume that the Web browser that has been pointed to www.bigco.com is running on a computer served by a different ISP from the one that connects the bigco.com domain to the Internet. This will force the inquiry to the Internet's top-level master DNS server, which will help illustrate how DNS works. It will also illustrate how renumbering hosts on a network may cause DNS changes to ripple all the way through the DNS structure.

The first place a DNS inquiry goes is to the local DNS (if there is one). The local network DNS usually only lists the address records for hosts on the local network, as well as for a few external hosts that are in the local domain. It usually isn't a very complete DNS, because it only serves the needs of users on the local network. Furthermore, it's usually positioned behind the firewall, so it is only accessible by internal systems. It's not practical for the internal DNS to list too many external hosts, the IP addresses of which might change without the knowledge of the DNS administrator.

An inquiry for address resolution for an Internet host usually fails on this first attempt on the local name server, but that's okay; there are better places to check. The most convenient place to start is the local DNS, so it is usually checked first. Since the local DNS can't resolve the name, the name resolver program resorts to plan B, which is to start at the top of the Internet's DNS hierarchy and work its way down to the bigco.com domain.

The top of the Internet's DNS hierarchy is a set of 12 DNS servers that contain the top- and second-level domain names for every known domain in the Internet. This set of 12 DNS servers, which are referred to as *root zone servers*, are maintained by both private and commercial organizations as an Internet service. The master root zone server, root zone server-A, contains the master set of records for all of the domains registered under the six top-level domains (.com, .net, .org, .gov, .mil, and .edu). That is, it lists at least the host name and IP address for the DNS servers for bigco.com, espn.com, nintendo.com. harvard.edu, army.mil, whitehouse.gov, nasa.org, and so forth.

Today, there are more than 4 million records like this in the root zone servers, which function as the master servers for the Internet DNS. The master DNS file on root zone server-A is maintained by Network Solutions, Inc. (NSI), which also acts as one of the registrars for Internet domain names in the .com, .org, and .net domains. Since it registers domain names, it also adds them to the root zone-A database, and distributes updates each day to the other root zone DNS servers.

Note that the root zone servers only point a DNS inquiry to a lower-level (or second-level) DNS server, or name server. That is, an inquiry to a top-level root zone server returns the IP address of the name server

(DNS) for the second-level domain. The IP addresses for a primary and a secondary second-level DNS server must be registered with NSI when the domain name, such as bigco.com, is first registered.

To repeat, the DNS service is a distributed service. This means that the responsibility for maintaining correct DNS records for the hosts in, say, the xyz.com domain, or, in this example, the bigco.com domain, falls on whoever maintains the DNS for any second-level domain. The root zone servers only keep the IP addresses for the second-level domain primary and secondary, or backup, DNS servers. Therefore, the top-level root zone servers only provide references to other DNS servers that may know about the IP addresses and names of hosts in second-level domains.

CHANGING NS RECORDS

Network Solutions maintains the master root zone server records on root zone server-A, changes to which are distributed daily to all of the other root zone servers around the world. Any changes to the host names or IP addresses of the DNS servers for a secondary domain must be submitted to the InterNIC, which is run by NSI, so that the root zone server-A master file can be updated.

Let's say that the bigco.com domain's name servers will get new IP addresses, as a result of renumbering BigCo's internal networks. The new addresses must be submitted to the InterNIC, which will update the root zone server-A records and, subsequently, the other root zone server files.

To make a change to the root zone server's DNS records for the bigco domain, the person who is designated as the administrative or the technical contact for the bigco.com domain must submit a change template. The change template is an electronic form on the consolidated NSI-InterNIC Web site, www.networksolutions.com. The same change template can be used to modify name server information, as well as to change the name, address, or phone number of the administrative and technical contacts for the domain.

Once it has been submitted through the InterNIC Web site, the form is processed automatically. An email message confirming the transaction is sent back to the administrative contact. To prevent an unauthorized person from making a change to the records, the email address of the administrative or technical contact must be a valid address. If the InterNIC system can't mail the transaction verification to either the administrative or technical contact, the system assumes that it may not be an authorized change request. In that case, the InterNIC must be contacted directly (through its 800 number, which is listed on the InterNIC Web site), to make changes to the name server records.

The implication of renumbering a network is that if the IP addresses of the secondary domain's DNS servers change, the records in the top-level root zone servers must also change. As a practical matter, DNS servers are usually located on a host or server that is external to the network or by an ISP that provides a DNS service to the customer. Consequently, a renumbering program that affects internal network addresses only, such as one undertaken on a customer network but not on the serving ISP's network, won't affect the DNS name server addresses.

Having failed to resolve the name at the local DNS—the name resolver program on the local DNS server—the local DNS creates its own DNS inquiry for www.bigco.com, and forwards it to one of the 12 root zone servers. The 12 servers are located around the world, though most are in the United States, so the DNS usually sends the inquiry to what it thinks is the closest root zone server.

The resolver will use the IP address for the name server for the bigco.com domain to send a second DNS request to the name server for bigco.com. The name of the DNS host for bigco.com is usually in the form of NS1.bigco.com, although it could be any name. As BigCo's externally visible, or public DNS, the NS1.bigco.com DNS will probably list the host name and IP address for www.bigco.com, and return the IP address for that host. If there are other second- or third-level domains under bigco.com, the name server may also point to another DNS to resolve the host name.

DNS Resource Records

The DNS files comprise a set of tables that map host names, or hosts that serve specific purposes, to IP addresses. The files are maintained as text tables, but the individual entries in the files are referred to as Resource Records, or RRs, which are maintained by the DNS administrator. Network managers or network administrators planning a network renumbering project should know something about the format of the DNS database records, because the records might have to be modified during renumbering.

There are several different types of RRs, to identify different types of hosts or aliases for host names. The most important and most commonly used types of RRs are:

- Hosts (A records)
- Aliases (CNAME records)

- Name servers (NS records)
- Mail exchangers (MX records)
- Pointer records (PTR records)

RRs of all types are simply lines of text, and most follow the same general format in the DNS database, which is:

<hostname>   <expiration>   <class>   <type>   <data>

The <hostname> field is the name of the host or the resource to which the RR refers. The data in the RRs in a DNS database may expire after a period of time, requiring secondary DNSes to get a fresh copy of the database. This expiration value is set in a Time to Live, or TTL, value in the <expiration> field. The type of record, such as A or CNAME, indicates whether this is an RR for a host, an alias, or another type of record. Finally, the IP address for the host is listed in the <data> field.

In addition to the resource records, the DNS database also has other information that indicates the domain or domains that the DNS serves, how long secondary DNSes should keep the DNS records before they should be updated, and so forth. This information is kept in a special kind of DNS resource record called a *Start of Authority*, or *SOA*, record.

The SOA record is usually the first in the DNS database (although it is not required to be at the start of the DNS data file), as it acts as an identifier for the other RRs. The SOA also lists the name and email address of the DNS administrator. The format of the SOA record is somewhat different from that of other RRs, because it contains more administrative and control information, as shown here:

<name>   <ttl>   <class>   SOA   <origin>   <person>

                  <serial>

                  <refresh>

                  <retry>

                  <expire>

                  <minimum>

The administrative information in the SOA record includes the <name> field, which describes the zone to which the SOA refers. The <origin> field lists the name of the primary name server for the zone, which is itself for the primary name server's SOA record. The <person>

field contains an email address, which is usually that of the DNS administrator or a mailbox to which DNS inquiries should be addressed.

For obscure historical reasons, the email address is listed in the SOA in the form mailbox.domain, not mailbox@domain. Listing an email address this way is just one of the many idiosyncrasies of the format of DNS files. These idiosyncrasies, all of which must be observed carefully, have perfectly valid explanations, but none of them is intuitively obvious to most DNS administrators or to casual observers. Another example is the <class> field, which is almost always IN, for Internet. There aren't any other choices for a <class> value, so it could, in fact, be ignored; however, there are some software programs that use DNS files that expect it to be there, so it's a standard part of the SOA record.

The rest of the information in the SOA record is control information regarding how long the RRs in the database can be considered valid and how frequently the zone file should be backed up. Most of these control values are for the benefit of secondary DNSes, which don't check back with the primary DNS until the SOA control values tell them to do so. A secondary DNS copies the entire DNS data file, including the SOA record or records, when it does a zone transfer to get the primary DNS's data files.

For example, the <serial> field is a number that specifies the version of the DNS database file. Whenever the DNS file is changed, the <serial> field should be incremented. That way, secondary DNSes know if the copy of the data file they have is the same one that the primary DNS has.

Secondary DNSes use the value in the <refresh> field to determine when they should get a fresh copy of the zone file from the primary. The value in the <refresh> field is an increment of time, expressed as the number of seconds to transpire before the secondary should ask the primary DNS for a new copy of the database. Note that even though the DNS database may have changed before the <refresh> interval expires, secondary DNSes won't necessarily know about it. They won't automatically check until the <refresh> value expires.

In a renumbering program, secondary DNS refresh intervals affect how soon IP address changes in DNS RRs will propagate to secondary DNSes. It's important that they do so, and that all of the affected DNSes have the new addresses, so that hosts that have been renumbered can be found by other Internet hosts, which will be unaware that some hosts' IP addresses have changed.

The <retry> field is another time value that tells a secondary DNS how long it should wait to query the primary DNS for a new copy of the zone file, if its initial or subsequent inquiries for a zone file update fail. That interval is usually set to 600 seconds, which is 10 minutes.

The <expire> field tells the secondary DNS when the data file it has should no longer be considered current. This is a "freshness date" for the secondary DNS's zone file. If the secondary can't get a fresh copy of the zone file after it has expired, it considers all its responses not to be authoritative, even though they may still be correct.

Finally, the <ttl> value is the shortest TTL, or expiration, value that is to be used in any RR in the DNS data file's RRs. The standard value is one day (86,400 seconds), although most versions of the standard Unix DNS program, BIND, impose a minimum value of 300 seconds. This is another one of those historical artifacts of DNS that can interfere with newer capabilities of DNS. Dynamic DNS services, for instance, want to update DNS RRs immediately, not after whatever interval the <ttl> value imposes. Sometimes, Dynamic DNS updates don't work properly because of the <ttl> value in the SOA, so DNS administrators and network managers should be aware of this problem.

A Records

An A record is the most common type of DNS record, because it lists a host name and its corresponding IP address. An A record is a general-purpose DNS record type. The format of an A record in the DNS database is:

<name>   <ttl>   <class>   A   <data>

Most hosts listed in the DNS have A records. A Web server, for instance, will have an A record, because as far as the DNS is concerned, a Web server is just another host, and a host name like www.bigco.com is just another host name. A mail server, however, may be referred to in an MX record, to identify the email gateway for a specific application, such as email. An A record can be used for anything with an IP address, so a host address referenced in an A record could be a router port or a dynamically assigned address in a DHCP address pool.

CNAME Records

Aliases, or other names, for hosts are listed in CNAME records. CNAME stands for the canonical name of a host, which means a secondary name for that host. If the name servers for a domain are renumbered, the DNS administrator may have to establish temporary CNAME records for the name servers. The CNAME records would list the new IP addresses of the name servers during a transition period, while the NS records would list the old IP addresses of the name servers. The reason for this is that most DNSes keep copies of DNS zone files for a period of time, and both the old and the new IP addresses of DNS servers may have to be carried in the DNS files during the transition.

NS Records

Name servers, which are DNS servers, are listed in *name server* (NS) records. It's essential that NS records be accurate, because they point to DNS servers for other domains. Note that though NS records are pointers to the DNS servers for other domains, they don't specify any host names for anything within that domain. For instance, even if you maintain your own DNS for your domain, your ISP probably keeps NS records in its DNS to point back to your DNS. The root zone-A record for your domain, such as xyz.com, would list the DNS of your ISP as an NS record. Your ISP, in turn, would have an NS record pointing back to your DNS. Inquiries to resolve host names to IP addresses for hosts in your domain would go from the root zone server to your ISP's server, which would point the inquiries to your DNS.

If your ISP maintained the DNS for you, the ISP's DNS would maintain the zone file for your domain and resolve DNS inquiries on your behalf. In either case, an Internet user who made a name resolution inquiry for a host on your domain would get the same result.

If a network is renumbered, it may not be necessary to change NS records in a DNS if the name servers themselves aren't renumbered. Internal DNS servers behind a firewall, which serve only internal hosts, would need updated RRs to reflect renumbered hosts. If there is a DNS that is external to the network, such as one maintained by an ISP, it may not be renumbered, because it may not be connected to a network that is being moved into new address space.

MX Records

Mail Exchanger (MX) records list mail servers or mail gateways. MX records usually point to externally visible hosts, so that mail arriving for internal users can be received from outside a firewall or a security barrier. Mail exchangers use external addresses, so MX records may not have to be changed in a renumbering project, as long as the next higher network provider, such as an ISP, is not also changing addresses.

PTR Records

In addition to resolving host names to IP addresses, DNSes can also do the reverse, resolving IP addresses back to host names. This is a useful capability for network interfaces that are usually identified only by their IP addresses, such as router ports. It is also useful for network services that want to identify hosts that are asking for certain types of connections or services.

For example, an internal Web server for the XYZ Corporation may have proprietary information that should only be seen by its employees. In order to provide some control over access to the Web server, the server may ask a DNS to translate the source IP address of the request back to a host name. Host names that are not in the xyz.com domain, for instance, could then be denied access to the Web server.

Reverse address resolution uses a special kind of resource record, called pointer records (PTR records). PTR records are maintained in a DNS database, but they actually belong to a special domain called the in-addr.arpa domain. For reasons too complicated to describe here, PTR records list the IP address of a host in reverse order. This creates a set of pointers that a DNS uses to locate the DNS that has the PTR record for the host.

Just as with other DNS records, the addresses in PTR records may change if networks or hosts are renumbered. It's easy to forget that the PTR records, too, have to be updated when addresses change, because it's not obvious to inexperienced DNS administrators what the PTR records are, nor how they work. In fact, many DNSes don't even have them at all.

DNS Zones

Most DNS services maintain the host name-to-IP address records for a single domain, such as for bigco.com, in which case, the bigco.com domain is referred to as a *zone*. In DNS parlance, a zone is the set of domains for which a DNS maintains host name-to-IP address records. So, if the NS1.bigco.com DNS only keeps records for the bigco.com domain, it is the authoritative zone file for the bigco.com domain. The list of RRs in the bigco.com DNS (or any DNS, for that matter) is referred to as the *DNS zone file*.

A DNS zone can contain the records for several domains. For instance, an ISP may run a DNS service for several of its customers that don't want to run their own DNS services. The ISP's DNS may be the DNS for the abc1.com, abc2.com, and abc3.com domains, all of which are its customers' domains. In that case, the zone served by the ISP's DNS file covers three separate domains.

In this way, a domain is an administrative concept for assigning names to hosts. The IP addresses assigned to those hosts are linked in the DNS. Otherwise, there is no relationship between domain names and IP addresses, because assigning IP addresses and assigning domain names are completely independent administrative procedures.

The DNS service for a zone is usually backed up by another DNS, in case the primary DNS is out of service or a failure of some network link renders it unreachable. That's why the InterNIC requires each domain name to specify two name servers. The primary is called the primary DNS and a backup DNS is called a secondary DNS (there may be more than one).

The secondary DNS servers download copies of the primary DNS zone file periodically, to get a fresh copy of the DNS zone files. The interval at which they look for a new copy of the zone file is determined by the <refresh> value in the SOA record of the zone file. The secondary uses that value to determine when to ask the primary for a fresh copy of the zone file. The <serial> value in the SOA record indicates the version of the zone file. A secondary DNS knows it has a new zone file when the new file has a higher <serial> value than the old one.

Downloading a new copy of the DNS database file from a primary DNS is called a *zone transfer*. For security reasons, it may be wise to restrict access to the DNS file so that only authorized secondary DNSes can do a zone transfer. Otherwise, anyone who wants to do so can take a copy of the DNS database file and determine the addresses in use on your networks. For this reason, most firewalls won't allow zone transfers to be done through the firewall, to prevent an intruder from gaining access to an internal DNS database.

Summary

A network administrator or network manager who is doing a network or host renumbering project may not have to make changes to DNS files. Nevertheless, the network manager should have a clear understanding of how renumbering affects DNS information.

At a minimum, renumbering affects the A records in the DNS database, because they map host names to IP addresses. But a large-scale renumbering or network engineering effort may also affect other DNS records, such as the CNAME or alias records for those same hosts, MX records, and even NS records for other DNSes. The latter changes can be particularly insidious, because the DNS administrator may not know all of the other DNSes that hold NS records for a DNS server that may have changed its IP address.

Modern operating systems, such as Windows NT, and the most recent versions of the Unix DNS, BIND, can relieve the administrative burden of maintaining DNS records. That said, administering a DNS can be as much an art as a science, particularly when renumbering the hosts and networks to which it refers.

Provider-Aggregated and Provider-Independent Address Space

If IP addresses only need to be unique for networks and hosts to be reachable on the Internet, it shouldn't matter what IP address you have, because they are all just more peas in the same pod, right? And once they're yours, they should be yours forever, right?

The first point—that all IP addresses are the same—is almost right. They are from the perspective of routing, but not from the perspective of connectivity. That is, IP addresses need only be unique, but their uniqueness is also tied to the ISP who grants their use to customers. The second point—about perpetual ownership of IP address space—was once widely assumed to be true, but it's false. IP addresses are only temporary possessions—you don't own them, you only rent them. They're loaned by ARIN and the other address delegation organizations. Perpetual ownership, or more correctly, use of IP addresses is only a goal, not a rule. Some things, such as changing ISPs or an ISP changing its relationships with other ISPs, may change address usage and may even require network renumbering.

Independent and Aggregated

Though it is true that IP addresses must be unique, there are different kinds of IP addresses. They're referred to as *provider-aggregated* (PA) addresses and *provider-independent* (PI) addresses. Both are unique, fully routable IP addresses. What distinguishes them is the degree to which an organization that uses them can relocate networks behind different ISPs, change ISPs, or affect routing to them from the Internet.

It's an important distinction for network administrators and system designers to make, because it affects whether networks using those addresses can be moved to different ISPs without renumbering or whether the networks will remain reachable from the Internet regardless of where the networks are located or which ISP connects them.

For system designers and network administrators, the key questions that must be answered are:

- What kind of address space do I need?
- From whom do I get address space?
- What are the requirements for getting the right kind of address space?
- Which one—PA or PI—will position me better for the future?
- Which one will give me the best Internet reachability and routability?
- Is PA or PI better for an ISP?

A general guideline, but one that is not always reliable, is that provider-aggregated addresses are those given by an ISP to its customers. ISP customers use provider-aggregated addresses to number hosts on their networks. ISPs, on the other hand, may hold provider-independent address space. It's referred to as provider-independent in that Internet routability to hosts and networks within the address space isn't dependent on its being part of the space used by any other provider.

Provider-Aggregated Address Space

Provider-aggregated (PA) addresses are IP addresses that are part of an address block that has been assigned to an ISP. Generally speaking, PA must remain with that ISP for Internet routability and reachability.

The ISP announces the addresses back to the Internet as part of its address block. Its route announcements ensure that the addresses in the PA space will be routable and reachable.

Because its customers look to the ISP to give them public address space, the ISP subdivides the address space it has been assigned into subnetworks, and assigns them to its customers. The customer who has been assigned PA space can do whatever it wants with that space, subdividing it into subnetworks to meet its network needs and its environment.

The addresses in PA space are called aggregated because the customer must advertise PA space back to the ISP that assigned the addresses. That is, the ISP must announce the entire block to its next higher ISP, meaning that the address space the ISP assigns to its customers must remain in that block.

For example, let's say that a local ISP is assigned the 172.16.0.0 Class B address block by ARIN. Today, the pressure to simplify Internet routing is driven by CIDR address blocks. CIDR, discussed in Chapter 3, simplifies Internet routing, because it requires that large, contiguous groups of addresses be advertised as a single route to the higher-level national Internet ISPs.

The local ISP may give one of its customers two subnets from that block, say the 172.16.1.0 and 172.16.2.0 subnets. The customer may configure and subnetwork those two Class C equivalent addresses any way he or she likes. However—and here's the provider aggregation part—the customer must advertise those two subnets back to the local ISP as a single route to 172.16.1.0 /23. This enables the local ISP to advertise its entire block back to its national ISP as 172.16.0.0 /16. In other words, they are provider-aggregated addresses because both the customer and the ISP must both announce the address space as a single route back to their respective providers.

More important, PA space must be announced as part of a higher-level provider's address space in order for the addresses in it to be reachable on the Internet. The New World Order of Internet routing now decrees that new address space that hasn't been consolidated into large, aggregated address blocks may find itself unreachable from the Internet. Why? Because top-level Internet routers may ignore it as a means of simplifying their routing tables.

PA space, particularly as it refers to the space given to an ISP's customers, is only loaned or leased. It is used and identified with a specific customer, but it isn't owned in any sense. It's like a license plate number. It's used by someone, and it serves to identify a vehicle and its owner, but the plate number is really owned by the state motor vehicle department.

Provider-Independent Address Space

Provider-independent address space is not dependent on being part of a larger aggregated block of addresses. They can stand on their own, and will be carried by the Internet's top-level routers, whether or not they are part of a larger ISP's address space.

There are three common reasons why PI space doesn't have to be part of another ISP's announced blocks:

- It has been delegated to a large ISP by ARIN, RIPE, APNIC, or one of the other address delegation agencies.

- It is a large enough block that even if it is advertised by itself, it is too large to be filtered out by the NAT routers.

- It has been grandfathered in as a legacy IP address, and also won't be filtered out.

Top-level ISPs usually have PI, and, in some cases, so do companies and organizations that own large blocks of address space. If the aggregated address block is larger than a CIDR /19, the address block may also be PI, depending on how the address block is seen from the perspective of Internet routing.

Let's say the local ISP has been assigned the 172.16.0.0 /20 address block. It announces that block to the national ISP at the next level above it in the Internet routing hierarchy. That address space, even though it has been assigned to the local ISP by ARIN, is still too small to be reachable anywhere on the Internet. It is routable anywhere on the Internet, but the top-level ISPs will filter it out because it's too small for them to carry. Consequently, the local ISP's address space is provider aggregated, but it's not provider independent.

For example, a company that has had a full Class B address for some time may have provider-independent space. Its space doesn't fall within the newer, small blocks of address space filtered out by top-level ISPs, so it is PI. It probably isn't aggregated by other ISPs, so it's not PA space.

Private Address Space

While it seems inconceivable today, not every TCP/IP system is connected to the Internet. Some are isolated from the Internet, either for security reasons or because they're intended to be experimental systems. Because TCP/IP has been the standard networking protocol for Unix and other systems, it has long been used on small, isolated networks of computers that run special-purpose applications or that are used for experimental or developmental purposes.

To accommodate these special-purpose, so-called private TCP/IP networks, RFC 1918 sets aside certain blocks of IP address space as private addresses. Host addresses and network addresses that fall within these special "no-fly" IP address zones are supposed to be on isolated networks that aren't visible from other TCP/IP networks, including the Internet.

To accommodate private networks of varying sizes, RFC 1918 sets aside these special IP address blocks for Class A, B, and C networks that will be isolated from the Internet:

Class A 10.0.0.0

Class B 172.16.0.0 to 172.31.0.0

Class C 192.168.1.0 to 192.168.255.0

Anyone who wants to can use any of these IP addresses for any network, as long as the network or networks that use them aren't seen by any other network. You don't even have to contact the InterNIC, ARIN, or anyone else to use these numbers. To ensure they aren't seen by any other network, IP routers are programmed to ignore traffic sent to or from IP addresses that fall within these private address blocks. In fact, routes to these networks are also dropped from routing table updates if they appear in routing table updates.

The result is that IP datagrams that have source or destination addresses within any of this private address space are unroutable. Unless they are specially programmed not to do so, IP routers will discard traffic that bears any address from within these blocks of private address space. They do this because they assume that traffic from any network that uses private address space has somehow "escaped" into the Internet and that they need to protect other routers and hosts from potentially harmful effects of an experimental protocol or application that might be running on one of those private networks.

One of the major benefits of private address space, as just mentioned, is that anyone can use the reserved addresses, as long as the networks that use them are not connected to networks that use public address space, such as the Internet. The address space may be reused by any company or organization that wants to do so, even repeatedly at different locations in the same company. The key is to use NAT to translate the private addresses into unique, "public" addresses for communications with anyone else on the Internet or at another location.

For example, a company with locations in New York, Los Angeles, Chicago, and London could use the same addresses from the private Class B address space (172.16.0.0 through 172.31.0.0) at each of its four locations. The only requirement would be that the private addresses would have to be translated to public addresses for traffic that was sent between locations or through an ISP gateway to the Internet.

The company's network administrator could even use the same addresses to designate routers, servers, and applications servers in each location. NAT would hide all of the private addresses, and allow traffic that originated in private address space to be routed across the Internet.

Maybe You Can Take It with You

As long as the addresses work, network administrators and systems designers usually aren't particularly concerned with whether their space is provider independent or provider aggregated, but the former certainly sounds better than the latter. Given a choice, most people would choose anything called "independent," perhaps even without knowing what that means.

The key issue for a corporate or organization network, or even for ISPs, is whether the address space is portable.. Specifically, the question is, if you change ISPs, or if your relationship to a higher-level ISP were to change, would you have to surrender the use of that address range and renumber your networks (or those of your customers) into a new block of IP address space? Address portability is like 800 telephone number portability. Until 1993, 800 numbers "belonged" to specific long-distance carriers (AT&T, then-Worldcom-less MCI, Sprint, and so on), which served specific 800 exchanges. For example, all 800 numbers in the 1-800-444-#### exchange were MCI numbers. If a business had

800 service from MCI, and used an 800 number in that exchange, changing 800 carriers meant changing 800 numbers, too.

As of May 1993, a Federal Communications Commission (FCC) mandate regarding 800 number address portability, gave 800 customers the option of keeping an 800 number, regardless of which long-distance carrier provided the service. As simple as the concept was, it took more than a decade to overcome the regulatory hurdles and make the technical changes in the way phone companies handled 800 calls to make 800 number portability a reality.

The answer to the address portability question is that some PI addresses are more equal than others. Whether address space is truly portable isn't so much a matter of who granted it or how long you've had it; provider independence is really a matter of whether traffic to your addresses will be routed there by everyone on the Internet.

In the IP addressing world, there is no central authority like the FCC to mandate IP address portability. IP address portability is dependent on whether a customer or an ISP has PA or PI. While there are exceptions to this rule, generally speaking, PA is not portable address space, and PI is.

I Want My PI

The key determining factor about PI space is whether Internet routing will work for it, regardless of where it sits in the routing hierarchy. Having an address block that has been delegated by an address registry such as ARIN doesn't necessarily mean the block is PI, because address assignments don't necessarily mean the space is reachable on the Internet.

Reachability on the Internet is really a question of whether the address space in which your networks are numbered is known by the rest of the Internet. And this is really a question of routing and reachability policies established by the top-level ISPs, particularly the ones that swap traffic at major Internet access points, or NAPs.

To keep their routers from being overwhelmed by large numbers of individual route announcements, some of the top-level ISPs have started to filter out address blocks smaller than /19 CIDR blocks (the equivalent of 32 Class C addresses). As mentioned in an earlier chapter, Sprint was the first to do this, and, as one of the largest of the top-level ISPs, its influence led other top-level ISPs to do the same thing.

Sprint's reasoning was that if it didn't do something to halt or reverse the growth of the size of the routing tables in its NAP routers, eventually, they wouldn't be able to maintain all of the routes to all of the networks on the Internet. Therefore, Sprint announced that CIDR blocks smaller than /19 in newly assigned address space would be filtered out of its address tables, effectively rendering them unreachable, because Sprint would no longer have a route to those networks. Sprint's routers would throw away datagrams destined for networks it couldn't locate, which would leave those networks unreachable from customers behind Sprint.

Although it was a controversial move, the logic and reasoning behind Sprint's policy was generally supported by large ISPs. Older address space wasn't affected, and the filtering policy forced many ISPs to try to consolidate the address space they had, in order to make it PI. One large ISP, for example, reduced the number of networks it announced to other ISPs from more than 3,000 to fewer than 800.

The point is, whether addresses are PI really depends on how they are treated by the routing tables in the Internet's routers, not who grants them.

The New PI Rules

Obviously, it's to anyone's advantage to have provider-independent address space. PI is particularly advantageous to ISPs who want to have the flexibility to change their relationships with top-level ISPs without affecting the connectivity, routability, or IP address usage of their downstream customers.

It's also advantageous to the smaller ISPs, but it may be harder for them to get PI. Even if a small ISP wants to have PI, it may not be large enough to ask for or to get a large enough block of address space that will make it PI space. That is, it may be harder for a smaller ISP to get what we consider to be PI today. The rules about Internet routability, including how large (or small) a CIDR block top-level providers will filter out, may change as the Internet grows.

To give smaller ISPs a better chance to get their own, provider-independent address space, in early 1999, ARIN changed its rules about address block allocation. Recognizing that a /19 CIDR block was the minimum size needed for an IP address block that would be provider independent and still qualify for global routing, ARIN initiated a "fast-track" program for small ISPs.

This program allows a small ISP that wants to get its own PI to do so, as long as it feels that it can grow quickly enough to warrant more space. The objective for the small IS is to get a large enough address block, which doesn't have to be aggregated by another, higher-level provider, so that it isn't dependent on global routability by virtue of being part of another, larger address block.

If the small ISP has made efficient use of a smaller, PA block from another, upstream ISP, the fast-track program allows the small ISP to apply for, and get, a /20 CIDR block. A /20 block only has 16 classful Class C addresses, and it isn't PI. However, ARIN will reserve the next contiguous /20 block of addresses for the small ISP, enabling it to advertise what is really its smaller /20 block as a /19 block.

The benefit of this is that the smaller ISP can now have (according to global routability rules as they stand today) a provider-independent /19 block, even though it really only has a /20 block from which it assigns addresses. The small ISP must use and assign the /20 block efficiently to its customers and, more important, agree to renumber everything into the new space.

It's considered a fast-track program because if the small ISP needs more address space within 18 months, ARIN will give it the second /20 block that was reserved at the time of the original grant. Once the small ISP has the second /20 block, which is contiguous to the first block, the no-longer-small ISP will have a /19 block, which will be PI.

Do I Need an Autonomous System Number?

An Autonomous System (AS) is a designator for a group of routers under a single routing administration. ASes are routing and administrative concepts that have implications for internal and external routing (they are described in more detail in Chapter 13).

Like IP address space, the number of ASes that are available for assignment to companies, organizations, and ISPs throughout the global Internet is finite. Consequently, ARIN and other address delegation authorities only issue AS numbers to organizations and ISPs that really need them.

The implication for the provider-independent and provider-aggregated addressing issue is whether you actually need your own AS number. It's not a PI or PA question, rather a question of how big your network is and how your network fits into the Internet routing scheme.

Generally speaking, you will need an AS number if your network has the following characteristics:

- It has its own internal routing protocol and routing policy.
- It uses BGP to exchange routing information with "peer" networks.
- It has more than one connection to the Internet (called multihoming), for redundancy and backup.

Since most networks are located behind other ISP networks, and those ISPs handle all of the details of BGP routing for their connected networks, it is fair to say that most networks do not need their own AS number. Network managers who run Autonomous Systems must accept a considerable amount of responsibility for running their own routing protocols (such as BGP) to neighboring networks. For most ISP customers, however, the ISP's network will have its own ASN, and your network will appear to the Internet as part of that AS.

Getting PI

Not everyone needs PI, and not everyone can get it, either. Unless you're an ISP, it's difficult, period. For most corporations and organizations that need more address space, PA space works fine. Having PA may mean that you might have to renumber your address space at some time in the future, but you may not have any control over that. Besides, your ISP will probably try to minimize the possibility of that happening. ISPs make every effort not to change address space unless there's some good reason to do so; they have nothing to gain by inconveniencing their customers.

Provider-aggregated address space is granted by whomever has PI to parcel out to users under it. In most cases, it's an ISP, which aggregates address blocks under it, and announces them to the rest of the Internet. That's the simplest and cleanest way to get address space that has both reachability and routability.

Given the constraints on the use of address space today, as noted, new provider-independent address space is customarily granted to ISPs, and less frequently to corporations or organizations. The three primary reasons for this restriction are:

- ISPs need address space to give to their customers.
- Most organizations or corporations that connect to the Internet do so through an IS that has been granted its own block of address space.

- ISPs understand the requirements for using address space efficiently and effectively.
- ARIN and other address delegation authorities charge fees for new address space delegations.

Companies and organizations that are expanding their networks, and that need more IP address space to do so, should look to their ISPs for more space, rather than try to get their own provider-independent address space. The address delegation organizations, such as ARIN, RIPE, and APNIC, see the ISPs, not necessarily end users, as their primary customers. For the near future, most new address space will most likely go to ISPs, because of the requirements for global routability and sensible address aggregation.

Summary

In a perfect world, all Internet users and ISPs would have their own provider-independent address space. Unfortunately, the Internet has become too complex for everyone to have completely independent space. Furthermore, not everyone needs PI space; and the reality is that companies and organizations that have been connected to the Internet for some time already have PI space.

It is true that the rules of Internet routing may change in the future as the number of Internet-connected systems grows. However, other techniques, such as the use of private address space, network address translation, and, assuming it occurs, the eventual adoption of IPv6, may change the addressing permanence and portability concerns of Internet users.

CHAPTER

11

Host Considerations

Traditionally, devices that have IP addresses have been referred to as "hosts." And though it is true that the second part of an IP address is called the host ID, it's not necessarily a host at all. In a renumbering project, finding and changing all of those host addresses, or references to them, can be a major piece of work.

The host ID identifies an endpoint in a TCP/IP network. However, as we have already noted, a host is not necessarily a host computer. It could be a PC, a mainframe computer, a minicomputer, a server, or one of any of the ports on a router. An IP address is a software identifier that we associate with a network interface, in order to route IP datagrams to it.

Different hosts and different types of network interfaces deal with and understand IP addresses differently. To develop a workable plan for changing or managing IP addresses, the network administrator must have some understanding of how different types of hosts, operating systems, and applications understand their IP addresses, where they are stored, and how they change them.

A Host Is a Host

Regardless whether they are PCs, workstations, servers, or mainframes, computers must have some mechanism by which they determine their IP addresses. IP addresses are configured on each network interface, either automatically by a network service, or by a network administrator, host administrator, or user who enters a specific host IP address.

The Dynamic Host Configuration Protocol (DHCP) and the bootP service are examples of network services that deliver a valid, unique IP address to a host at bootup time. The IP address assigned by DHCP or the IP address manually entered to a PC or workstation may become part of a configuration file. The configuration file may be a text file, such as the HOSTS or LMHOSTS files in Windows PCs. A static address in a Unix system is typically embedded as a parameter call to ifconfig in an /etc/rc file, or indirectly to another file in the /etc directory.

The simplest and most reliable way for a host to determine its IP address is to take it from a configuration file stored on a local disk. Windows systems use this method when they create a LMHOSTS file, from which the Windows PC can get its own IP address, as well as the IP addresses of other key network services, such as the Primary Domain Controller.

While it assumes network connectivity, DHCP is a far more flexible and efficient way to assign IP addresses to hosts than static addressing. DHCP is particularly helpful in a renumbering effort, because it eliminates many, but not all, of the problems of assigning IP addresses from new address space.

HOSTS File

Windows 95 and Windows NT systems create a small text file, which is usually C:\windows\hosts, to cache frequently used or essential IP address-to-host name mappings. For example, the IP addresses listed in a HOSTS file might include:

- The local loopback address (127.0.0.1), by which the PC tests its network interface connection.
- The IP address of the Microsoft Exchange Server that maintains the user's Exchange mailbox.
- Addresses of applications servers, and the names by which they are known.

- Addresses of clients and their workstation names.
- Addresses of Windows Primary and Secondary Domain controllers.

The names of hosts listed in the HOSTS file may be dot-com style addresses, or they could be the NetBIOS names of hosts and their corresponding IP addresses. In either case, the HOSTS file provides a simple, easy-to-use local file that can be accessed locally.

Today, it is safe to assume that most networks have a DNS service. So, the inclusion of dot-com to IP address mappings is less important than it was before the DNS became an essential part of the network infrastructure.

The entries in a HOSTS file are much more useful for mapping IP addresses to NetBIOS names. Many devices in Windows networks, including NT servers, still use NetBIOS names to identify themselves. If, however, those devices also have IP addresses (as most do), something must map NetBIOS names back to IP addresses.

WINS and NetBIOS

In a Windows network, the Windows Internet Name Service (WINS) provides a network-accessible service to map IP addresses back to NetBIOS names. So Windows devices may discover IP addresses either by consulting a DNS or by requesting the IP address that corresponds to a NetBIOS name from the WINS service.

NetBIOS is a network naming protocol that was devised by IBM in the early 1980s as a way to map Token Ring MAC-level addresses to "named" network objects. The idea was to simplify locating network devices and services in the relatively small, simple networks that were created in the 1980s. NetBIOS address broadcasts aren't normally passed by routers to other networks, so this protocol couldn't scale well when interconnected, routed networks became the standard form for local networks.

To ensure backward compatibility with older versions of Windows networking and with the Windows concept of workgroups, Microsoft retained NetBIOS naming as the default network naming convention for Windows networks. It even continued to use NetBIOS after it introduced Windows 95 and Windows NT, both of which used NetBIOS as their default naming conventions.

Then when Microsoft introduced Windows NT, it also introduced TCP/IP as the protocol for routed Windows networking, meaning that smaller, "flat," bridged networks could use NetBIOS, while complex, routed networks could use TCP/IP. To support these two different environments, and to eliminate the need for every Windows PC to maintain separate local files that had IP-to-DNS-style host names and IP address-to-NetBIOS names, Microsoft introduced WINS.

The idea behind WINS is that it functions as a DNS for NetBIOS names. Routers will pass WINS requests, so a workstation on one network can make a request for the NetBIOS name of a server on another network segment. The WINS server can answer the request and pass back the IP address of the server to the client, so that the client can make a standard TCP/IP address request of the server.

Microsoft has taken pains to integrate its NT DNS service with WINS. Its goal is to make the existence of WINS transparent to the client, so that it always uses the routable TCP/IP protocol (and the correct IP address) to communicate with servers and services. For example, in NT 4.0, all requests for either dot-com names or NetBIOS names go to the NT DNS service. If the DNS can't resolve the name to an IP address, it can pass the request to the nearest WINS server for resolution. In either case, either the DNS or the WINS server can return the correct IP address.

Some versions of other DNS services, such as those running older versions of the BIND DNS service on Unix computers, do not pass unresolvable name requests back to a WINS server. However, the newest versions of BIND can pass a NetBIOS name request to a WINS service. In order to do this, there must be a resource record in the DNS for the WINS server, mapping its name to an IP address so the DNS can find it. Windows NT DNS services need the same IP address, but theirs can be configured when the Windows NT DNS service is set up.

Unix System Configuration Files

Unix systems maintain IP address information in configuration files. They may be managed or accessed through a graphical interface, but they're kept in text files that can be edited with a standard text editor. The location of the configuration files that contain IP address configurations will vary by system, but a common directory for them is inside the /etc directory.

The Unix command to configure IP addresses is ifconfig, assuming the interface IP addresses weren't already configured by the installation script that installed the Unix OS in the first place. The ifconfig command allows the user or system administrator to specify the interface on which the IP address is being assigned, the IP host address, a netmask, and, if needed, a directed broadcast address.

A directed broadcast address may be specified if the network broadcast address is not an all-ones address (host .255). Even if it is the standard all-ones broadcast address, some Unix system administrators prefer to set the broadcast address explicitly to avoid any confusion about it.

The ifconfig command also allows the system administrator to use the name of the host that is being configured, instead of specifying (and possibly mistyping) the IP address of the host. However, the system administrator must have entered the name and IP address of the host in the /etc/hosts file, because ifconfig usually executes first, before the DNS is running.

The netstat command will show the configuration of all of the interfaces on the Unix system, including their IP addresses.

On Unix systems that get their addresses dynamically from DHCP, some versions run two separate processes to handle IP address configuration information. The IP host address is managed by one process and the other information, such as the DNS address, is handled by another process.

Readdressing with Configuration Files

Host configuration files can be a particularly problematic issue in an IP readdressing effort. They are hard-coded into PC, workstation, and server configurations, and therefore they are likely to be difficult to inventory and to replace.

One strategy for dealing with local configuration files, particularly on Windows networks, is to replace them as part of the renumbering task plan with a batch file distribution system. For example, Symantec's Ghost, the HP Desktop Administrator, Intel's LANDesk, and Network Associates' Zero Administration Client (ZAC) Suite can all distribute files to networked PCs, in order to overwrite, replace, or distribute files.

Many HOSTS files on Windows PCs contain only one entry: the IP address for the Exchange server. The Exchange client must be pointed to whichever Exchange server maintains the user's mailbox. The Exchange server's NetBIOS name is usually resolved back to an IP address by the WINS server and cached back in the HOSTS file.

DHCP

The Dynamic Host Configuration Protocol, defined in RFC 2131, performs four important functions for networked hosts. Through DHCP, a host or a PC can get:

- Its own IP host address and subnet mask, either for temporary or permanent use
- The IP address of the nearest DNS service
- The IP address of a WINS server
- The IP address of a default gateway to the Internet or to other networks

As its name implies, DHCP is a dynamic IP address assignment protocol for configuring hosts for network connectivity. In this case, dynamic means that a host's IP address may change from time to time. If we accept the principle that any IP address is just as good as any other IP address (as long as it is part of the network address space to which a device is attached), it shouldn't matter what address a PC or host has. As long as the address is routable and unique, it won't matter.

In practice, the *dynamic* part of DHCP refers to its ability to reassign an IP address that is no longer in use to a different host. Whenever possible, DHCP tries to assign the same address to a host. Under normal circumstances, a DHCP client will use the same address as long as it is connected to a given network.

Furthermore, if hosts don't have fixed or static IP addresses, it simplifies network administration, and particularly renumbering. DHCP simplifies greatly the tasks of network and host address renumbering and network configuration.

DHCP Server, Where Are You?

Instead of knowing at bootup what its IP address is, a host, workstation, or PC broadcasts on the local network for a DHCP server. The DHCP server responds, verifies the identity of the PC or workstation, and returns an IP address to the host. If it is configured to do so, the DHCP server can also return other useful (or essential) IP addresses, such as that of the preferred DNS server, and the default gateway to the Internet.

The preferred DNS server may be any DNS server, as long as its IP address is routable by the internal network and its gateway. Some networks may have a split DNS, with an internal DNS for protected, internally known hosts, and a second DNS for externally visible hosts. The DNS address returned by DHCP may be either one, but the administrator of the DHCP server will probably configure the DHCP service to return the internal DNS server address to protected hosts on the protected inside networks.

DHCP is related to the earlier bootP Bootstrap Protocol (RFC 951), which is the more common address-assignment protocol for Unix systems; it is a subset of DHCP. Both bootP and DHCP clients and servers use the same UDP port numbers (67 for the DHCP or bootP server and 68 for their respective clients), so a bootP request may be able to go to, and be answered by, a DHCP server.

DHCP Scope

One of the parameters that DHCP services use is the DHCP *scope*. The DHCP scope is the set of subnets on which client machines are connected, to which a pool of IP addresses will be assigned. That is, the scope is a way of fixing a range of IP addresses that will be assigned to specific clients. The scope is defined by the subnet range in which client addresses will be assigned.

In the Windows NT DHCP service, scopes are assigned names so that they can be referred to logically. The DHCP service also allows the DHCP administrator to set the duration, or length, of an IP address lease. The lease is the specific amount of time a computer may use an IP address until it must ask DHCP for another IP address. DHCP-assigned addresses may be assigned permanently or they may be assigned for limited periods of time, such as a day or a week.

The readdressing implication of the DHCP scope is that it enables the network designer or administrator to control which IP host addresses will be assigned to which subnetworks. It really doesn't matter how long the DHCP lease terms are, but it is usually determined by how many extra addresses (if there are any at all) exist in the address pool available to a specific subnet. The closer the address space is to the number of IP addresses that will be assigned, the shorter should be the lease term. In other words, if there are just enough addresses to go around, make the lease period a day or so. That way, when users are traveling or just haven't logged in to the network, their DHCP-assigned addresses go back into the pool sooner and become available for reassignment to other users.

Displaying DHCP-Assigned Address Information

Windows PCs must go to the DOS shell to display their DHCP-assigned P addresses. Instead of marching through the Control Panels...Network icons, a user of a Windows PC that has been assigned an IP address by DHCP can display the address by invoking the ipconfig or winipcfg command from the DOS command line.

The result of running these DOS commands is, curiously, a Windows box that displays the currently assigned IP address and subnet mask, as well as the IP addresses of the Default Gateway, the DNS server, the Primary WINS server, and the DHCP server. Because this information comes from DHCP, and is not entered by the user or the network administrator, it does not appear in the Control Panels...Network windows. That set of tabs is for entering static IP address information; it's overridden by the DHCP-assigned addresses.

DHCP can be configured to assign all of the most useful "utility" IP addresses a PC user needs, such as the IP addresses of the DNS, the WINS server, and the default gateway, not to mention the PC's own IP address. Its capability to give a networked PC all of its necessary IP address information at bootup makes it particularly useful in a network renumbering effort.

DHCP is the easiest and simplest way to renumber the workstations and many of the hosts on a network. Network administrators who are considering doing a renumbering task and who have not yet used DHCP should install it and work with it before starting the renumbering project. Provided it is configured properly, DHCP relieves the network administrator of many of the gory details of renumbering. In addition, DHCP scopes control the allocation of address ranges to specific subnets. Furthermore, the DNS, default gateway, WINS, and other IP addresses downloaded along with the client IP address establish a level of consistency for network utility addresses, thereby reducing problems arising from misconfigured workstation addresses.

Configuring a PC to Use DHCP

By default, Windows PCs must be configured with hard-coded IP addresses, although configuring a PC to use DHCP is relatively simple. Assuming that a DHCP server has been set up on the network, the simplest way to configure Windows PCs to use DHCP is:

Select Settings...Control Panels...Network

In the Configuration tab, choose the TCP/IP adapter that is being used as the network interface and select the Properties button. There may be more than one, such as a dial-up adapter and an Ethernet adapter, but it's usually the Ethernet adapter for desktop PCs.

1. In the IP Address tab, turn on the radio button for Obtain an IP Address Automatically.
2. Select OK on all the open windows.
3. Remove any entries for default gateways and DNS servers, as they may override parameters supplied by DHCP.
4. Reboot to get the DHCP server to assign an IP address to the PC.

As is usually the case with Windows, there's also a hard way to do it, through editing the Windows NT Registry entry that controls the use of the DHCP client. The Registry entry that controls the use of DHCP on a Windows NT machine is in:

```
HKLocal_Machine\SYSTEM\CurrentControlSet\Services\DHCP\Start = n
```

The default value of n is 1, which means do not start DHCP. If you change the value to 2, the DHCP client will start automatically on bootup.

The Registry may also already hold a static IP address. The static IP address, as well as the subnetwork mask entry, must both be changed to 0.0.0.0. In addition, the EnableDHCP = n value must be changed to EnableDHCP = 1.

Note that both the IP address and the subnetwork mask numbers must be changed to 0.0.0.0, not just highlighted and deleted. Both are part of the Registry entry:

```
HKLocal_Machine\SYSTEM\CurrentControlSet\Services\DHCP\Parameters\TCPIP
```

Hosts with Multiple Interfaces

Some hosts and workstations have more than one network interface, and therefore need separate IP addresses for each interface. These hosts are connected to different networks because they act as servers on different network segments or they have some special-purpose need for multiple network connectivity.

At bootup, each network interface will send out its own DHCP request and be assigned a different IP address. If the requests go to different DHCP servers, the addresses the host receives for other network services, such as the DNS or the default gateway, may be different. The questions that must be addressed are which one is the best one to use and, assuming that both work, which one will the host use?

The answer is system- and operating system-specific. NT machines will most likely use whichever address is bound to the network interface in use. On Unix systems that get their addresses dynamically from DHCP, some versions of Unix run two separate processes to handle IP address configuration information. The IP host address is managed by one process, and the other information, such as the DNS address, is handled by another process.

Part of the configuration of some Unix systems, such as Sun Solaris, is the designation of one interface as the primary interface. Solaris considers only one of its network interfaces (in a system with multiple interfaces) to be the primary interface for DNS and other parameters. The purpose of a primary interface is to establish which interface will be the one whose parameters for DNS server, default gateway, and other network service addresses will be used by the system, instead of interface-specific ones.

Ethernet Switch Problems

As simple as DHCP sounds, there are some network conditions that can prevent it from working properly. For example, some vendors' Ethernet switches that can detect Ethernet port loops may prevent a Windows PC from getting an IP address from DHCP. A loop occurs when traffic is fed back to the sending station through its network interface.

Loopback tests are common in TCP/IP networks as a means to test the network interface. However, in an Ethernet switch, a loop means that the device is on the network, but can't communicate. When a PC is powered on, some Ethernet switches can take from 10 to 15 seconds to test a port for a loop condition, if the spanning tree feature is turned on.

When this occurs, the PC sends its request to the DHCP server as a connectionless UDP broadcast. However, the switch may not pass any traffic from the PC when it is testing for the loop condition, so the DHCP address assignment request may be lost.

The fix is to make sure that during or before a renumbering task, either Ethernet switches can handle DHCP requests properly; or, if the switch has a problem with passing traffic during a spanning tree loop test, that the spanning tree discovery switch configuration option is turned off.

The DHCP Downside

Using DHCP to assign IP addresses is a tremendous help in an address reengineering program, but it can't resolve all IP address references in other systems. Though DHCP automates the process of assigning new IP addresses to hosts in a readdressing exercise, it doesn't also put those new IP addresses everywhere else they should (or do) appear.

For example, the network administrator who is contemplating an IP address reassignment project may have to look in some of these places for fixed IP addresses. A network management system that uses the Simple Network Management Protocol (SNMP) may rely on static, not dynamic, IP addresses in the devices it is managing. As a practical matter, however, workstations may not be SNMP-managed devices in the same sense that servers, routers, or other networking gear are. If a workstation goes out, it's a local user concern; but if a router goes out, that's a problem. Consequently, DHCP is best used with devices that can change IP addresses frequently without affecting anything else, such as networked workstations. That said, IP address transience can affect other network management programs. Microsoft's System Management Server (SMS) uses static IP addresses for some functions, although it can also handle dynamically assigned IP addresses for workstation management.

In order to identify devices that can pass access control list checks, firewalls and screening routers may need to see specific IP addresses in devices for which they run access controls. Firewall administrators may be able to circumvent the problem of requiring specific IP addresses by specifying a range of IP addresses that can gain access. This is a security risk, of course, but it may be the only way to manage access control while taking advantage of the benefits of DHCP.

Unless a network has a DNS that is updated dynamically by DHCP (a dynamic DNS), the IP addresses in the DNS won't match the IP addresses assigned by DHCP. For most PCs, which may not have entries in the DNS anyway, this will not be a huge problem. However, this may be an issue if a host that receives a connection request from a workstation does a reverse name lookup on a DNS, to determine whether the IP address matches a host name. Dynamic DNS services can update in-addr records as well as standard A resource records, but not all DHCP-dynamic DNS combinations are as thorough as others.

IP addresses in a WINS server also may not match the IP addresses assigned by the DHCP service. Again, for PCs and workstations, this may not be a critical issue, unless users are part of Windows workgroups or are trying to attach to a workstation to share a disk drive or a local printer.

Summary

DHCP can solve many of the problems of assigning new IP addresses during renumbering, but it can't necessarily find and resolve all host address references. IP address references on other hosts or network services, such as the DNS, WINS, or in SNMP applications, may be difficult to root out. In fact, many may not become apparent until after renumbering has been completed, and users or network administrators find out that certain things that once worked no longer do.

You and Your ISP

As far as your network is concerned, renumbering may not change anything but the IP addresses your hosts and networks use. As long as all references to the previous address range that were embedded in DNS resource records, applications, servers, hosts, network management systems, and workstations have been changed (that's enough of a list) changing IP addresses won't change the operation of your network. What it might change is your connectivity to the Internet or to other networks with which you have become accustomed to communicating. When you change your IP address range, it's as if you had changed your phone number. On the Internet, nobody can reach you if you've changed your IP addresses.

In this chapter, we'll look at some of the things that you or your upstream (toward the Internet) providers may have to do to accommodate the use of a new set of IP addresses. These primarily involve changes in routing or in routing announcements. These changes may be simple, but they may also involve more complex reconfigurations of network or Internet connectivity. The latter might be true particularly if you are *homed*, or connected to, more than one ISP, or if you are connected to the same ISP through more than one connection.

Other factors that might affect your network connectivity after renumbering include whether you are using provider-independent (PI) or provider-aggregated (PA) address space. Each has its own considerations, as we will see. In addition, the interior and exterior routing protocols that you and your upstream provider are using may influence your relationship and routing strategies. Finally, you may be your own Autonomous System (AS) or need to be designated your own AS after renumbering.

The situation may be markedly different if you are an ISP and are renumbering to get a larger block of address space. Though the changes that an ISP may have to make when renumbering are similar to those an ISP's customers may have to make (they also involve route announcements and Internet reachability), they may be complicated by traffic carriage agreements with other ISP peers or by agreements to act as a transit network for passing traffic to other ISPs.

Stub Networks

The connection between a stub network and an ISP is the simplest case to discuss. It's also the most common, because it covers most of the typical instances of connecting to the Internet through an ISP.

A customer's network is frequently called a *stub network* because there is no other network behind it. Traffic destined for other parts of the Internet originates in the customer's network, and inbound traffic from the Internet terminates there. There isn't anyplace else for traffic to go, because the customer's network doesn't connect to anything but the ISP.

The routing from a stub network into an ISP may be as simple as the topology of the connection. The ISP feeds traffic for the customer's IP address space through its router connected to that customer, and the customer feeds traffic destined for the Internet back to that same router. So both sides of the connection—the ISP's router and the customer's router—can be configured with static routes to each other's networks, as shown in Figure 12.1.

The connection between the customer's network and the ISP may be a leased line or a frame relay connection. It's the single entry point from the ISP to the customer and, in the router's view, it is the "stub" through which the ISP sends traffic for whichever networks are in the customer's routing domain.

The customer's boundary router, which is the router at the customer's premises that terminates the leased line link to the ISP, has a static route that points to the ISP as its default route. All hosts and routers

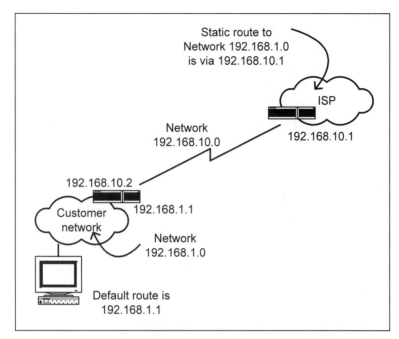

Figure 12.1 Static routes between a customer's router and an ISP's router.

within the customer's network use the interior interface of the boundary router as their default route.

The ISP does the same thing, pointing a static route to the customer's address space to the inside interface of the ISP's boundary router to the customer's networks. This, too, can be a static route, which directs traffic from the Internet (or from elsewhere in the ISP's network) back into the boundary router and then back to the customer's network.

Static routes aren't the most flexible choice for a customer connection to an ISP, but they are the simplest choice. In addition, static routes help insulate the customer's routing domain from that of the ISP because the customer's internal network routing information isn't passed to the ISP's routers. Static routes separate the routing domain of the customer's networks from the routing domain of the ISP.

The benefit of this forced separation is that it helps ensure that routing errors or problems in one routing domain won't affect routing in the other and that neither can pollute the other's routing space. Networks that use static routes usually don't pass routing updates to each other in routing table updates; consequently, static routes require manual configuration and updates. The advantage to static routes is that they are the most stable and the surest means of connecting customer and ISP routing domains in stub networks.

If a customer changes IP address space, and both the customer and the ISP are using static routing, the static routes must change. But the impact of the address change will be far greater on the customer than the ISP, because more customer hosts, applications, and network services may have the old address space embedded in them than do ISP routers.

Multiconnected Networks

Many customer networks are linked to ISPs through more than one connection. That is, the same ISP connects back to a customer network at more than one interconnection point. There could be several reasons for having multiple ISP connections, including:

- Local ISP connections for branch or field offices
- Redundant connections for reliability
- Different network access line requirements for different-sized networks
- Single-supplier ISP contracts for subsidiaries or wholly owned entities of a business

Given the importance of Internet connectivity to all types of businesses and organizations, multiple connections to ISPs are becoming more and more common.

A multiconnected network is different from a multihomed network. A multiconnected network has more than one connection to the same ISP. A multihomed network has more than one Internet connection, but the connections are carried to two or more ISPs. The routing issues are similar, though not exactly the same, because a single ISP may see more than one connection to a customer's routing domain as equivalent or alternate routes. In a multihoming situation, which we will discuss next, different ISPs may not be able to balance routing so well.

As in the case of a stub network, the simplest way to configure multiple connections to the same ISP is for both the customer and the ISP to establish static routes to each other, as illustrated in Figure 12.2. If there are two links to the ISP from the customer's network, some of the hosts in the customer's network point to a default gateway at one of the routers connected to the ISP; the rest point to the other. In effect, the customer network is subdivided into two parts, with each pointed to one of the two ISP gateways as a default route.

There are limitations to this configuration, however, similar to those in a singly connected stub network. Static routes are still static routes, and hosts in the customer's network that point to the router on the first connection to the ISP will lose Internet connectivity if the link goes down.

That said, as long as the customer's two gateway routers know about each other and are linked by an interior routing protocol, traffic to the Internet won't be cut off permanently by the loss of a router link to the customer's ISP. When the customer's gateway router recognizes that the link is down, it will see a second route to the ISP via the second gateway link, and forward traffic there. This route will appear as a secondary link, not the closest, primary link, but it will provide a backup to the primary link.

The same type of static route relationship may be configured on the ISP side, pointing Internet traffic to the customer's networks through one of the two gateways from the ISP's network. The difference may be that the customer might not want inbound traffic to come through whichever gateway is convenient to the ISP, instead preferring traffic to

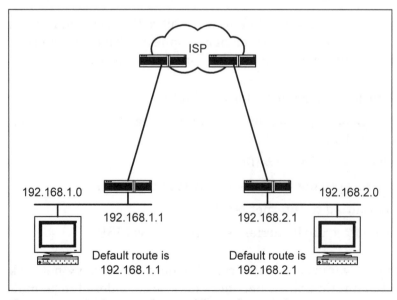

Figure 12.2 Static routes for a multihomed connection.

be directed through whichever gateway is closest to the destination network within the customer's routing domain. For example, a customer who has ISP connections in Los Angeles and New York will probably want Internet traffic destined for hosts on networks in the Los Angeles office to go through the Los Angeles gateway, not the one in New York, and vice versa.

To route the traffic to the correct customer network, the ISP can configure static routes to the networks in the Los Angeles and New York office networks on the ISP's gateway to those offices. At the same time, more general, aggregated routes to all of the customer's networks can also be configured on the gateways. The static routes will be more specific than the aggregated routes, so under normal circumstances, inbound traffic from the Internet will go to the correct field office.

If one of the links fails, the more general, aggregate routes will determine routing, and direct traffic into the customer's networks over the single remaining link. Once inside the customer's network, the customer's internal links will have to backhaul traffic to the correct branch office. Even if this isn't exactly what the customer wanted, at least his or her traffic is reaching his or her network, though it may take longer to arrive at the correct destination network.

Multihomed Networks

A multihomed network is connected to two or more ISPs, or it may be an ISP network that peers with two or more top-level ISPs. The motivations for having connections to more than one ISP include:

- Redundant ISP connections, for reliability
- Maintaining backup links in case one provider has Internet connectivity problems
- Fault tolerance for high-traffic sites
- Advantageous pricing for a low-bandwidth backup link
- Alternate routing to Internet NAPs
- ISP peering for transit carriers and higher-level ISPs

Companies or organizations with complex networks, heavy network traffic, or that maintain transit networks may be considered to be multihomed networks.

Multihoming poses particular challenges, because each ISP or network is treated as a separate routing domain by other ISPs. Therefore, advertising only those networks that are supposed to be reachable through the ISP connection, and not all others, is tricky. The reason is that, unlike single homed stub networks and multilocation homing to a single ISP, multihoming usually implies that the company, organization, or smaller ISP has a routing plan. The routing plan defines how the customer will balance the routing to and from the networks to which it is multihomed. The objective of multihoming may be a simple principle, such as balancing Internet traffic between two different ISPs to spread the load over two different access circuits. Making that work is another issue. The routing plan specifies only how that traffic is balanced, either by specific route announcements, routing by AS, or some other means. The problem is that hosts and routers in the customer network will see two routes to the Internet, unless they are configured with a default route to one of the two providers. Conversely, the rest of the Internet will see two routes—one through each provider—back into the customer network. Most traffic will choose one rather than the other, defeating the strategy of load balancing.

The other potential problem is *asymmetric routing*. Assuming there are two ISP connections, through ISP1 and ISP2, this occurs when outbound traffic for some Internet destinations goes through ISP1, but return traffic comes through ISP2. This can be a problem if the bandwidth on the two connections is different; there could be congestion on one connection and wasted bandwidth on the other.

Most, but not necessarily all, multihoming scenarios assume that the customer network is using the BGP4 protocol (version 4 of the Border Gateway Protocol, usually referred to as BGP) to communicate with its providers or its neighbors. BGP gives a customer's network a great deal of flexibility in handling load balancing and alternate routes. The other option, static routes, will work, but, as mentioned, they're much less flexible. In a multihoming situation, the justification is often flexibility and reliability, both of which imply the use of BGP.

Primary and Backup

If a customer network has two Internet connections, each to a different ISP, the customer may want most traffic to go over one link, rather than the other. The second link may be a low-bandwidth circuit that is used primarily for backup, being held in reserve in case the primary, high-bandwidth link goes down. Note that this is not load sharing or load balancing. In most cases, most of the Internet traffic will go over the primary link, leaving the secondary circuit as a backup in case the primary fails.

In many cases, the ISPs, not the customer, do most of the configuration for a primary and for backup links. For example, many ISPs give routes that they learn from their customers' networks a higher preference than those that they hear from other ISPs. If there are two links to a customer network, as illustrated in Figure 12.3, ISP1 would list two routes to the customer network. The first would be through its own connection to the customer network; the second would be in the routes announced to ISP1 by ISP2.

Because the customer's network is one of ISP1's own customers, ISP1 would treat the routes that it learns from its customer networks at a higher preference than the routes it hears from other ISPs. The customer would also have to tell ISP2 that the link to ISP1 is to be the primary path. ISP2 would then configure its routing so that it gives preference to the routes to the customer through ISP1, rather than through its own, direct link to the customer.

This configuration will force most inbound traffic coming from the Internet to go through the link to ISP1, not to ISP2. Whatever traffic

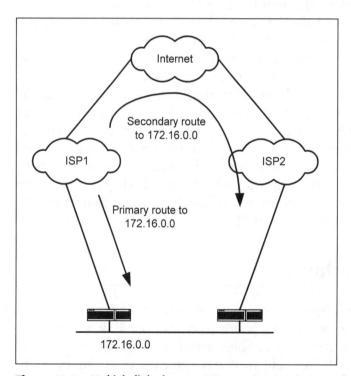

Figure 12.3   Multiple links from an ISP to a customer's network.

ISP2 receives for the customer's networks will be passed back to ISP1 for delivery to the customer.

If the link between ISP1 and the customer fails, ISP2 will still show a route to the customer. When the routing table updates between ISP1 and ISP2 are updated to remove the link between the customer network and ISP1, inbound traffic will be directed across the link from ISP2 to the customer.

On the customer network side, the customer wants to direct most of its outbound traffic to ISP1, still leaving the connection to ISP2 mostly unused. The simplest thing for the customer to do is to configure two static routes to ISP1 and ISP2, giving the route to ISP1 a lower-cost metric than that to ISP2. Routing decisions between the two routes will favor the ISP1 link because of its lower cost, directing most outbound traffic over the link to ISP1.

Configuring a primary and backup links to different ISPs depends heavily on how the ISPs configure their routing back to the customer network. The administrator of the customer network must make it clear to both providers which one will be primary and which one will be the backup. The ISP connected over the primary link may also prefer to configure its routing in some provider-specific way, which may affect how the exterior routing from the customer network is configured.

Sharing the Load

Sharing the load between two connections to two different ISPs is more complex than the primary/backup scenario. It involves coordination and cooperation among three entities—both ISPs and the customer network routers—as well as the customer routers sharing route table entries with each ISP. In this case, the customer's routers connecting to ISP1 and ISP2 must have enough memory to handle each ISP's route table entries, instead of the simple, default routes described in other situations.

Note that with two active connections to two different ISPs it still may be difficult to achieve routing symmetry or a relatively equal distribution of traffic over both connections. Doing so may require that the customer network be split into two Autonomous Systems, or configured so that outbound traffic defaults to one of the two ISP connections.

One way to configure a two-connection setup for load sharing is to have the customer's router connecting to ISP1 take (via BGP) ISP1's routes to its own customer set and ISP2's routes to its customers. For all other destinations to the rest of the Internet, the customer network would have default routes to ISP1 and ISP2, but different weights would be assigned to each connection.

This configuration would work best if ISP1 and ISP2 were large, national ISPs, such as Sprint and UUNet. Their routes to their customer sets would cover large numbers of Internet destinations. Other destinations not reachable through Sprint or UUNet would be reachable through whichever IS link had been given the higher weight by the customer's routers. The logical choice would be the link with the greatest bandwidth.

Even so, load sharing for inbound traffic can't be guaranteed in this situation. Other ISPs connected to ISP1 and ISP2 will hear routes to the customer's network announced equally by ISP1 and ISP2. There's no way to control which path inbound traffic will take, unless other ISPs weight their routing accordingly. That may be too much to ask of an ISP that doesn't serve the customer's network directly anyway (and receives no revenue from it). Besides, the links could change. Frankly, other ISPs are more concerned with maintaining their own links to other ISPs correctly, passing off traffic as quickly as possible and protecting their networks from being overwhelmed by Internet traffic. In either the multiconnected or the multihomed examples, renumbering any of the networks (the customer or the ISP networks) will force changes in the static routes.

Transit Networks

Above the level of the customer networks and the local ISPs that serve them, larger ISPs function as transit networks, carrying traffic between ISPs and into the Internet's core traffic exchange points. At this level, most of these networks are commercial ISPs or large university or government networks that operate like ISPs, providing Internet connectivity for their customers.

Transit networks may run internal networks that provide national or international connections. They also have agreements with other ISPs and networks, which have contracted with the transit networks to provide long-haul connectivity or connectivity to the Internet core NAPs.

When the Internet was far smaller, transit networks frequently carried traffic, for which they received no revenue. Today, transit networking is a business, so transit networks carry only traffic for networks that are reachable through them, specifically to their customer sets, as shown in Figure 12.4.

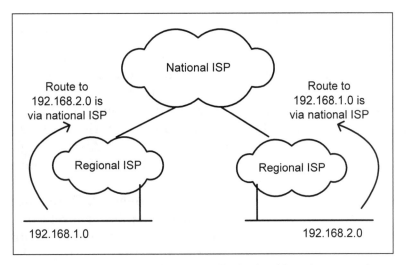

Figure 12.4   Transit networks carry traffic destined for other networks.

Transit networks, like ISP networks, are Autonomous Systems that use BGP to announce routes to networks for which they have routes. BGP also provides a second important capability for transit networks: the facility to announce networks reachable through them for which they will carry traffic.

So, a transit ISP, such as Sprint, AT&T, MCI, UUNet, or Cable & Wireless, may announce routes to a customer network behind another ISP. However, a transit ISP's BGP announcements will indicate the ASes for which it will accept traffic. To back up this routing transit "policy," the ISP will also filter outgoing AS reachability announcements, so that the transit ISP is seen as a viable routing path to networks for which it has agreed to take traffic.

Transit ISPs are like multihomed networks, in that they have multiple connections to a number of other ISPs, either directly or through Internet network traffic exchange points (NAPs). The difference is that transit ISPs frequently act as conduits, carrying traffic through to other ISPs, instead of terminating it at their customers' own stub networks. Transit ISPs erect routing policy filters to honor the revenue-generating contracts they have established with their peer networks. At the same time, they want to preempt their being used as Internet doormats, potentially carrying traffic across their networks for which they receive no revenue.

BGP and Transit Networks

BGP is the key protocol exchanging routing and reachability information between the Autonomous Systems that constitute the major networks of the Internet. BGP also links the ASes that carry traffic to a specific destination network and network routing information to a path vector. That is, BGP will carry to a distant AS not only the networks that are reachable in another AS, but also the sequence of ASes through which the traffic passed to get to that AS. This is illustrated in Figure 12.5.

BGP's reachability information is important to top-level ISPs that act as conduits for lower-level ISPs to pass traffic to other lower-level ISPs. The top-level ISPs use BGP's reachability and routing announcements as a defensive mechanism to prevent "traffic dumping" by other ISPs. The BGP routing and reachability announcements allow them to announce not only which networks can be reached through them, but to which networks they are also willing to carry traffic. This allows ISPs to accept traffic for other ISPs with which they have an agreement to carry traffic and to filter out traffic that they aren't willing to carry.

Take, for instance, a top-level ISP that serves both North America and Europe. This ISP probably has a number of circuits, which it has to provide and pay for, running across the North Atlantic to link its net-

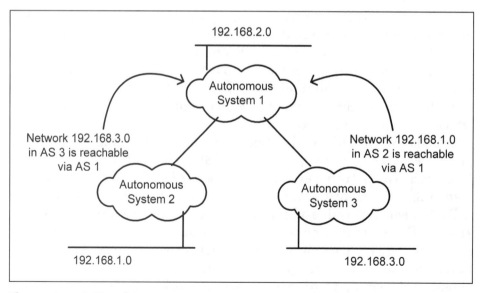

Figure 12.5   BGP and Autonomous System sequence routing data.

works on both continents. In a perfectly fair and balanced routing world (which we know does not exist), those links might be seen by other, lower-level ISPs as pathways to get from customers in North America to Web sites and servers in Europe, or vice versa.

In practice, the top-level ISP would probably not see it that way. Instead of allowing itself and its costly North Atlantic circuits to be used as a doormat by every other ISP in the world, it would probably want to restrict the use of those links to itself and its own customers. BGP lets it do this, thus forcing other ISPs to find their own way to get to other locations they don't serve, usually by contracting for "transit service" with a top-level ISP, like the one in this example.

Summary

The good thing about ISPs is that their business is to connect your networks to the Internet, and, for the most part, not to bother you with the gory details. However, if you're trying to do something tricky—such as connect to the Internet through more than one ISP—the network manager may have to gain more than a passing acquaintance with routing, and with interior and exterior gateway protocols.

Today, ISPs have far less flexibility than they used to have in accepting any and all address space from their customers. The rapid growth of the Internet has put many ISPs under pressure to advertise only the addresses in their assigned CIDR blocks. Because it adds extra routes and extra work, ISPs don't like to make holes in their address blocks to accommodate portable addresses.

As we will see in the next chapter, many large organizations may have to manage exactly the same kinds of problems if they act as an ISP for their own organizations.

You as ISP

If you are the MIS director of a large organization and you are reengineering the addressing of the networks in your organization, your relationship to your "customer networks" may be the same as that of an ISP. That is, the organizations or units of your corporation may get their Internet connectivity through a corporate Internet connection. Like an ISP, you may acquire and assign IP address space for them and run DNS services for them. In addition, their network routers may maintain default routes to you for addresses they can't identify.

You may also be a "real" ISP, connecting many smaller customer networks to the Internet. A real ISP performs many of the same functions: assigning address space, maintaining default routes to the Internet, and running essential network services, such as a Domain Name Service.

In Chapter 12, "You and Your ISP," we examined some of the network connectivity issues a customer must manage when renumbering networks or hosts that affect the customer's relationship with an ISP. In this chapter, we will look at the considerations an ISP must take when one or several of its customers are renumbering their networks. We will examine this topic from the perspective of the MIS or IS organization, rather than from that of an ISP, because most ISPs have a good handle on what they have to do in these circumstances. (If they don't, they probably won't be in the ISP business too long.) MIS organizations, on the other hand, may be accustomed to dealing with ISPs, but not with dealing with their own, internal customers as if they were the service provider for them. They may also be unfamiliar with managing the administrative, address delegation, and network service change issues for their customers. So in this chapter, we'll address the requirements of the network customers' service provider, whoever that may be.

NOTE Because the audience for this discussion is the IS crowd, rather than actual ISPs, we refer to the two parties as "customers," and to the "provider" as either a "real ISP" or an "IS provider."

Drawing the Line of Demarcation

One of the first issues the provider must address is drawing the demarcation line between what the provider will do before, during, and after a renumbering program, and what the customer will do. Both the customer and the provider must agree on the actions, controls, and equipment each will be responsible for, and who will call the shots regarding the sequence of events and priorities when renumbering occurs. Most important, they must understand and agree how troubleshooting will be done in case something doesn't work right. Conflicts between customers and providers are a lot less intense when an agreement has been reached beforehand about how problems will be resolved and when each side knows what the other is doing.

The simplest way to draw the line of demarcation is to make an arbitrary division between the hardware and software that the provider and the customer control. If the provider is a real ISP, the division will clearly fall between the customer's equipment and the provider's router. Only the control of the local telco circuit connecting the two may be in question; generally, whoever pays for it should decide "ownership."

If the provider is the IS department, the line may be easier to draw, because many IS departments control all of the networking infrastructure in the organization. It will be more difficult to draw this line in organizations where IS acts as a holding company for more loosely controlled operations that act as independent companies.

The line of demarcation must be drawn between hardware, software, and administrative matters that are controlled by the customer and those that are controlled by the provider. Some of these matters include:

- Router configuration
- Exterior and interior routing protocols
- Multihoming
- Autonomous System designation
- Host addressing
- DNS
- Reverse address domains (in-addr.arpa)
- Firewalls
- Network Address Translation (NAT)
- Router access controls
- Addressing plans
- Address delegation and assignment
- Documentation
- Administrative control over readdressing

Not all of these issues needs to be addressed by the provider, whoever it is. In this chapter, we will address some of the issues that providers must handle to provide Internet connectivity for the networks they serve. These are many of the same issues they must handle when their customers renumber their networks, too.

The role of a provider may be filled by a real ISP or it may be done by an IS department that acts as a provider for other parts of the company, agency, or organization. As a provider, the IS department may do many of the same things that an ISP does for its customers. If IS acts as a provider, it may do many of the things for its customers that an ISP may do for the IS department. Control of router configurations, default routes, and router-to-router protocols may be centrally managed by IS, only because IS may have the expertise to do the job, whereas its subordinate organizations may not.

Address Space

The provider, whoever it is, must determine the type of address space that will be best to use for renumbering its customers' networks. For example, a small ISP that is projecting significant growth in the next year or two (and all ISPs should be) will want to qualify for provider-independent (PI) address space, instead of provider-aggregated (PA) address space, as discussed in Chapter 10.

Provider-independent address space gives the provider, whether it is a real ISP or an IS department, the flexibility to change addressing one time to get networks numbered in that address space. As long as the rules about holding PI don't change, that address space should stay assigned to that provider for the foreseeable future.

An IS department that has a large enough network may qualify for PI, but it will be more difficult for a private organization to do so than an ISP. Usually, it's the IS that qualifies for PI, only because it has a need for a large address block, and so can make a case for being able to subdivide it among its customers as efficiently as possible.

In either case, PI offers both providers and their customers the prospect of a stable, fixed address space, free from the threat of renumbering if the provider's next-higher provider changes. In the case of an ISP, it might be a national ISP that interconnects with other top-level ISPs as an Internet NAP. In the case of an IS department, it would be the organization's ISP, through which it gets Internet connectivity.

The bottom line is that the provider is usually in the position of acquiring the address space for its customers, and thus, of determining how much address space any of its customers gets. Remember that providers are responsible for justifying their address space requests and for making sure that their customers use it efficiently. Even if the IS department is the provider to other parts of the organization, the company's real ISP still must make sure the address space it delegates to the company is used efficiently.

Route Aggregation

Customers have some responsibility for aggregating routes they announce to other networks, in order to reduce the size and complexity of Internet routing tables. However, this responsibility falls more heavily on providers, to whom the core Internet ISPs look to maintain high levels of route aggregation.

For example, customers may have only a few networks. Customers who have only a small number of hosts may only have a subnetwork of a Class C address, which has been assigned to them by their provider. In that case, the customer can do little to effect route aggregation. In essence, the customer's address space has been as aggregated as it will ever get. In the case of a customer with a small network, only the ISP can do anything about route aggregation, because probably the ISP subnetworked the Class C in the first place.

In larger networks, the responsibility for route aggregation starts with the customer, but weighs more heavily on the provider. The provider may have a number of customer networks for which it provides Internet connectivity. This is the business of real ISPs, of course, so their route aggregation issues, particularly when their customer networks renumber their networks, are more complicated.

First, providers are under pressure to aggregate routes by the higher, top-level providers. As we discussed in Chapter 3, some top-level ISPs filter out address blocks smaller than /18 (32 Class C addresses) from their top-level NAP routers. This proscription most affects real ISPs, which pass their aggregated route statements to other, higher-level ISPs.

An IS department that acts as an ISP may not have a responsibility to aggregate routes for networks it serves. The real ISP the organization uses may do it for the networks controlled by the IS department. However, since ISPs are usually the entities that are assigned address space, they are ultimately responsible for aggregating routes to their next higher providers.

A real ISP's customers may have a mix of address space from the ISP's assigned address space and their own address space. Some of the latter may be legacy space that they have been permitted to carry with them, even though it is not part of the ISP's address space. An IS department-as-provider may face the same problem if its customers' networks are numbered from a collection of legacy addresses, or if the company has been assembled from separate companies that have been allowed to keep their old address space. The problem is the same, but the urgency is diminished. For the IS department, responsibility for aggregation may be passed up to the real ISP.

Static Routes

Customers sometimes have the impression that static routes are an easy way out for providers. They think of static routes as a dodge, in that they free a provider from doing the real work of routing effectively between networks and to other providers.

The truth is that static routes work just as well for providers as for the providers' customers. They work very well, in fact, as long as the provider has a single, primary route to the Internet. Providers that

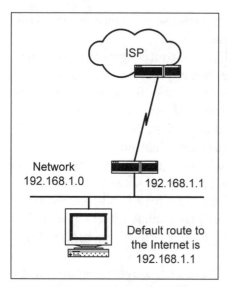

Figure 13.1   Directing Internet-bound traffic to the ISP.

have a single, primary route to the Internet use static routes because they simplify routing. Static routes can relieve them of responsibility for maintaining more complex routing schemes to higher-level providers, such as the Border Gateway Protocol (BGP).

For example, an IS provider that provides Internet connectivity for other parts of its organization will find it simpler to maintain static routes for outgoing, Internet-bound traffic. If the IS provider only has one path to the Internet, why not direct IP traffic for any address that isn't internal to the organization's network to the real ISP, as shown in Figure 13.1?

Static routes may make sense for real ISPs that have the same kind of relatively simple static routing arrangements with a single upstream provider. For the real ISP, as well as the IS provider, the downside of static routes is that to be changed they require manual intervention; they don't receive routing updates from other, neighboring routers. Furthermore, they're not dynamic. If network conditions change, such as a failure of a link to a primary, higher-level provider, static routes must be changed manually to forward traffic to a backup path.

Multihoming

Providers, unlike their customers, are usually homed, or connected, to more than one higher-level provider, instead of being a stub network to a single provider. It is not unusual for the IS department, if it acts as a provider to its customers, to be a single-homed stub network back to its main provider. That said, a real ISP, which serves a number of customers, usually cannot afford to operate a network with one Internet access path, which can be a single point of failure. Real ISPs need multihoming more than IS providers, because their customers can go elsewhere for Internet service—though doing so may imply renumbering customer networks; but there's more than one reason to leave your ISP.

From the perspective of either a provider or a customer, there are a number of reasons for multihoming, including:

- Redundant links to the Internet
- Alternate routing
- Backup circuits for increased reliability

As a provider, whether or not you are multihomed to another higher-level provider is not apparent to your customers. To them, you provide Internet connectivity; how you provide it is your decision, not theirs. Their only concern is that Internet connectivity be provided reliably. Multihoming is one way by which providers increase the reliability of their Internet connections.

The issues in multihoming for a provider are similar to those faced by a customer. As we discussed in Chapter 10, the trick in multihoming is to try to balance traffic between two or more higher-level providers. Another strategy is to favor one higher-level provider's connection over another. A link to one provider may offer higher bandwidth than another. Or, you may have a link to another, higher-level provider that is intended to be used only as a backup. In that case, you may want to steer traffic away from it because it is only a low-bandwidth backup link, or because a second higher-level provider may not offer the most direct routing to an Internet interconnection point.

Autonomous Systems

The concept of an Autonomous System (AS), first discussed in Chapter 10, may be lost on customers; in any case, creating an AS is usually the responsibility of the provider. An Autonomous System is an administrative entity that defines a set of routers that fall under a common routing administration. Autonomous Systems are administrative constructs, but they also have technical implications for network routing. Exterior routing protocols, such as BGP, use *Autonomous System Numbers* (ASNs) to advertise addresses contained within the AS.

Autonomous Systems are assigned unique ASNs that identify each AS. Because they are unique numbers, they are assigned by the same organizations that assign and ensure the uniqueness of IP address space—ARIN, RIPE, APNIC, and the other organizations discussed in Chapter 2.

An ISP usually maintains its own AS, whereas an IS provider may not. The requirements for maintaining a separate AS, specified in RFC 1930, are complicated. But for the purpose of this discussion, they can be reduced to a few general principles. A provider may need its own ASN if:

- It uses a dynamic exterior routing protocol, such as BGP, to talk to neighboring networks or providers.

- It connects to the Internet through two or more other providers or networks, each of which advertises its own ASN.

- The provider's network is not seen by the Internet through another provider's network.

In most cases, customer networks do not need their own ASNs, though many administrators of customer networks think they do. The reason is that a customer's network is usually part of a provider's AS. The network addresses within a customer's network are seen by the Internet through the provider's AS.

Providers have two fundamental responsibilities with respect to the AS that has been assigned to them:

Advertise the networks that are reachable through their AS.
Route announcements of networks reachable through an AS is done by BGP advertisements. Routers on the borders of ASes update each other on network reachability within their respective ASes through BGP updates. BGP consolidates route advertisements within an AS, and simplifies the process of AS-to-AS route advertisements.

Determine whether the addresses that they are advertising for their customer networks—but that are not actually assigned to them—really belong to their customers. It's not unusual for the administrator of a customer network not to know where the address space it has been using came from originally. The administrator may have inherited control of the address space from another administrator, or the current network administrator may be under the impression that its address space was permanently assigned. In many cases, it actually belongs to a provider's address block, and if the customer changes providers, so too may its address usage.

If a customer network renumbers, its new address space may not come from address space that has been delegated to the provider. For example, a customer may have applied for and received provider-independent (PI) space from AIR, RIPE, APNIC, or another address delegation organization. That address space is not part of the provider's address space, but it must be advertised to the Internet by the provider as if it were. Even though the provider doesn't "own" the address space, the Internet thinks it does; therefore, responsibility for verifying customer-owned PI space must be verified by the provider.

Note that there is no absolute requirement imposed on providers to verify the addresses they advertise. However, advertising address blocks that don't belong to a provider screws up Internet routing. It can render the real user of the address block unreachable from the Internet, because the address block may be in use elsewhere by a provider that advertises it legitimately.

Other providers also consider advertising routes incorrectly to be bad form. The larger the provider is, the worse the form, because bad routing advertisements can cause *route flap*, when the advertisement of a particular route to a network or address block changes frequently. The cause can be an unreliable circuit that renders networks unreachable intermittently or bad routing advertisements.

In general, providers don't mind adding and deleting networks from their routers' routing tables; it's part of the business of routing. But the now-you-see-it, now-you-don't effect of appearing and disappearing network advertisements causes extra work for their routers. In addition, it takes time for a change in a route advertisement to reach every router that keeps the route. By the time the change reaches all of the affected routers (which is called reaching "convergence"), the route may have changed again. Providers like stability, and route flap constitutes a form of rocking the boat.

Some providers, particularly those at the top level, close to the Internet's core traffic exchange points, may reject address blocks whose ownership they can't verify in the Routing Arbiter Database (RADB). The

RADB is a centralized database of new address block assignments, created under U.S. federal government sponsorship by MERIT, a group at the University of Michigan.

The purpose of the RADB is to simplify the exchange of routing information among the top-level providers at the Internet traffic exchange points, or NAPs. Participating providers add new addresses assigned to them to the RADB database. The RADB distributes the new address announcements to Routing Arbiter (RA) servers at the NAPs. Top-level NAP routers can refer to the RA to pick up newly assigned address space.

Using the RA is an alternative to receiving routing updates for newly assigned address space from other top-level providers' routers, but many top-level providers don't use it, either because they prefer to get routing updates directly from other providers or because they have private peering arrangements with other providers, which allow them to exchange Internet traffic directly with other top-level providers, instead of at one of the common Internet exchange points. Some providers have declined to use the RADB because they feel that other ways of getting route advertisements are more efficient or more effective.

DNS

Maintaining DNS registrations for customer networks is usually another responsibility that falls to the provider. Most customer networks have their own DNS services, but the customer's DNS may only maintain host-to-IP address mapping for hosts inside the customer's network. The provider, either an IS provider or a real ISP, usually maintains the address records in the externally visible DNS. Networks that do not have separate inside and outside DNS services may have only a single DNS located on a firewall. In that case, the firewall may actually maintain two logical DNS services, one a DNS database that can only be accessed from inside the firewall and a second that can only be accessed from outside the firewall.

Whatever its configuration, the provider usually has responsibility for the external DNS. It is the name server (NS) to which the top-level root zone servers point for name resolution for second-level domain names. For example, let's say that XYZ Company has the right to use the domain name xyz1.com. The company's IS department has arranged to get its Internet connectivity through a small, regional ISP,

BORDER GATEWAY PROTOCOL

Providers that maintain their own Autonomous Systems (ASes) use the Border Gateway Protocol (BGP) to pass routing and network reachability information to other ASes. As defined earlier in this book, BGP is an exterior routing protocol; it governs the router-to-router communications between ASes so that routers in adjacent ASes know where to send traffic for networks in other ASes. It is the "glue" that holds the ASes in the Internet together.

More specifically, BGP controls *path selection*, the process by which an AS determines the best way to get traffic to a destination network. It usually means passing traffic from one AS to another; BGP helps the border routers in interconnected ASes determine and select the optimum path to other networks.

It is the responsibility of providers to configure and maintain BGP on the routers that connect providers' ASes to other ASes. An IS provider that operates its own AS, for example, may only run BGP on the border router that connects the AS to the organization's ISP, which runs its own AS. In that case, the IS provider's customers will be included in its AS. Internal router communications within the AS would be governed by an interior routing protocol, such as OSPF, RIP, or IGRP.

BGP can control three types of routing:

- Routing between other ASes
- Routing between BGP routers within an AS
- Transit routing through other ASes

BGP maintains routing tables, transmits routing updates, and uses routing "weights," which are assigned by the BGP administrators to make routing decisions. BGP routers create routing tables of all feasible paths to other networks, but they make routing decisions based on the weights assigned to specific routes or paths.

Providers play a key role in Internet connectivity, by properly maintaining BGP configurations, routing announcements, and path variables. Unless they run BGP themselves, customers rarely see the work that providers do to make inter- or intra-AS communications function—unless, of course, it doesn't.

which we will call ISP1. ISP1, in turn, gets its connectivity to the rest of the Internet through a larger, national ISP, which we'll call ISP2.

Name server pointers can refer to second-level DNSes anywhere, as long as the IP addresses in the NS resource records are correct. Since

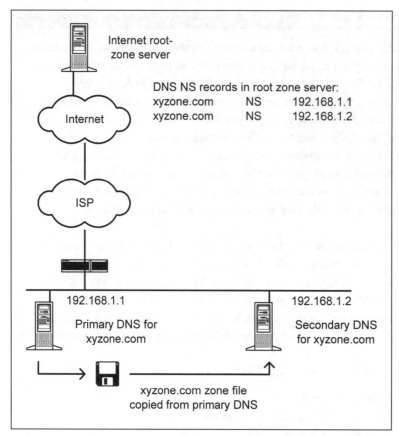

Figure 13.2 Root zone DNS server pointers to ISP's DNS servers.

the smaller ISP, ISP1, maintains the external DNS for XYZ Corporation, the Internet's root zone servers will list an NS record pointing to ISP1's primary and backup name servers, as illustrated in Figure 13.2.

Note that the name servers for the national ISP, ISP2, are not referenced at all in the root zone servers for the xyz1.com domain. There's no need, because they probably don't have any resource records for the xyz1.com domain. They could have them, because it is possible that ISP2 could in turn maintain a DNS service for ISP1, but it's unlikely that even a smaller provider would not maintain a DNS for its customer networks.

This is not to say that an IS provider might not delegate the responsibility for maintaining external DNS records to its ISP. It may be simpler for an IS provider to delegate this responsibility to its ISP, particularly if the IS department is small or not technically proficient.

Even though its customers think of it as a provider, an IS provider may not offer the same types of services as a real ISP.

If a customer renumbers some or all of its networks, the DNS implication for both IS providers and real providers is that the IP addresses in the external DNS must be correct. The DNS resource records will not necessarily have to be changed, but they do have to be checked to ensure they are correct. A customer who renumbers into provider-independent address space, or even a different block of provider-assigned address space, may renumber the networks and host addresses of externally visible hosts or only internal ones, or both.

For example, take a customer that uses RFC 1918 private address space (such as 192.168.1.0 through 192.168.255.0) for numbering its internal networks. The customer would still need a real, routable network address, such as a single Class C network address from its ISP, for externally visible hosts. The internal DNS would list the private network addresses, while the external DNS would list hosts numbered from the ISP-assigned Class C address. A network address translator, most likely configured as part of the customer network firewall, would also draw addresses from the external network address pool.

If the customer switched to a different provider, and retained its internal network private addressing scheme, only its external network address would have to change. So, too, though, would the resource records in the new ISP's DNS; but they would most likely be re-created by the new ISP. Since the maintainer of the company's external DNS would also have changed, the resource records in the Internet's root zone servers would also have to be modified, to point to the new ISP's DNS.

It may be that the resource records in the external DNS may not have to be changed at all. A customer could renumber internal networks behind the firewall and leave unchanged the address of an external, DMZ network on which a Web server, an anonymous FTP host, and a mail exchange server reside.

The renumbering implication for a customer is that if the internal network addresses change, the resource records in the internal DNS must be changed to incorporate the new, correct addresses for internal network servers and services. The internal DNS probably also has a resource record pointing to the external DNS, so that address resolution requests the internal DNS can't resolve (such as those for Internet URLs) can be passed to the external DNS for resolution. If the external network address changes, this too must be changed to specify the new, correct address.

Documentation

Documenting the changes that have been made in a customer network by a provider, particularly when customer networks have been renumbered, is one of the easiest things to forget or to ignore. It's also a detail that can bring what might otherwise be very well-managed networks to grief.

Documentation should be the responsibility of the provider, particularly if it's an IS provider. An IS provider has a much clearer picture of its customer networks and connections than a real ISP provider does. The IS provider is closer to the end user, and it often controls its customers' access to the Internet. The IS provider is responsible to the entire corporation or organization, so it must document its services to its customers within the organization.

The documentation should include the following:

- Diagrams of network connectivity to the provider
- Address assignments for customer networks, router interfaces, and circuits
- Address delegation authorities and contact names, phone numbers, and email addresses
- Service-level agreements with providers
- Access circuit designations or identifiers
- Special service arrangements
- Static routes used
- Routing to and from customer networks
- DNS responsibility and locations
- DNS resource record changes
- Assigned but unused address space

Real ISPs, though they may not have as much detailed knowledge of customer networks as IS providers do, must also keep accurate records of customer network connections.

Summary

Acting as an Internet access point for other parts of your organization may put a network manager in the same position as an ISP, less the revenue and the glory, such as it is. The "organizational ISP" may be connected with address aggregation, subnetworking, and address assignment, as well as network security, network address translation, multipoint routing, and a host of other concerns.

However, large organizations may find that it is more economical, and gives them greater control over the organization's security perimeter, to direct all Internet access through a few select points. It may mean backhauling a lot of Internet traffic across the organization's internal network to a few Internet access points, but the security, control, and cost issues are usually worth the effort.

Renumbering Routers

IP addresses are associated with network interfaces, and the network manager may develop an addressing plan based on assigning network numbers to specific locations, LANs, or areas. Routers are the devices that connect the networks; they are responsible for passing traffic between networks and for passing traffic to other networks for delivery to the correct destination.

To perform their primary routing task, routers build and maintain a logical view of router and network connectivity. Routers maintain routing tables, which are the maps they use to understand where other networks, which are not connected to them directly, are located.

Though many networks use routers produced by networking equipment vendors, such as Cisco or Bay Networks, routers are in fact special-purpose computers that perform functions that were originally carried out by general-purpose hosts. Unix hosts, or their close relatives in the Linux family, for example, have the capability to do routing. In fact, most routers use a Unix-like interface or have an operating system built on Unix concepts. Windows NT servers can also route traffic between different networks, and it appears that Microsoft intends to build more routing functions into future versions of the Windows NT operating system. Hosts, network hubs and switches, and servers may implement many of the same functions as "pure" routers.

The point is, a router doesn't have to be a special box that does only routing. But because networks have proliferated wildly in the past decade, dedicated routers have become widely used as an economical solution to network connectivity. It's also simpler to manage network connectivity through devices that are dedicated to that task. General-purpose computers, such as Unix, Linux, or NT machines, have all kinds of file management systems, utilities, device drivers, and other software modules that are unnecessary for single-purpose routers.

Again, routers are special-purpose computers that interconnect networks and forward traffic; they aren't usually considered to be hosts, because they typically don't provide network services, although sometimes they do. Routers are assigned IP addresses for each of their network interfaces. They can be thought of as collections of network interfaces, each of which bears an IP address.

In this chapter, we will examine some of the considerations in assigning IP addresses to routers, both under normal circumstances and when the networks they connect are being renumbered.

Router Interfaces

IP addresses are assigned to network interfaces. A network interface could be a connection to a local area network (LAN) or a connection to a wide area network (WAN) leased-line link. A network interface could be either a physical interface or a logical interface; that is, there may be a one-to-one relationship between network interfaces (which are physical network connections) and IP addresses, or IP addresses could be assigned to logical network interfaces. Thus, IP addresses may be assigned to interfaces that don't really exist, but that serve a diagnostic purpose. The loopback interface is an example of this type of interface. A third possibility is that more than one IP address may be assigned to a physical interface, if more than a single IP network address is in use on a single physical network interface.

Routers may also support dial-up ports that permit remote access to the network, as well as special-purpose ports for connecting a terminal for router administration and configuration. Dial-up ports may have a number of IP addresses assigned to them, while terminal ports may have none.

There are several different types of router interfaces, most of which will be assigned IP addresses. The types of ports or interfaces on routers include:

- Serial ports
- LAN interfaces
- Secondary addresses
- Loopback address
- Terminal ports

Serial Ports

Router serial ports are typically used to terminate WAN connections between routers. A router in Cleveland, for instance, may be the interface between a LAN located in a company's Cleveland office and the company's WAN. A router on a second LAN in another office in Baltimore may connect over the company's WAN to the router in Cleveland. Serial ports on the two routers establish the WAN link between them.

The WAN link could be any of a number of types of connections, including a traditional analog or digital leased line, frame relay, X.25, or ATM service. It could also be a Virtual Private Network (VPN) link, established over the Internet or through an ISP network to another location.

Serial ports on routers also terminate links to the Internet. Internet access circuits are usually router-to-router links, running from the customer network site to a serial port on a router at the ISP's site. As with internal network router-to-router links, the IS connection could be a leased line, a frame relay link, or an ISP-provided VPN.

Though it may not seem to fit the typical definition of a network, the WAN link between two routers' serial ports is a network. As such, the link itself is assigned an IP network address, and the two serial ports are assigned host addresses from that network range. In addition, the WAN link itself may also be assigned an IP host address from the same address range. If an IP host address is assigned to the link itself, it serves only as an identifier for the link.

Instead of using an entire Class C network address for the link, the most common practice is to use the smallest Class C subnetwork (a /30, with four host addresses) from a whole Class C address to assign host addresses on the link. Two of the four addresses go to the two serial ports, and one host address (host 0) is used for the network identifier. The fourth address, host 4, is reserved as a broadcast address.

For example, an ISP link to a customer network may be assigned the Class C subnetwork address 192.168.16.0 /30 (mask 255.255.255.252). This subnetwork includes the following four IP host addresses:

192.168.16.0

192.168.16.1

192.168.16.2

192.168.16.3

The ISP may elect to assign 192.168.16.1 to its router port, 192.168.16.2 to the customer's router port, and 192.168.16.0 to the link. The last available address, 192.168.16.3, is a reserved network broadcast address.

There are three common reasons for assigning IP host addresses to router ports, even though router ports aren't hosts in the common sense of the term. As we have noted, IP addresses really aren't assigned to hosts, but to their network interfaces. Routers have network interfaces, therefore those interfaces must have IP addresses.

Assigning an IP address makes the router port an addressable network interface. This means that a ping command can be directed to the router port, to verify that the port is alive, and that the network connecting the ping source to the port is available. Ping is a simple utility program that sends an inquiry to a specific IP address. If you can ping an IP address, you know that the network can connect to the destination IP address, and that the network interface at the IP address is alive.

Assigning IP addresses means that router ports can be specified as default gateways. The default gateway for a customer network may be the ISP's router, which will pass traffic to other Internet networks that aren't known to the customer's routers.

A router port's IP addresses can be mapped to host names in a DNS service. This is not necessarily what most users think that DNS is intended to do, but it's a useful capability for network troubleshooting. If router ports are assigned host names, they can be identified in a routing path (using the traceroute utility) through a network.

For example, the traceroute utility identifies the router and host ports through which network communications pass from source to destination. The traceroute utility also attempts an inverse address lookup on each router or host port it encounters. Router ports that have been assigned host addresses (and for which exist in-addr records in the right DNS) appear by host name and IP address in the traceroute results. Otherwise, all the traceroute display shows is the IP address of each port, which is not as useful as some indication of where the port is actually located.

UNNUMBERED SERIAL ROUTER INTERFACES

Most router vendors support the concept of unnumbered router interfaces, which are network interfaces on routers to which IP addresses are not assigned, as shown in Figure 14.1. The purpose of unnumbered interfaces is to bind the two routers into a single "logical router," so that traffic can pass over a point-to-point link between them, as if they were really only one router.

If two routers have a serial link between them, and no IP addresses are assigned to the serial ports on each router, the router software associates the IP address of a LAN interface with the router's corresponding unnumbered serial interface. Each of the routers uses dynamic routing updates to inform the other router of the networks behind them. Each router sends traffic it receives over the serial link to the interface or software process associated with the LAN interface behind it.

An ancillary benefit of unnumbered interfaces is that neither the routers' serial interfaces nor the link connecting them use up IP addresses. Neither interface can be addressed directly with the ping command, and network management systems that use SNMP may not be able to poll the ports, so some functionality may be lost on unnumbered interfaces. However, it's a useful technique if address space is very tight. It's also useful if joining two networks through routers wasn't planned and there isn't another network from which a small subnetwork to number the interfaces and the link can be carved.

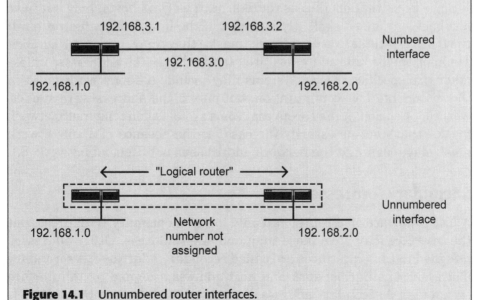

Figure 14.1 Unnumbered router interfaces.

LAN Interfaces

Routers map network traffic to router interfaces, so their primary interest is in the network portion of an IP address, not the host portion of the address. However, router interfaces are connected to networks, so router LAN interfaces also take host addresses. Assigning an address to a LAN interface on a router means giving it at least three things:

- Network ID
- Host ID
- Subnetwork mask

A LAN interface on a router is a good example of a network interface that has a host IP address, even though it obviously isn't a host in the traditional mainframe or minicomputer sense of the word. Conversely, a LAN interface is the easiest thing to associate with the network portion of an IP address.

LAN interfaces on routers take both a host address and a network address, as well as a subnetwork mask. Routers use the subnetwork mask to identify the network part of the IP address assigned to the port, as was described in Chapter 7. If the mask indicates that the network is a subnetwork of what would otherwise be a larger network address space, the mask is called a subnet mask.

Some hosts that operate as routers, such as Unix hosts, may not have a subnetwork mask explicitly included in the interface configuration. If they don't include a subnetwork mask, they may make an implicit assumption that all addresses are standard classful addresses, unless otherwise specified. Those systems may include a subnetwork mask in the router interface configuration, but only if the address were subnetworked. So though it may seem that some systems don't have subnetwork masks, that's not necessarily the case, as the absence of a subnetwork mask may mean that the network address has not been subnetworked.

Secondary Addresses

A LAN interface on a router can only have one primary IP address, but the interface may have more than one other address. Other addresses assigned to LAN interfaces are called secondary addresses. A secondary address is another network and host address assigned to an interface on a router. A secondary address can also expand the number of IP networks reachable through a router port.

There are three common reasons for configuring secondary addresses on router LAN ports:

- Additional network addresses
- Separated networks
- Transition from bridged networks

Of course, the router software must support secondary interfaces, but that's not a problem since all the major router vendors' software do so. Some routing protocols may treat secondary addresses differently when they send routing table updates. For example, some routing protocols may not recognize secondary addresses at all.

Additional Network Addresses

The drive to conserve IP address space has become so strong today that most networks are assigned Class C network addresses. The effect of Classless Inter-Domain Routing (CIDR), described in Chapter 3, is to make most network addresses Class C addresses, even though a single Class C may not be adequate for the number of hosts on the network. A single Class C address is sufficient for a network with 254 hosts, but many networks need more than that.

One solution is to assign a secondary address for a second Class C address to a router interface. This doubles the number of hosts that can be on the physical LAN cabling behind the router interface. For example, a network that has 400 hosts on a LAN will need two Class C addresses, or a subnetted part of a larger address space. The simplest solution is to assign a second network address to the interface, so that there are two networks on the same interface.

When configured with a secondary address, the router advertises to other routers that the network is reachable through it, just as it would any other network. As long as the router configured with secondary addresses directs traffic to the correct interface, and uses Address Resolution Protocol (ARP) mechanisms to deliver that traffic on the LAN, it's no different from having a single IP address on each interface.

Separated Networks

Two subnets of the same network address can span two routers that are separated by another network, by assigning secondary addresses to routers that serve both subnets. This allows a single network address to be served by more than one router. Using secondary addresses for this purpose can extend a single network address over more than one location.

For example, an organization may have 100 hosts on a LAN in one location and another 100 hosts on a LAN in another location. The hosts on both LANs can share a single Class C network address, which has enough host address space for both networks, by configuring secondary addresses on the routers that serve each LAN.

This configuration, illustrated in Figure 14.2, subnets the Class B address 172.16.0.0 between two routers, which are connected by a point-to-point link with another subnet address, 172.16.5.0 /30. All of the subnets connected to both routers are part of the 172.16 address space, but it spans two routers.

The secondary address 192.168.1.0 /30 is assigned to the network connecting the routers, using 192.168.1.1 on the interface on Router A, and 192.168.1.2 on the interface on Router B. The link between the routers gets the network address, which is 192.168.1.0 /30. In each router's routing tables, the separated subnets of the 172.16.0.0 network that are attached to the other's router are listed as being reachable via the 192.168.1.0 /30 subnet.

Transition from Bridged Networks

Older networks, particularly those connecting LANs in a campus environment, were frequently connected with Level 2 bridges instead of routers. When these networks are upgraded, the bridges are usually replaced with routers. Routers allow the network to be separated into dif-

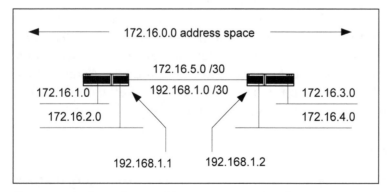

Figure 14.2   Secondary IP addresses on router interfaces.

ferent networks, so that it can grow and change. By contrast, all of the interfaces in a bridged network must be numbered from the same IP address space, so it can't scale beyond the size of the address space. However, the older bridged networks frequently must be assigned IP network addresses, in order to transition the networks into a routed environment.

The problem in moving from a bridged environment to a routed environment is that bridged networks often encompass a single IP subnet. Moving to a routed environment, particularly for large networks, means that the network must be broken up into distinct IP subnets. Secondary addresses can be assigned to the router interfaces of the former bridged network segments to facilitate the transition to the new router environment.

Loopback Address

One of the addresses that is assigned to a router interface is the loopback address, 127.0.0.1. The loopback address isn't an address of a network; it's a special, reserved Class A network address that points to the router or the host itself, and is used for testing and diagnostic purposes on IP routers and hosts.

A router is a set of network interfaces, each of which has one or more network addresses assigned to it. A router isn't a host in the sense that a PC is a host, so the router needs an IP address to refer to itself. That's what the loopback address does. It serves as an address for the router hardware to test network connectivity.

Some routers, such as those made by Cisco, allow the router administrator to configure several loopback addresses, in addition to 127.0.0.1. For example, the router may need a separate loopback address for Novell IPX/SPX Service Advertisement Protocol (SAP) broadcasts or for a router ID for OSPF broadcasts.

Terminal Ports

Most routers have a separate RS232 port for connecting a local terminal. The bulk of router administration is done from a PC running a Telnet client to the router, but it may be more convenient to connect a real terminal to the router to configure and administer the router. Local administration policies for highly secure environments may require that all router administration be done from a locally attached terminal, rather than over a network.

The terminal port is usually not assigned an IP address, because it is not intended to be a network interface. A network client initiating a Telnet session to a network interface would use the network interface's IP address.

Dial-Up Port Pools

Routers that also serve as remote access servers may maintain their own pools of assignable host addresses for dial-up users or they may get them from another server on the network. Routers may assign the addresses directly or they may act as the middleman between the address assignment server and remote users. A remote user doesn't necessarily have to be a user who dials into a local port, as the connection could be made over a Virtual Private Network connection or an encrypted channel over the Internet.

There are three different ways in which a router can handle address assignment for a remotely connected user:

Router address pool. The router may maintain a pool of addresses for remote users and assign an address from the pool directly. The advantage of this approach is that the router doesn't have to depend on any other network device to handle a remote connection request. The disadvantage is that the router may also have to be configured with user IDs and passwords for every remote user, or just for the set of users who will connect to that router.

DHCP server assignment. If the number of remote users is large enough, it may be more practical for the router to forward requests for host addresses from remote users to a DHCP server. That's the role that the DHCP server is supposed to fill anyway. Networks that depend heavily on DHCP may find it simpler not to split the address assignment tasks between a router acting as a remote access server and the network's DHCP service.

Access validation server. A router may forward remote access requests to an access validation or authentication server. The server validates the remote user's ID and password credentials and logs the remote access request and grants access to network resources. The authentication server may be running the RADIUS or XTACACS protocols (described later) to handle authentication between itself and the router. The authentication server may then get an IP address from its own pool of addresses or forward the request back to a separate DHCP server.

All three approaches work, but the more a network utilizes DHCP, the more likely it will be to direct all transient address assignment requests to it. Administrators of small networks may find it useful to have the router do its own address assignment, until such time as remote access usage grows large enough to justify a separate back-end DHCP server.

DHCP Services

Hosts that do not have permanent IP addresses usually are temporarily assigned addresses from DHCP or bootP servers. Many networks of PCs, for instance, do not have fixed addresses. Instead, they are assigned an address "lease" at bootup by a DHCP server. The server draws from a pool of addresses from within a specific host address range, which it leases to networked workstations.

The implication of DHCP services to router and network renumbering is that routers usually have to know where the DHCP server is, so that it can forward DHCP and bootP broadcasts. At bootup, a PC is configured to use DHCP broadcasts for a DHCP server. To prevent DHCP broadcasts from being propagated everywhere, they are usually not forwarded by routers. However, a router may be configured to forward a DHCP broadcast to a network segment on which a DHCP server is located, so that the broadcast can be directed to the network on which the DHCP server has been positioned, rather than everywhere on the Internet.

If network or interface numbering changes, the router configuration must be changed to indicate where the DHCP server is located. The DHCP server may not have moved at all, but if its address changes, the router needs to know it to direct DHCP and bootP broadcasts correctly. The router may direct DHCP broadcasts from a specific router interface directly to a specific DHCP server; if that server's address changes, the router needs to know the new address, too.

DNS Implications for Router Renumbering

Routers don't provide DNS services, but they can keep host name-to-IP address translation tables for their own use. When networks are renumbered, the name resolution entries in routers (if there are any) also must be changed or deleted from the router.

Routers may, for instance, cache names and addresses of the routers or hosts they use as default gateways. In a renumbering program, the addresses of router default gateways may change. Router configuration files may contain the IP addresses of dial-up servers and DNS servers. These hard-coded addresses must be changed if the networks on which services referenced in router configuration files change.

The router interfaces may also be listed in DNS resource records (RRs), with separate A records that map the IP address of each router interface to a host name. Either in the same DNS or in a different DNS, there may be pointer (PTR) records that map the IP addresses back to host names. Recall that the purpose of PTR records is to resolve IP addresses back to host names. Reverse address resolution is particularly useful for router interfaces. Router interfaces are usually only identified by their host names in network traces, such as those collected by the traceroute program. Traceroute results are much more useful if they identify the router interfaces between an Internet client and a server by name, rather than just by IP address.

Renumbering networks may also force changes in DNS resource records that refer to router interfaces. Usually the problem is finding all of the references to router interfaces in DNS records. It's relatively simple if there's only one DNS; however, sometimes reverse address resolution records (the PTR records) are maintained by an ISP, not by the organization. It also happens that the organization inadvertently solves the problem by never having created the PTR records in the first place.

If router interfaces are assigned new IP addresses, it may help the transition to keep the old address as the primary IP address of the interface and add the new address as an additional network address. Router interfaces may take more than one IP address, although there is usually a vendor-specific limit of, for example, six or fewer addresses per interface. If this is done, DNS records for the router interfaces have to be changed to reflect the old and the new addresses.

Authentication Server Access

Some of the ports on a router may act as terminal server ports, to permit remote users to dial into the network. Dial-up users may be authenticated on the router, if the router keeps a list of their user IDs and passwords. An alternative method of authenticating dial-up users is to have the router, which acts as a terminal server for dial-up ports, pass user IDs and passwords back to another server on the network for authentication.

Remote access terminal servers and authentication servers often use a separate authentication protocol to exchange remote user authentication requests and responses. Two of the most common authentication protocols are the Remote Access Dial-up System (RADIUS) and the Extended Terminal Access Control and Communications System (XTACACS). Both RADIUS and XTACACS control communications between the remote access server and a separate access authentication server. The widely used, open RADIUS protocol was devised by Livingston Systems, a firewall and remote access server vendor, now part of Lucent Technologies. XTACACS is a Cisco-developed version of the older TACACS protocol.

Both protocols govern how remote access servers pass user authentication data back to an authentication server, as well as how the authentication server manages the database of remote user access information. RADIUS and XTACACS servers differ slightly in how they manage the authentication process and the level of security applied to user IDs and passwords. The benefit of a RADIUS or XTACACS authentication server is that it can serve several remote access servers, freeing users from having to dial into a specific access server for authentication, as illustrated in Figure 14.3.

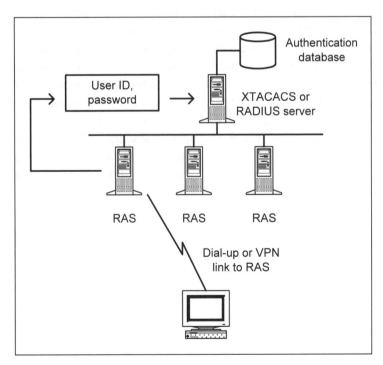

Figure 14.3 XTACACS or RADIUS server authentication for remote users.

However, the configuration files for the dial-up ports on a router that acts as a remote access server may contain the IP address of the authentication server, rather than its name. Many remote access server administrators feel it is more reliable to embed the IP address of the authentication server instead of its host name in a router configuration file. They feel this way because DNS information may change, the name of the authentication server may change, or the DNS may not be available at all times. IP addresses, on the other hand, are less likely to change for servers and hosts, unless, of course, their networks or hosts are renumbered or they are moved to other networks. If the configuration file contains the IP address of the authentication server, the remote access server will always be able to reach the server, and reduce the possibility of leaving a legitimate remote user unable to log on to the network.

Summary

Most network managers think first of the host addresses that will change in a renumbering program, leaving considerations of renumbering routers and router ports as an afterthought. As we have seen in this chapter, router ports are assigned a number of different uses, each of which may be affected differently in a renumbering program.

Furthermore, changing the IP address assignments of router ports used for specialized applications, such as remote configuration or dial-up remote access, may imply other changes to back-end security or authentication systems. If the latter depend on user access or an authentication request from a specific IP address, or a range of IP addresses, renumbering routers may imply other changes elsewhere. The ripple-through effect of changes to router, host, or applications addresses again emphasizes the need for detailed, current documentation of the current state of the network.

CHAPTER

15

Renumbering Steps

The keys to a successful renumbering program are organization and planning: Get organized, then plan the operation. The execution should be easy. At least that's the theory, but like all theories, it has a way of not working out quite so simply in practice. Things go wrong. Some unexpected difficulty arises with configuring addresses, routing, or connectivity that stops the process cold. Welcome to network administration.

The inevitable glitches aside, network administrators still need a road map to guide them in the process of converting a network to a new numbering plan. That's the purpose of this chapter: to delineate the steps to take to renumber a network.

In an earlier metaphor, we likened renumbering a network to painting a house, saying that most of the work is in the preparation, not applying the paint. Similarly, new host and network numbers can be configured on a router and on hosts relatively simply. It just takes time, because it has to be done router by router and host by host. Some network administration tools, such as the Dynamic Host Configuration Protocol (DHCP) can simplify parts of the process, but not to the extent that it becomes automatic.

In practice, the most difficult part of a renumbering effort is making sure that other services, specifically the DNS services, are updated to incorporate the new addresses. All of the DNS services that are affected by network renumbering may not be controlled directly by the organization. Consequently, it may take several days for new addresses to propagate to all of the affected DNS services.

Process Steps

The exact number of steps of the process of renumbering depend on how many networks and hosts are being renumbered, how those networks are connected to the Internet, and the number and locations of the DNS services that will be affected by renumbering. As we will see, changing the records in DNS services and, more important, propagating that information to other DNS services, will probably take the most time. And a large, organizationwide renumbering effort that involves hundreds or thousands of hosts and PCs may take several weeks to complete, particularly if address assignment automation tools, such as DHCP, are not used.

The most significant steps of a renumbering effort are:

1. Plan renumbering effort.
2. Get address allocation assignment.
3. Update and upgrade DNS servers.
4. Start renumbering rollout.
5. Enable routing.
6. Update DNS and test.
7. Complete rollout.
8. Reset DNS services.
9. Do administrative cleanup.

This list is not intended to be a complete, cookbook approach that will meet every network renumbering effort; it's meant as a overall guide. Some organizations don't run their own DNS services, for example, so they will have to coordinate DNS updates with their ISP or whoever does it for them. Other organizations may only be renumbering a small part of their network, so the implications for network infrastructure may not be so large. In any case, a network administrator may have to vary the procedures to meet specific circumstances.

Plan Renumbering Effort

Football games begin with a game plan, a set sequence of plays that will be executed during the contest, in conjunction with an offensive and defensive strategy for defeating the opponent. A renumbering project should have a game plan, too, and drawing it up is the first step in renumbering.

The game plan is a scenario that the network administrator thinks will play out in the renumbering project. It's not the master plan, but the way the renumbering will proceed to achieve the readdressing design.

The readdressing design will identify the parts of the organization or enterprise that will be renumbered and the new address space into which the networks will be numbered. It will also specify how (or if) the new routes will be summarized.

The readdressing plan will also specify who is responsible for the renumbering tasks and how that personnel will be coordinated. For example, renumbering will involve the administrators of all of the networks involved, as well as DNS administrators, DHCP administrators, and router administrators. All of these may be different people, working in different locations. They have to be informed *before the project launches* as to what their responsibilities will be, and which devices, such as routers and hosts, the project manager may need access to during the project.

The game plan should also specify the order in which tasks will be done and who will do them. It's difficult to identify up front what might go wrong, nevertheless it's a good idea to think through the troubleshooting and diagnostic techniques that might be employed if something does.

The game plan may be specified in a document, a Gantt chart, or a project plan document. Whatever form it takes, it will specify the steps of executing the renumbering project. The rest of this chapter outlines the general steps that must be taken, and Chapters 16 through 18 give examples of renumbering projects on different size networks and organizations.

Get Address Allocation Assignment

After the game plan has been drawn, the next step is to confirm the address space that will be affected by renumbering. This step includes determining both the new address space and the old address space, as well as what will be done with the address space that will be vacated.

The issues in getting new address space have been discussed in Chapter 8, "Network Address Translation." The network administrator must determine whether address space assigned from an ISP will be suitable for the organization's needs or if it should get address space from another address allocation organization, such as ARIN. The choice comes down to provider independent (PI) and provider-aggregated (PA) address space, which were discussed in detail in Chapter 10. In most cases, provider-aggregated address space, assigned by an ISP, will be suitable. Provider-independent address space fixes the assignment of address space with an organization, but the assignment must be fully justified.

Establish Current Address Usage

The first thing to do at this stage is to determine which IP addresses are in use in the organization's networks. The detailed requirements for conducting an address inventory were discussed in Chapter 6. In brief, again, the inventory may be obtained from several sources, including:

- Network documentation
- DHPC address ranges
- ISPs or service providers
- Router configuration files
- Routing tables

Of the sources given here, the most reliable and comprehensive listing of network addresses in use will come from the router configuration files and routing tables. Routers must know which networks exist behind them and which networks are reachable through them. If a network is reachable, it must appear in router tables, particularly those in the highest levels of the organization's routing hierarchy.

In addition to a list of all of the network address space in use in the organization, the router administrator needs a comprehensive list of all of the address space that has been assigned but is not in use in the organization. Such space may not appear on network documentation. Additional unused but assigned addresses, if they exist, can be obtained by asking the ISP or service provider to confirm the address ranges that have been assigned, and if any other addresses have been assigned. It is possible that the ISP or service provider may have addresses that have been assigned to your organization that you don't use. Either they were assigned some time ago and weren't ever put into use, or they were assigned, used, and then taken out of service, and never used again. Anything is possible.

The other sources for information on assigned addresses are the Web sites of address assignment organizations, such as InterNIC, ARIN, and other address allocation organizations. Each runs a Whois database that can be searched by organization name. Whether IP address assignments can be gleaned from the Whois database depends on whether the database lists assigned addresses and if the address assignment organization assigned the addresses. Here are the Whois Web sites and their respective URLs:

InterNIC: www.networksolutions.com

ARIN: whois.arin.net

RIPE: whois.ripe.net

APNIC: whois.apnic.net

U.S. military: whois.nic.mil

U.S. government: whois.nic.gov

For example, an inquiry on the ARIN Whois Web site (whois.arin.net), using the keyword *Microsoft*, shows more than 100 network address ranges and host addresses listed in the ARIN database. Some of the addresses are actually assigned to ISPs that serve Microsoft. For example, the network address 205.163.62.0 is used by Microsoft; however, the address block from which it is derived, which is composed of the address in the range from 205.160.0.0 to 205.163.255, is assigned to US Sprint. Sprint delegated that address to Microsoft for its use, but Sprint announces the address as part of its bigger address block to other ISPs.

The DHCP servers on the network should also be checked to determine the address ranges that they are using, and if they match the address ranges assigned by the provider. Configuration files for remote access servers and routers that handle remote access requests should also be examined to determine that their address ranges are in assigned address ranges, too.

Determine Address Usage

It's one thing to have address ranges assigned to an organization and it's another to determine which ones are really in use. An interesting exercise for a network administrator to run is to do a ping test against all of the addresses in the assigned address ranges, just to see how many are really in use. The network administrator may have a good idea how many hosts are in the organization's networks, but not how the address space is being used.

To conduct this test, the network administrator can write a simple script that pings each address in a network address range, logs the results in a file, and parses the file for used and unused addresses. The ping test should be run daily over the course of two weeks, to get a good idea of actual address usage.

This is not to say that running a ping test is necessarily the easiest thing in the world to do, but it may be the only way to determine just what is and what is not in use. For large networks, or even one with a single Class B network, ping tests can chew up a lot of time. Pinging all addresses on a single class B means pinging more than 65,000 separate host addresses, which is not exactly fun, but that's why there are computer script files to do it for us.

Address usage is helpful for determining exactly how much of the assigned address space is in use and how fully network address ranges are utilized. The network administrator will have to match address usage against a diagram of network connectivity, showing where networks have been located and how many hosts are on each network. The immediate benefit of gathering this information is to determine whether address assignments can be consolidated or address announcements summarized. The benefits of both will be to simplify internal network routing and, for providers, route announcements for Internet connectivity.

A secondary benefit of understanding address usage will be to set an address usage baseline, from which the network administrator can estimate how much the network may grow in the next five years. If all or part of the network is being renumbered, enough new address space should be secured to accommodate network growth for at least five years. While network growth will most likely continue beyond five years, a five-year horizon is one of the address usage measurements utilized by address assignment authorities to estimate providers' address needs. Providers' customers should use the same time period to estimate their needs.

If everyone in an organization has a PC or a workstation, a reasonable estimate is to double the number of addresses in use today. This will accommodate a second network device for every current user. The more difficult estimate will be the expected user growth in the next five years. It's anyone's guess, but a network administrator may anticipate that Internet companies and ISPs may double in size each year. Other organizations may not project much growth at all, or plan to downsize, outsource, or shrink the size of the network.

As with any forecast, it's a guess, so it's more art than science. It's best if it errs on the high side, although not too high. Either the network administrator or the provider may have to justify the estimate of network growth.

Get Address Assignments

Once the network administrator has estimated address usage and identified the networks to be renumbered, a request can be made to the provider for new address space. If the organization is moving to a new ISP or provider, and it doesn't have provider-independent address space, address space will be assigned by the new ISP.

It is possible that a new ISP may be willing to advertise an organization's old address space, but only if responsibility for that space can be transferred from the previous ISP. Before IP address space became a scarce and highly regulated commodity, it wasn't unusual for a new ISP to advertise a new customer's space, even if it fell outside its address blocks. It's less common today, now that ARIN and other address assignment organizations charge for address space. Besides, the provider must treat the additional space as an exception to what may be carefully controlled blocks of its own, CIDR-ized address blocks.

Update and Upgrade DNS Servers

Renumbering isn't hard to do for those aspects of the process that the network administrator can control. Renumbering hosts or assigning a new address scope to DHCP might be a lot of work to have to change each host address in its Windows or system configuration, but it's a manageable problem. It's those uncontrollable parts of the job that can cause all of the trouble.

Take, for instance, the DNS. In Chapter 9, "DNS Considerations," we examined the DNS implications of renumbering. Host and interface addresses are embedded in various types of resource records in the DNS. DNS records aren't hard to change, but often the DNS is administered separately, by another group in the organization or by an ISP. Furthermore, a number of servers may be running DNS; there may be internal and external DNS services, each with its own view of what is visible to inside and outside clients. And the primary DNS may have one or more secondary DNSes that take copies of its database periodically.

Before revising to the DNS resource records, the network administrator or the DS administrator should think about upgrading the DNS to the most current version of the DNS code. For Windows NT machines, it could be Microsoft's DNS Service or a third-party product like MetaIP. For Unix machines, it's the most recent version of the Unix DNS program, BIND. If all of the DNS servers that have resource records that will be affected by renumbering are controlled by the same administrator, it might be advisable to upgrade all of them before changing the DNS database records.

Upgrading the DNS may be part of a more comprehensive operating system upgrade, such as a changeover to Windows NT 5.0 (Windows 2000). Whether it's a change of operating systems or DNS code, the same principles apply: Upgrade the operating system on a given server, then test it to make sure it works right. Once it works right and stabilizes, change or upgrade the DNS service programs and load the old resource records again, if necessary. Test that configuration and let the DNS services stabilize for a few days before changing the resource records.

Changing NS Addresses

A comprehensive renumbering effort may change externally visible IP addresses, in addition to internal addresses. If externally visible networks and host addresses change, the name server (NS) resource records in other DNS services may also have to change.

Let's say that the XYZ Two Corporation (xyztwo.com) changes ISPs and then renumbers all of its networks into address space controlled by the new ISP. If the company runs its own external DNS, that DNS address will also change. Because the address of the host running the DNS has changed, any NS records in other DNSes must also be changed, so that inquiries on hosts in the xyztwo.com domain can be resolved successfully.

The key issue is to determine where those NS records are and who has the right to request a change to the records. The NS records are probably only in the Internet's root zone servers, which maintain the NS pointers to name services for all second-level domains. If the ISP had secured the domain name for XYZ Two, the ISP could request the change, as it would be the administrative contact of record. Otherwise, it would be the administrative or technical contact at the XYZ Two Corporation.

In either case, a change in the NS records would have to be made through the Network Solutions Web site (www.networksolutions.com). NSI maintains the root zone server database, and only the official administrative or technical contacts of record may make changes to its domain name registration records.

Changes to the root zone server records take effect each night, so changes in the addresses listed for the primary and secondary name servers' NS records should be made only after the DNS servers have been renumbered. The addresses of hosts on renumbered networks won't be visible until the following day, so the changes should be made to the root zone NS records late in the day when the DNS servers are actually renumbered. If the primary and secondary servers aren't renumbered at the same time, their corresponding NS records may be changed one at a time, too.

Changing the SOA

Changing the root zone server NS records means the DNS services can be found. If the records in the primary DNS are changed to reflect the new addresses, DNS name resolution will work fine. However, updating the records in the primary DNS doesn't mean that they will automatically be updated in the secondary DNSes.

Recall that a secondary DNS is a backup to the primary DNS, providing the same text name-to-IP address resolution services as the primary. That's why registering a domain name requires a primary and at least one secondary name server, although more than one name server may be listed. There may be any number of secondary name servers to a primary name server, although most organizations usually only have one or two secondaries to each primary. A DNS can be the primary for several domains, and it can also serve as the secondary for more than one domain. To make matters more confusing, a DNS can be the primary for one domain and the secondary for another. Usually, though, a DNS is either a primary or a secondary. It's easier for DNS administrators to keep things straight if they stay away from exotic primary and secondary DNS relationships.

The secondary name servers have resource record databases that are identical to those in the primary name services of the domains they serve. The domain, such as xyztwo.com, is called a zone, and the resource record database for a zone is called a *zone file*. Secondary name servers periodically copy the zone files from their primary name servers.

Secondaries copy zone files at intervals defined by the Start of Authority (SOA) records in the primary name server. Secondaries also have the IP address of any primary name service for which they serve as secondaries. So, if the IP address of the primary changes, it must be changed manually in any secondary, so that the secondary can find the primary to copy the current primary zone file, through a *zone transfer*.

The primary's zone file SOA record contains three values that influence when the secondary picks up a fresh copy of the primary's zone file. The point is that these values will determine how quickly the secondary name servers will pick up a fresh copy of the primary's zone files after renumbering. The SOA values should be set artificially low for long enough to enable the secondaries to get a new, revised copy of the zone file, then return to their normal values after all of the secondaries have been updated.

The three values in the SOA record that should be adjusted after the primary name service's resource records have been changed after renumbering are:

Time to Live (TTL). The part of the SOA record that is copied by the secondary DNS. The purpose of the TTL is to tell a secondary DNS how long the zone file will be good. This value is expressed in seconds, and it might be set to one week (604,800 seconds), if the zone is relatively stable. This value should be changed to a short value, such as one hour (3,600 seconds) just after renumbering, so that the zone file "ages out" quickly. This will force secondaries to get a new zone file quickly, and update their DNS databases.

Refresh. A value usually set to one hour (3,600 seconds) that tells the secondary how frequently it should ask the primary if the zone file has been changed. If it's been changed, the secondary will FTP a copy of the zone file. This value should be reset to a much shorter interval, such as 15 minutes (900 seconds) after renumbering, to force the secondary to ask for a new zone file.

Retry. A time value expressed in seconds that a secondary DNS should wait if it can't contact the primary DNS, before trying again. A typical value is 10 minutes (600 seconds), which should be reduced to five minutes (300 seconds) after renumbering.

Remember that the purpose of changing the DNS records at this point isn't to change any of the data in the primary and secondary DNSes. The point is to force all the DNSes that are affected to pick up the TTL, Retry, and Refresh values in the SOA. Once they have those values, they will pick up changes to the master DNS quickly. When renumbering is done and the affected DNSes have the new address records, the values will be restored to their old values, so DNS updates can occur normally again.

Start Renumbering Rollout

Presumably, at this stage, the network administrator has already considered all of the parts of the address rollout, such as which networks should use which numbers, how many subnetworks should be set up, and so forth. (Chapters 16 through 18 give examples of renumbering plans for different types of networks.)

To draw on the painting metaphor again, painters usually do what they call a "test patch" in an inconspicuous part of a wall or a room to see how the color looks and how the paint goes on the surface. Likewise, renumbering should be started on a test patch network that is as far away from the Internet as possible, to make sure routing works to the new numbering scheme and that DNS records are updated properly.

The best place to start a renumbering effort is on a LAN that is as far away as possible from the Internet; that is, a network in the organization that must go through several other routers to get to the ISP connection. The idea is that such a network is most likely isolated from most other networks, and changes to its numbering won't affect other networks. Since renumbering will start on this network, the network administrator will want to know that routing to and from the renumbered network works, and that it can be replicated safely on other networks.

If a spare router port, a few extra computers, and an unused, valid network address are available, it's also a good idea to set up a new network on which renumbering can be tested. If renumbering works on the test network, it should work elsewhere. In addition, mistakes and problems on the test network won't affect the operation of the other production networks.

The unused, valid network address could be one of the network addresses into which the networks will be renumbered. If the new address space has come from an ISP, the ISP has probably already advertised a route to that address space to the Internet at large, even though the address really isn't in use. It's likely that new, ISP-assigned address space falls within its summarized addresses or CIDR blocks anyway, so the new space is fully routable from the Internet, even if it isn't being used.

Enable Routing

Before renumbering any computers, the new network will have to be reachable from the Internet. That is, routers will have to be made aware of its existence, so that they can route traffic back to it. How this is done depends on the interior and exterior routing protocols in use in a network. The network administrator should ask the ISP that assigned the space if the new address space is being advertised on the Internet. The idea is to first make the address space reachable from within the organization's networks and then out to the Internet. If the former works, so should the latter.

The network administrator should enable internal network routing to the new network on the organization's internal routers. If dynamic updates are propagated among the organization's routers, the existence of the new network will be known to the organization's internal network shortly after the router port is configured with the new network. If the routers use static routes, routers can be configured with static routes that point to the new network.

Even if there are no computers on the new network at this point, it's a valid network. The next step is to test a real machine on the network, to see if it can reach the Internet and, more important, *be reached* from the Internet. These tests will use IP addresses, not host names, because the DNS records haven't been updated yet to include anything on the test network.

To conduct this test, connect a PC to the test network, and configure it with a host address within the address range of the network. The router port for the network will also have a host address, so the PC will be the second host on the network. At this point, the PC should be a fully reachable, fully routable host. Run a ping test from the PC to known addresses on the internal network, then to addresses on the border router, and then the Internet.

Ping is a simple test, and if it works, it means the address works, and that routers are aware of the address and know how to route traffic to it. Working outward from the test network's router port, ping should be done on a number of IP addresses, including the following:

- Backside and frontside ports of the router on the LAN
- Router ports on the border router or firewall to the IS
- The ISP's router
- Internal and external DNS servers
- Internet root zone servers

A second, more important test is to check if the network can be reached from outside the network. To do this, run a ping test from somewhere else on the Internet to see if the network can be reached externally. This test can be run from another site or through a dial-up connection to an ISP.

Be aware that firewalls or screening routers may stymie the ping test and other connectivity tests. Firewall rules or filters that screen out unknown source or destination addresses, or that only permit certain kinds of traffic to certain address ranges may make it appear that the new address space isn't routable from the Internet. In addition, those same firewalls or screening routers may not allow internal hosts to ping external hosts. Consequently, the network administrator may have to coordinate tests of the new address space with the firewall administrator. Traffic to and from the new address space may have to be configured on the firewall rulesets, just to make the routability tests work properly. The firewall *rulesets* specify the types of traffic the firewall admits or denies, as well as the networks and addresses that that may be reached through the firewall.

Update DNS and Test

Once the network has been found to be routable, the DNS records for any hosts on the test network should be updated. The DNS A records for any hosts on the network will reflect the hosts' old IP addresses. However, a second A record can be entered for each host that lists its new address. Even if the first record lists an old, now-incorrect record, the second record will be correct, and DNS inquiries for the host name will be resolved correctly. The DNS will return both records for the host, but only one will be correct.

The original A records for each host will be deleted when the new numbering plan has been proven to work properly. To help the DNS administrator keep straight which DNS records should be deleted, it is helpful to add a comment to both the original and the new A records for renumbered hosts. Anything that appears after a semicolon (;) in a DNS resource record is treated as a comment. A comment may be added to each record that will be dropped, to indicate that it is the old record, as well as to the following, new record, as in this example:

```
Renumbered_PC1 A     192.168.1.5 ; original record
Renumbered_PC1 A     192.168.50.5 ; new record
```

The DNS administrator should take care to update the reverse address resolution records, too. These are the in-addr PTR records, which map IP addresses back to host names. Both the primary and the reverse address records may be maintained locally or by an ISP. The in-addr records may be kept only on an external DNS, not on the internal DNS. External DNS changes may have to be coordinated with the ISP or with whomever maintains the external DNS.

As the renumbering proceeds, updating internal and external DNS services and coordinating their entries may be one of the tasks that will take the most time. If there are few hosts listed in the DNS, there will be few DNS entries to update. If the organization is using Dynamic DNS, and creating a host record for every PC or workstation on the network, the DNS coordination effort will be correspondingly more complicated.

If the organization has its own DNS server, one of the internal network addresses that may change during renumbering will be that of the internal DNS server. Each host in the network must know the address of the DNS. When its address is changed, the address configurations of every machine will have to be changed so they can find the DNS.

This issue is another reason for using DHCP to assign addresses to PCs. In addition to giving PCs and workstations their IP addresses, DHCP also gives them the address of the DNS. It's simpler to change the DNS address in the DHCP server than it is to do so individually for a large number of PCs.

Once the DNS records for the hosts on the test network have been updated, the updates have to be propagated to the secondary DNSes. This is why the TTL and other values were changed in the primary DNS before any renumbering started. If the TTL, Reset, and Retry entries were changed to values similar to those suggested in step 3, the new DNS records should propagate to any secondary DNSes within a few hours.

Depending on the number of secondary DNSes, it will probably take a few hours for all of the modified entries to propagate to other DNSes. Using the new TTLs and Retry values, the secondary DNSes should copy the revised zone files from the primary DNS within a few hours. Again depending on the number of secondary DNSes, the network administrator should wait at least two hours for all of the secondary DNSes to update their zone files.

The test network should be left to run for at least a day, to make sure that the routing tables in all of the network's routers don't purge their routing tables of an entry for the new network. If they do, something is wrong with the advertisement of the route. It could be that route announcements for the new network or its subnets aren't being announced, that they have been dropped by a router that has been rebooted, or some other problem.

Finally, the original A records for the hosts on the newly renumbered network can be deleted from the primary DNS zone file, leaving the new records as the primaries. If comments were added to resource records, they can be deleted or left in place, to indicate that the old record has been deleted. Some documentation fanatics may want to add each old address to the comment field of the resource records that remain, but that is probably unnecessary if a backup of the original zone file was kept.

Complete Rollout

If the renumbering on the first or test network has worked, and it can reach Internet hosts, and Internet hosts can reach hosts on the new network, renumbering can proceed to the next part of the network. If renumbering started at the most distant parts of the network, it should proceed inward toward the Internet connection. This is particularly useful if subnets are being aggregated in the new routing scheme, because updated route announcements from renumbered networks will contain the aggregated addresses.

In each case, a renumbered network should be tested as the first test network was. Once the network administrator and the DNS administrator are confident that they understand exactly which steps they take and what problems may occur, they may renumber more than one network at a time, as long as they coordinate their efforts.

Reset DNS Services

When the network has been completely renumbered, DNS records have been updated, and the new network numbering plan has been fully tested, the DNS SOA values can be reset to their original values. The TTL, Refresh, and Retry values should be set back to their original values, so that DNS updates between the primary and secondaries take place on a normal schedule.

Though there's nothing wrong with leaving those values alone, it may create a lot of unnecessary network traffic and DNS activity if they aren't changed back to higher values. The TTL, for example, can be set back to its old value, which might have been anything from a day to a week or longer. Keep in mind that server load-balancing schemes that are based on multiple DNS records for the same host name may rely on relatively low TTL values to work properly. So reset the SOA values to whatever they should be, which is not necessarily what they had been.

Do Administrative Cleanup

Finally, when everything is working properly, the network administrator can notify the address space provider that the old address space is no longer in use. This assumes that the old address space is being given up, which would be the case if an organization were switching ISPs. If the new address space is to be reused in another network, no notification is necessary, except to revise routing announcements.

One last task: documentation. If missing or incomplete documentation made the renumbering effort more difficult than it had to be, this is the time to correct the problem for future generations of network administrators. Document the new network numbering arrangement, as well as how routing works in the renumbered networks. Create diagrams of the new network renumbering plan; print out a copy and hang it on the wall near the router that runs to the ISP. Documentation is probably the last thing that the network administrator wants to do at the end of a project, but it's the best time to do it, and it must be done.

Summary

The cookbook approach of this chapter has been designed to organize the structure of a network renumbering project. But, to paraphrase those disclaimers made about fuel economy in car commercials, your exact steps of renumbering may vary, depending on network conditions, address ranges, and address aggregation policies. The purpose of this chapter has been to lay out a generalized sequence for renumbering, not a network-specific plan.

As in any complex process, a renumbering program places a great deal of emphasis on organization, documentation, and planning. It may not be possible to simulate the new, renumbered environment on an existing network, so the process described in this chapter emphasizes trying renumbering in a small part of the network, then moving it out to the rest of the network. Even that approach may not be suitable for some networks, or for organizations that can build the renumbered network in a lab environment, and then test and plan the renumbering process.

In the next three chapters, we will look at case studies of renumbering small, medium, and large networks. We'll use the pattern described in this chapter to do the renumbering, although, as we will see, there are plenty of opportunities and reasons to deviate for specific network conditions.

CHAPTER

16

Small Network Case Study

For the first case study, we will look at a renumbering project for a relatively small network of about a hundred hosts. The objectives are to analyze the network, determine a new numbering plan, and outline the steps, introduced in Chapter 15, which include designing the new addressing plan and realigning the network, if necessary, for that plan. Some of the considerations in the new addressing plan may be economy of address use, route summarization, or future growth, or all three.

In this case study, and the renumbering case studies that follow in subsequent chapters, we'll use IP address space from private address space, which is the space set aside by RFC 1918. Recall from our discussion in previous chapters that private address space is not routable in the Internet at large. It can be used on intranets, as long as private addresses are translated to public addresses with network address translation (NAT) at a firewall or gateway. So though we will use private address space as an example of a renumbering plan, a real network would use routable address space, unless there was some reason to use private address space and NAT.

> **NOTE** Renumbering plans may also be applied to new networks or to networks that are being joined, separated, or otherwise realigned. However, the larger the network, the more likely it is that it is not new, but is being renumbered to achieve some other objective, such as better address space usage or route summarization.

Situation

SmallCo is being forced into renumbering its network because it is moving to a different ISP. Today, changing ISPs may require renumbering, whether or not (probably not) the customer wants to do so. Leaving one ISP's assigned address space may take the network out of the ISP's CIDR block. For the sake of efficient routing on the Internet, ISPs advertise only their own address blocks.

The SmallCo network is composed of about 150 computers and 8 servers, all of which are in a single location. The company recently decided to switch ISPs in order to get better service and a faster Internet connection. The company has a part-time network administrator, and even though it depends on its computer systems and its Internet service for email with its customers, its managers would prefer to let the IS handle most of the details of its Internet access.

The company's current network, which is depicted in Figure 16.1, uses three different Class C networks. The new ISP has told the network administrator that since there are fewer than 250 PCs in the network, SmallCo will get a single Class C address, into which it will renumber all of its PCs.

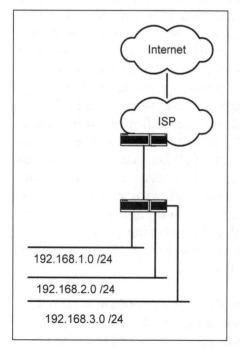

Figure 16.1   The original SmallCo network, before renumbering.

Scoping the Project

In this case, determining which address blocks to use for the renumbering plan is easy. As is typical today, the address space is assigned by the ISP, which gets address space from its higher-level providers or directly from ARIN. There's no need for SmallCo to have to justify private address space, because its network is small. Changing ISPs again sometime in the future may force another round of renumbering, but that's another issue for another day.

Since SmallCo has only one location and fewer than 250 hosts in use, and no apparent plans to expand significantly the number of hosts anytime soon, the IS will probably assign SmallCo's network a single Class C address. The address space may well be part of the IS's CIDR block, so it will be designated with CIDR notation, such as 192.168.1.0 /24. That refers to the single Class C network address of 192.168.1.0, including all of the hosts in the address range from 192.168.1.1 through 192.168.1.254. That's plenty for the SmallCo network, and it leaves some margin for growth, too.

Project Plan

The plan for renumbering, depicted in Figure 16.2, will be as follows:

1. Split the network into two parts at the central LAN switch; put the workstations on one part of the network and the servers on the other one. Everything will be numbered from the same address block, so it will appear to be one big network, but the servers will be on their own LAN segment.

2. Add a DHCP server to the server segment, so that PCs will get their addresses dynamically at bootup from the DHCP server.

3. Assign static addresses to the servers, so that server IP addresses don't change.

4. Establish a single DNS for the company, maintained by the ISP. Except for an email server, there are no internal servers that are accessible by Internet names. The ISP will act as a mail exchanger for the company, receiving its Internet email and forwarding messages to the internal mail server.

5. The ISP will run a firewall service for the company, instead of SmallCo installing and operating its own. It will add to the cost

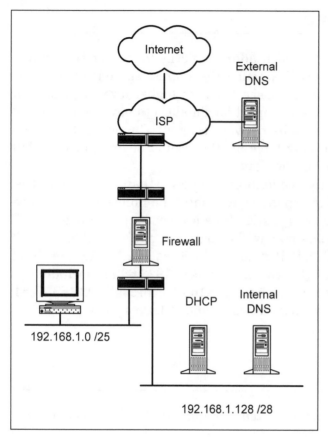

Figure 16.2   The plan for renumbering the SmallCo network.

of ISP service, but the company's security and Internet access requirements are simple. SmallCo won't be using private address space, so network address translation on the firewall isn't necessary.

6. Collapse all of the addresses into a single Class C address space, so route summarization won't be an issue. The address will be advertised by the ISP to the Internet as part of its address space. The ISP will most likely assign a small, /30 subnet (two hosts) from the Class C space for the link, leaving the rest of the Class C space for host addressing.

Preparing for Renumbering

This is a simple renumbering operation, so most of the preparation work will involve changing the configuration of the workstations for DHCP and reestablishing the static addresses on the servers within the new address space.

With the exception of the internal email server, none of the company's internal servers is listed in a DNS service anyway. However, the top-level root zone servers on the Internet list the name service for the smallco.com domain as the DNS service that the company had formerly maintained by itself. This registration will have to be changed, so that DNS address resolution attempts are redirected to the ISP's DNS. The request to change the root zone server name service resource record for the domain must be done by the person listed as the administrative or technical contact in the registration listing.

SmallCo is switching from static workstation IP addresses to those assigned by DHCP, so the network administrator will have to set up a DHCP service. The company wants to outsource as much network administration as possible, but it's not practical to outsource DHCP. The company already runs Windows NT servers, so it must establish a DHCP service on one of its NT servers and assign a range of addresses from the new address space as the dynamic address pool.

If the network administrator wanted to do so, the DHCP address range could be subdivided so that sales and marketing would get addresses from a specific range of addresses, administration would get them from another address range, and so forth. That's a local configuration option that would be an administrative convenience for the network administrator, rather than an operational necessity.

Addressing Rollout

Rolling out the new renumbering plan can be done over a weekend, as long as all of the preparation work has been completed beforehand. Once their Windows configuration has been changed to use DHCP for address assignment, users will receive a new address from the address range from the DHCP service. Since the company will be adding DHCP, it's a good idea to have users start working with the DHCP service with the old address range before the company switches over to the new address space and to the new ISP.

To ensure that the address rollout works properly, the administrator will test the operation of the DHCP service on a small number of machines before doing the big cutover. For the purpose of the test, addresses will be assigned by DHCP from the old address pool. This will establish that renumbering will work and that the DHCP service works, too.

SmallCo is moving responsibility for its DNS services to the new ISP, so the new ISP will be adding new resource records to its DNS for the SmallCo mail exchanger. The ISP is also the logical place for SmallCo to put its Web server. Giving the ISP responsibility for a number of services increases the cost of Internet service for a small company, but it also decreases the resources and effort the company must spend on network administration and management.

The routing for the new address space is also a simple matter, as most of it is managed by the ISP. The ISP's routers point inward to the SmallCo router, passing to it all traffic destined for any address in the 192.168.1.0 /24 address range. Except for the two addresses on the link between the ISP and the SmallCo router, the SmallCo router maintains all of the addresses in the rest of the address range. The SmallCo router has a default route to the ISP for all addresses except those in its own network range.

Administrative Cleanup

After the renumbering has been completed, the administrative wrap-up is relatively simple. Because the old DNS service has no role in the new network arrangement (DNS functions have been taken over by the ISP), the resource records in the old DNS should be deleted and the service made inactive in the NT server.

The address ranges from the old ISP's address space used by SmallCo's networks belong to the old ISP, so their disposition is the responsibility of the ISP. They will most likely be recycled to other customers of the old ISP after a number of months of inactivity (although because they were stub networks of the old ISP, they could be recycled sooner than that). They are still part of the old ISP's advertised address space, so as long as the ISP's routers direct traffic to the new networks that use those addresses, network routing will work properly. The old ISP will, however, have to change the resource records in its secondary DNSes to purge the SmallCo addresses from its DNS services.

Future Growth

Fortunately, the SmallCo network isn't so big that it occupies all of the address space that the IS has given it. If the SmallCo network had more than 250 hosts, the IS might have given it three /25 blocks, which would have been enough for 384 hosts. SmallCo's hosts consume about 175 of the 254 addresses in the block, leaving it room to grow its network by 79 more hosts. Even if SmallCo added a second location, it could still use additional addresses from the same block, if the second location had about 10 hosts in it.

One convenient aspect of the new network configuration is that using those addresses in a second location wouldn't affect routing from the ISP at all, and only minimally from the SmallCo router. The second location could be configured on a port on the SmallCo router, and its subnet could be configured on that port, as illustrated in Figure 16.3.

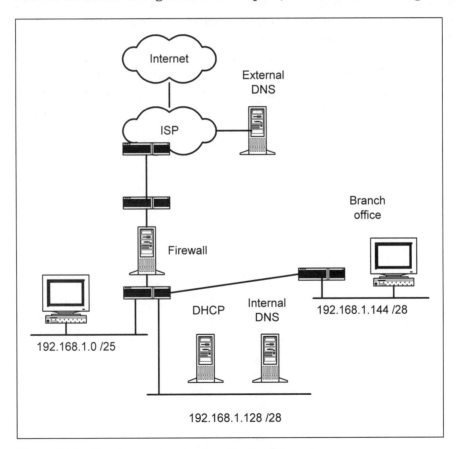

Figure 16.3 Creating a new subnet on the SmallCo router.

The second location could take a /28 subnet of the address space, which would allow it to have up to 14 hosts in the second subnet (disallowing the first and last addresses).

Summary

The case study of renumbering a small network illustrates the methodical steps of executing a network renumbering plan. This case study illustrates a relatively simple renumbering program, which has been required because the company is changing ISPs.

The case study has followed the cookbook approach to renumbering specified in Chapter 15, taking steps like analyzing the situation, scoping out the project, developing an project plan, and so forth. The SmallCo network was small enough that it gave us a chance to see how a complete renumbering process would be carried out. At the same time, the network was not so complex that it was difficult to keep all of the parts and considerations in mind.

The next case study, that of a medium-sized network spanning several locations, is more complex, and adds the complication of changing the interior routing protocol. While the next case study is more complicated, the same general planning and project execution steps will apply.

Medium Network Case Study

The second network case study addresses a medium-sized network, consisting of about a thousand workstations and servers, spread out over three locations. We will use the renumbering steps that were discussed in Chapter 15, as we did with the first case study of a small network. These steps include analyzing the scope of the project, designing a new addressing plan, and renumbering hosts in the new address space.

In this case study, as in the previous one, the objectives are to increase the flexibility of the addressing plan and to make most efficient use of assigned address space. In addition, we will try to summarize routes that are announced to other networks, such as to the company's ISP.

Situation

Unlike SmallCo, MediumCo isn't renumbering its networks because it is changing ISPs. In this case, the company wants to reorganize the way it is using the address space it already has, so that addressing conforms to a comprehensible plan.

Another, more significant motivation for MediumCo to be renumbering is that its IS organization wants to change the interior routing protocols that its routers use within its Autonomous System. MediumCo has been using the older Routing Information Protocol (RIP-I), only because it has been using an older generation of routers that couldn't run other interior routing protocols. MediumCo is upgrading its routers, which are capable of running more efficient routing protocols. The network manager would like to move to the newer Open Shortest Path (OSPF) protocol, described in RFC 1583. OSPF would make routing more efficient and give the network managers a chance to restructure the network so that it is easier to manage.

In order for OSPF to work, networks must be designed and arranged to summarize routes into a core area. The core area, in turn, summarizes all of the routes in the OSPF areas and announces them to a higher-level network. In this case, the higher-level network is the Internet, which MediumCo reaches through its ISP.

The MediumCo network is composed of about 1,000 computers, scattered over a single main office and two branch office locations. MediumCo's network now uses about 15 separate Class C networks, all of which have been allocated to it by its ISP. In line with the principle that any IP address is just as good as any other IP address (as long as no one else is using it), the separate Class C addresses work fine. The problem is that they're not quite so fine for OSPF. The MediumCo network manager has decided that things would work better with OSPF, particularly since the company is planning to add offices for acquired companies and, consequently, scale up its networks in the future.

Another reason rearranging the network to accommodate OSPF makes sense to the IS manager is that, for security reasons, the company is moving all three offices under a single, heavily monitored connection to the Internet. Currently, the company has a separate Internet connection in each of the three locations. The western division has a 56Kb connection to a local ISP, the central office has a 512Kb connection, and the eastern office has a 128Kb connection.

In addition, the IS manager wants to centralize security responsibilities in the central region office, which is the site of the company's headquarters. The company has firewalls on each of its three Internet connections, but the IS manager wants to establish a standard, corporatewide set of filtering rules for the firewalls, and manage the rulesets from one office. So the western and eastern ISP connections are being taken away, and all Internet traffic from all three offices will go to a single ISP through a new T-1 connection at the central region office.

MediumCo's current network, depicted in Figure 17.1, has about 1,000 workstations and servers in all; the central office has about 700 workstations and servers, the western branch has about 200, and the

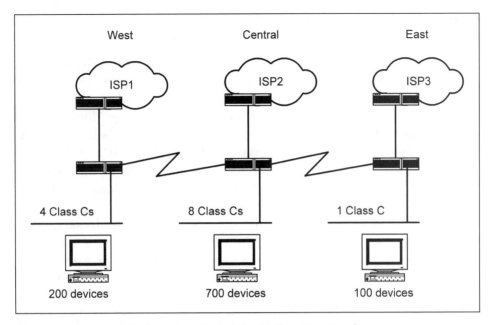

Figure 17.1 The original configuration of the MediumCo network.

smaller eastern branch about 100. Each office has its own servers, but the company's main administrative and financial systems are consolidated in about 25 servers and hosts in the central office.

As the network has grown, address space has been allocated on an as-needed basis by the local ISPs to accommodate the requirements at each office. For example, the central office is now using addresses from eight different Class C address ranges, the western office is using four Class Cs, while the Eastern office has its hosts numbered from a single Class C network.

Each location has its own DNS server, which resolves text host names to the IPS addresses of hosts in each branch. Address resolution requests for everything else go to the central office DNS, which is both the public (outside) and private (inside) DNS for the company. MediumCo already uses DHCP, which runs on separate servers in each of its three locations.

MediumCo would also like to add a dial-up remote access server (RAS) in the central office. About 50 salespeople, telecommuters, and some suppliers would communicate through the RAS, so the RAS would also need its own address space.

Scoping the Problem

MediumCo doesn't have its own provider-independent address space, because its addresses have all come from its ISPs. Now that two of its three ISP connections will be discontinued, MediumCo will have to request address space from what will be its sole ISP. The MediumCo IS department will have to allocate that address space to its internal networks. Moreover, because the company will be using OSPF as its internal routing protocol, it will have to allocate and organize that address space so that all routes collapse into a nice, neat route summary before they reach the ISP.

As Figure 17.2 shows, there is no consistency to the addressing plan currently in use at MediumCo. The addresses in each of the three regions were assigned some time ago as the network's addressing needs expanded, and no thought was given to Internet routing table efficiency or route summarization. Bringing each region under the same ISP will change all that; the ISP in the central region will most likely want to advertise only the address from its delegated address space, not the addresses assigned, and presumably owned, by other ISPs.

Consequently, the MediumCo IS department will have to request enough address space from its single ISP to cover all of its locations. Projecting its growth over the next five years, MediumCo's IS managers estimate that the company may need twice as many IP addresses as they use today.

After assessing the company's current addressing needs and its projected future growth, MediumCo's ISP assigned the company eight Class C network addresses, all of which were part of a single, continu-

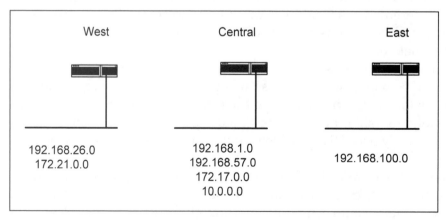

Figure 17.2   The original addressing plan for the MediumCo network.

ously numbered /21 address block, running from 192.168.1.0 through 192.168.8.0. The company's IS managers expect growth in the number of computers at each location, but they can't be sure exactly when or where the growth will be concentrated. The network address assignments, therefore, are intended to accommodate current usage and to allow for growth, wherever and whenever it occurs.

Having all of the network addresses in the same CIDR block from a single ISP also works in favor of the plan to use OSPF. Since all of the networks will collapse into a single route announcement, which is 192.168.8.0 /21, they can be advertised back to the ISP as a single routing announcement. The MediumCo network is a good example of how route aggregation can work to everyone's benefit.

Project Plan

The plan for renumbering MediumCo's networks is as follows:

1. Divide up the Class C addresses among the three locations, so that there is enough address space at each location to number the existing hosts. With more than 700 hosts, the central region offices need three of the Class Cs (three of the /24 blocks), just to renumber its current host count, with little room for continued growth, so it gets four of the /24 blocks. Three will be used to number the current hosts and the fourth will be held in reserve, to allow the central office host count to grow by 25 percent before it needs more address space.

2. Keep the addressing plan as simple as possible. A single Class C address block can accommodate all of the hosts in each of the eastern (100 hosts) and western (200 hosts) offices. To conserve address space, the eastern office can be given a /25 block from one of the Class Cs, the equivalent of half a Class C, capable of accommodating 128 hosts.

3. Devise an address assignment plan to allow for growth in both the eastern and the western offices. This is particularly important for the western region, which would exhaust the remainder of its /24 block if its host count were to grow by only 20 percent. If the eastern region were given an entire /24, it would have more than half the block unassigned, allowing the office to double in size without affecting the addressing plan.

4. To meet the need of the central location for another /24 block for the RAS server, each of the dial-up ports would need a single address from the /24 block. The RAS server needs to support as many as 50 active remote users at a time. While a smaller address block would be suitable, an entire Class C address block (255 addresses) may be assigned to the RAS. This will allow for plenty of growth in RAS usage in the future.

The address allocation plan plays nicely against the OSPF issue. The routes advertised by all three offices will be summarized at the central office, at OSPF Area 0, which is also the OSPF route summary area, as depicted in Figure 17.3. The networks in each of the three offices will be in their own OSPF areas. For example, the central office will be in Area 1, the western office in Area 2, and the eastern office in Area 3. The networks in each area will be summarized at Area 0 at the central office site and advertised as a block back to the ISP.

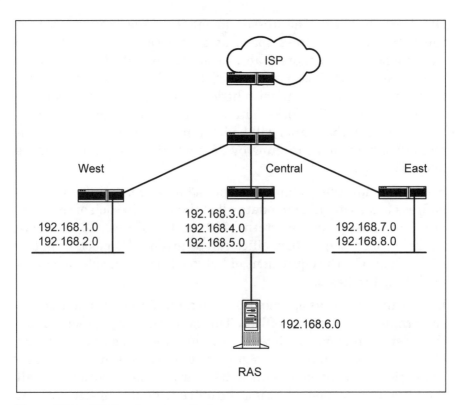

Figure 17.3   OSPF route summarization area.

DNS

MediumCo maintains its own external DNS, as well as an internal DNS at the central office site. The internal DNS will be upgraded to a Dynamic DNS, so that addresses assigned by DHCP are linked to host names, and resource record updates for each address assignment are sent to the internal DNS.

DHCP

Each of MediumCo's regional offices will have its own DHCP server, to assign addresses dynamically to workstations in the zone. The servers in each regional office will have static addresses, because their addresses will not change.

Preparing for Renumbering

It's a bigger network, so of course MediumCo network is more complicated than the SmallCo network, but many of the same principles apply when preparing to renumber its network. Static addresses assigned to routers and hosts have to be discovered and changed, a rollout plan must be devised, and changes must be made to DNS services that reference MediumCo services and servers.

The most significant amount of work prior to the actual renumbering will be to configure the network for OSPF. As we have noted, preparing a network for OSPF means arranging networks in a hierarchical fashion, so that routes collapse into a central OSPF area. Fortunately, the MediumCo network consists of three locations, which can be organized under a central, core network at the central office location. Consequently, the network can be arranged hierarchically relatively easily; it won't require reorganizing the network structure to accommodate OSPF.

Adding OSPF routing means that the router administrator will have to enable OSPF routing on the MediumCo routers. To avoid complications in using OSPF, a network must be organized to summarize routes into a core network. Once this has been done, OSPF routing can be configured on the routers. OSPF routing won't be configured on the MediumCo network routers until after the networks have been renumbered.

Since there will be a network "core" at the central office, a new, but small, network will have to be set up there to act as the network core, as illustrated in Figure 17.4. The purpose of this network will be to act as the OSPF core. All of the networks assigned to the regional offices will be summarized there and redistributed to the other OSPF areas. The networks within MediumCo will also be summarized there, and advertised to the Internet, via MediumCo's ISP.

Using OSPF usually implies that an organization's network is contained within and identified by an Autonomous System Number (ASN). The entire MediumCo network will be part of its own Autonomous System (AS), so the IS department must request an ASN through the company's ISP. Like IP addresses, ASNs must be unique, so they are also controlled and assigned by ARIN. ISP customers who need an ASN request it through their ISPs.

MediumCo maintains its own DNS service, so changes to DNS resource records need not be coordinated with the ISP, but with the internal organization that controls the MediumCo DNS services. As part of the preparation for renumbering, the DNS controlling authority within MediumCo must examine the DNS resource records in the primary and any secondary DNSes to determine which addresses, if any, will change during renumbering.

MediumCo's primary DNS is on an external network segment, and its IP address need not be changed, so the NS records in the Internet's root zone servers that point to the DNS for the mediumco.com domain won't have to be changed.

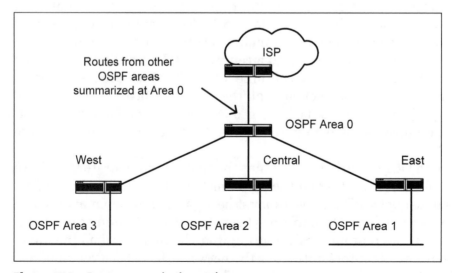

Figure 17.4 Route summarization at the core area.

Unlike SmallCo, which had to set up DHCP servers and then change all of its PC configurations to use DHCP, MediumCo is already set up to do dynamic address assignment, because even before undertaking its renumbering project, MediumCo used DHCP in its networks. The network administrator will, however, have to determine the range, or scope, of addresses to be assigned by DHCP. Any static addresses that have been assigned to router ports, servers, or workstations will have to be determined before renumbering begins. Since DHCP has been in use in the MediumCo networks, it is most likely that static addresses have only been assigned to servers and routers.

Dial-up devices will continue to have IP addresses assigned dynamically by the RAS, so their address assignments will be under the control of the RAS administrator. The RAS server will have a different set of addresses for its ports, and it must be configured with the new address range.

Addressing Rollout

The best places to start the renumbering rollout on the MediumCo network are at the smaller eastern division office and at the RAS network in the central office. They can be used as the testbeds for renumbering rollout.

To keep the network routers' routing tables clear of "pollution," static routes to and from the new network ranges will be configured on routers in the other regional offices. This will enable the network administrators in each region to test connectivity across the MediumCo network to and from the renumbered segments.

Once the internal connectivity tests have succeeded, static routes for the network numbers from the new address ranges will be configured on the routers in the central and eastern regions, to make the MediumCo network aware of the existence of the new networks. If the tests work, network renumbering can be rolled out to the other networks in each region.

To make sure that the renumbering works properly, and to simplify troubleshooting, renumbering will be completed throughout all of the networks in the eastern division before renumbering starts in the western region or in the networks in the central region. The principle is to renumber from the outer networks inward toward the core of the network in the central region, leaving the central region networks for last.

After the eastern regional office networks have been renumbered, the renumbering program will move to the western region. Again, a small network segment at the edge of the western region office network will be renumbered, tested, and operated for several days, to make sure it works properly and is reachable from elsewhere on the network.

Once the central network has been renumbered and the new OSPF core network has been set up, OSPF routing can be turned on in the routers. This will collapse the network route announcements in the Area 0 network and summarize the announcement of the entire 192.168.8.0 /21 network to the ISP. The /21 block is part of a larger block that belongs to the IS, so the ISP will announce the summarized networks to the Internet.

Administrative Cleanup

Most of the administrative tasks related to the use of the new address space will belong to the ISP, which has responsibility for advertising the address space to the Internet. The new ISP isn't responsible for the old address space that had been used by the eastern and western divisions. That address space came from the ISPs that provided the individual Internet connections from the eastern and western division offices, and so belongs within larger address blocks advertised by those ISPs. Keeping that address space, even if it isn't used, will not do MediumCo any good, because routes to it point from the Internet to the networks of its former ISPs. Therefore, when renumbering is complete, and the addresses from those networks are no longer in use, MediumCo's IS department should turn back that unused address space to the old ISPs.

As the networks in the regional offices are renumbered, the resource records in the internal DNS services will have to be changed accordingly. As for the SmallCo network, both the old and the new A records for each server should be kept on the internal DNS services, with appropriate comment lines in each resource record. When renumbering is complete, the new A records will be uncommented, and the old A records may be deleted.

Most of the DNS changes will affect the internal, not the external, DNS services. So, as a final rollout step, addressing changes will have to be propagated to any secondary DNS services on the internal network. The time-out and retry values on the primary internal DNS should be changed to low values, as discussed in Chapter 9, to force the secondaries to copy the zone files. When the updated zone files have been propagated to all of the other secondary internal DNSes, the SOA values can be changed back to their original values.

Future Growth

The new addressing plan for MediumCo has been set up to allow the networks to grow by 20 percent, not a huge allowance, but enough to give the company some room to expand the network within its new address space.

Any new address space will have to come from MediumCo's ISP. It probably won't be address space that will be contiguous to the 192.168.8.0.21 address block; most likely it will come from another part of the ISP's assigned space. If new address space is needed for future growth, it may be assigned as part of a larger address block by the IS or as individual /24s. In either case, the new address space might be assigned by MediumCo's network managers as subnets of the newly assigned space or as an entire network to each location.

In either case, the networks will be advertised back to the OSPF Area 0 in the central office location, then advertised back to each regional office. It will not be necessary for all of the address space in the entire MediumCo network to be part of the same address space, as long as each individual network is advertised both internally and externally.

Summary

The MediumCo network posed a special renumbering challenge because it involved both renumbering and arranging the network to accommodate a new routing protocol, OSPF. While adding two new elements at the same time—new network numbering and a new routing protocol—can be a recipe for disaster, it may be more efficient to do both at the same time, rather than change the addressing, then change the routing protocol later.

Adding something like OSPF, which assumes route summarization and careful, hierarchical network design, complicates this project tremendously. Changing routing protocols also requires the skills of experienced OSPF network designers, and a clean, comprehensible design. This case study has emphasized the renumbering aspects of the program, not the OSPF side, although both were part of the case study.

In the last case study, we will examine how a large company will renumber the network of an acquisition that will move from private network numbering to routable, public numbering.

CHAPTER 18

Large Network Case Study

The third and final network case study deals with a relatively large network, consisting of more than 5,000 workstations in several locations. As for the small and the medium-sized network case studies, we will use the methodology for renumbering the network introduced in Chapter 15, including analyzing the network design, specifying a new addressing plan, and renumbering the hosts in the new address space.

In any renumbering project, often renumbering is not an isolated event. As demonstrated in the medium network case study, renumbering often implies a number of other changes in the structure of the network. For instance, in the medium case study, renumbering was a consequence of an effort to reorganize the network to accommodate another routing protocol, OSPF.

In this case study, renumbering will be an incidental consequence of integrating some new networks into an already established larger network, and of changing the network's routing to accommodate Internet access and traffic flow requirements. The objectives will be to attach several new networks to an existing network and to control how data is routed to those networks. Route summarization and efficient use of address space will be less important than controlling routing and Internet access, and access between the old and new networks.

The point is that renumbering is rarely an end unto itself; it is more likely to be a result of other factors that enable other capabilities, such as route summarization. Renumbering can rarely be justified unless it is a means to achieve a more important goal.

Situation

BigCo has recently acquired the offices and factories of a smaller company (which we will call TinyCo) in another part of the country, and it wants to integrate the acquisition into its network. However, BigCo doesn't want to integrate too closely the networks and information processing systems of the smaller company. (Often, when a large company acquires a smaller one, network renumbering, if it is done at all, maintains a separation between the two networks, rather than effecting a complete integration.) BigCo's longer-term game plan is to keep TinyCo and its networks at an arm's length, in effect, operating as a wholly owned subsidiary. The goal is to have TinyCo stand on its own as an independent profit center, to potentially become the nucleus of a completely separate line of business that could be spun off as an incorporated entity. From a technical, networking standpoint, such a spin-off could be done by separating the network links between the two entities.

In short, then, BigCo wants to bring its new acquisition into the corporate fold, but only so far. TinyCo is to share certain of BigCo's key business applications, such as payroll, accounting, and general ledger. Its manufacturing operations will also be controlled by BigCo's centralized process control applications.

On the network side, TinyCo's networks in its four locations, depicted in Figure 18.1, are to be connected to BigCo's corporate network. The network connections between the two networks, as well as the extent to which they will control their respective information processing destinies, will mirror the business relationship between the two companies. Though connected, TinyCo's network will retain its own identity. TinyCo will keep, for instance, its own, separate Internet access points. BigCo also wants to control how traffic flows across the long-haul network that links the two companies, to balance the use of the wide area network.

Connecting the two networks implies renumbering, but only because today, TinyCo uses private address space. In itself, that's not a problem. Its networks are numbered with RFC 1918-compliant 10.0.0.0 addresses.

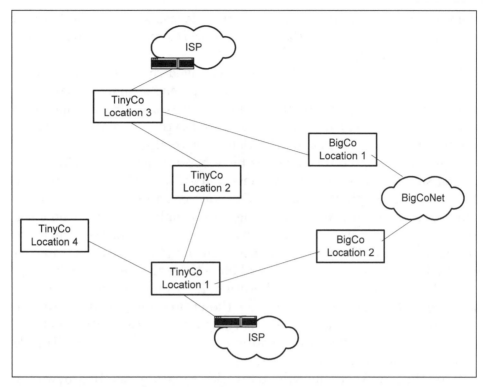

Figure 18.1   The TinyCo network, prior to being integrated into the BigCo network.

Because it will be a separate but equal network, the TinyCo network could continue to use 10.0.0.0 address space, as long as BigCo's network administrators were willing to use network address translation (NAT) between the two. However, there is some concern that certain of BigCo's key applications might not work with systems that use private addresses. To preclude this glitch, and to eliminate the possible complications that NAT may introduce, TinyCo's 500 hosts will be moved into routable, public address space. Furthermore, BigCo is contemplating other acquisitions in the future, some of which might already use 10.0.0.0 addresses. Its IS policy is to use public address space instead of private address space wherever possible.

Another addressing issue is that while BigCo has its own, registered Class B address, the BigCo network runs under the RIP-I routing protocol. The address space is subnetworked, but because the network is using RIP-I and a /16 subnet mask throughout the network, even point-to-point links consume a Class B subnet. As a result, BigCo's network administrators don't have enough extra address space in the Class B network for TinyCo. Thus, the TinyCo networks will have to use public, routable address space from their ISPs.

BigCo has its own Internet access, managed through a multihomed connection through a single ISP. However, instead of sharing that Internet connection, TinyCo will have not one, but two Internet connections from its network. The first will be dedicated to the use of the company's purchasing and electronic distribution departments.

In recent years, both companies have become active participants in online supplier bidding for materials and subassemblies; they've also taken on the supplier's role in online auctions to customers for their manufactured goods. As a result, the TinyCo online traders, who use a small group of 25 computers in Location 3, will need their own, separate Internet access. The other 475 users in TinyCo also need Internet access, but their Internet traffic will have to be directed through a separate Internet access point at Location 1, to preserve the use of the Location 3 Internet access point for the online auction users. And to make things interesting, if the important Internet connection at Location 3 fails, the auction unit's traffic is to be redirected to the TinyCo Internet connection at Location 1.

Note that to keep the two networks separate, as BigCo wants, TinyCo's Internet traffic won't flow back across the WAN to BigCo's Internet connections. Those circuits don't have enough capacity to handle another 500 users. Furthermore, BigCo's network managers don't want to clog up the WAN by backhauling Internet traffic to the BigCo network.

TinyCo will also have its own network services, connected to but distinct from those of BigCo. For example, the two companies' email systems, though separate systems, will forward mail to each other. DNS and DHCP services will exist in both networks, but TinyCo's DNS won't be a secondary to the BigCo primary. TinyCo's primary DNS will be backed up by a secondary DNS in another TinyCo location.

The most problematic issue will be controlling the flow of data across the network. The online auction traders will use BigCo's production management system, located at BigCo headquarters. The WAN link running from Location 3 to BigCo is to be used for that purpose alone. All other traffic between BigCo headquarters and TinyCo will use the link to TinyCo Location 1, leaving the link to Location 2 as a backup. In itself, that's not a serious problem, except that, as mentioned, the BigCo network uses the old RIP-I routing protocol, which works well, but it's not that efficient and it has a limited amount of flexibility.

Scoping the Problem

The separate-but-equal nature of TinyCo's status in the BigCo network means that its addressing plan won't have to be integrated with that of the BigCo network. As long as TinyCo has its own address space, its networks can exist as if they were part of any other separate network, reachable through routed WAN connections.

The significant issues that must be addressed in this case study are renumbering out of private network 10.0.0.0 address space, routing, and the traffic management through the two ISPs. Remember, though the TinyCo network will be connected to the BigCo network, the two will operate somewhat autonomously.

The first issue, renumbering from 10.0.0.0 address space, will be simplified by the use of DHCP (TinyCo networks currently use DHCP). For workstations that don't need static addresses, the DHCP servers can be configured to use address ranges from the new, public address space. Servers, hosts, and router interfaces that have static addresses will have to be readdressed manually within the new address space, but that will be a one-time task.

One of the issues that will have to be resolved is justifying TinyCo's use of the new address space it is requesting from its ISPs. TinyCo will have two Internet access points, each from a separate ISP. TinyCo isn't so much interested in backup as it is in reserving the traders' Internet access for their use only, so there is no need for traffic to be balanced between the two network access points.

In some ways, TinyCo's Internet access scheme simplifies the entire Internet access issue. Unlike the two other case studies, in which Internet access was to be consolidated across the company's main ISP connections, BigCo's desire to operate TinyCo as a separate entity means it can have its own, separately routable Internet connections.

Since TinyCo wants its own Internet access, it will have to request IP address space from its ISPs. This will solve the problem of where the address space will come from, and it will differentiate the routes to get from the Internet to TinyCo from those to get to BigCo. But, again, TinyCo will have to justify the address space that it will be requesting. Its offices are small, and only the office in Location 1, which has about 300 users, can justify even two Class C addresses. However, TinyCo wants at least three Class Cs, which it must get from the two separate ISPs. TinyCo needs two Class Cs from the ISP serving Location 1 and another from the ISP serving Location 3.

Project Plan

The plan for renumbering TinyCo's networks, depicted in Figure 18.2, is as follows:

1. Request address space for the TinyCo networks from the two ISPs. There are four locations, only one of which (Location 1) will have a significant number of users (about 300 users). Locations 2 and 4, which are smaller offices, only have about 50 users apiece. The traders' location, 3, has about 100 users and servers.

2. Get public address space from each of the two respective ISPs. TinyCo will have Internet access from Location 1 and Location 3, so the address space will come from two ISPs, in order to manage Internet routability to the two different locations. If the address space were advertised by the same ISP, TinyCo wouldn't have any control over how Internet traffic would reach any of its locations; that is, the traders in Location 3 might go to the Internet through their local connection, but they would have no way of ensuring

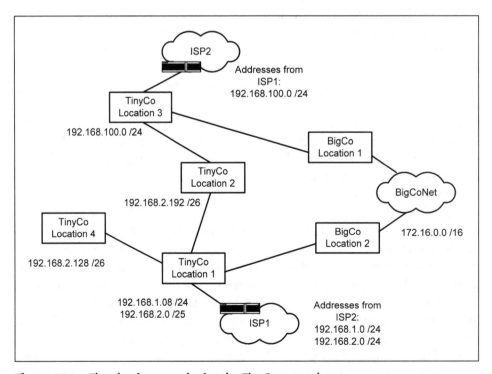

Figure 18.2   The plan for renumbering the TinyCo networks.

that inbound traffic from the Internet wouldn't come back through the ISP connection at Location 1, and be backhauled across the TinyCo network to Location 3. A single ISP could manage traffic to and from both Internet access points, but TinyCo has decided to go with two ISPs so that it isn't dependent on a single ISP for its Internet access.

3. Leave BigCo's network essentially untouched by the renumbering in TinyCo networks. In the greater scheme of things, it could be argued that this is an opportunity for BigCo to move from RIP-I to a more capable, modern protocol, such as OSPF. However, in this case, the BigCo IS department isn't going to start a migration to OSPF in the TinyCo network. That's a completely separate project, and integrating TinyCo by renumbering only the TinyCo networks is a workable solution.

4. Have TinyCo network use RIP-II as its internal routing protocol. This will give the TinyCo network administrators more control over its internal routing, and it will allow them to use VLSM to set up smaller subnetworks in Locations 2 and 4.

5. Get Locations 2 and 4, each of which has about 50 users, a subnet of the address space from the Location 1 ISP's space. Each location only needs 50 addresses, so each can be assigned a /27 subnet from one of the Class Cs assigned to Location 1. The addresses will be summarized up to Location 1, and the subnet masks propagated by RIP-II.

6. Enable BigCo to manage traffic flow back into the TinyCo network by having different IP address ranges for Locations 1, 2, and 4 and Location. The BigCo network uses RIP-I, which sees adjacent networks according to their full, "natural" address masks. If the TinyCo network had retained its 10.0.0.0 private address space, the BigCo routers would have seen the entire 10.0.0.0 network as equally reachable through the connections to Locations 1 and 3. With separate Class Cs in Locations 1 and 3, the BigCo network's routers will see the two Class Cs that cover Locations 1, 2, and 4 as reachable through Location 1, and the Class C in Location 3 as reachable through the link to Location 3.

7. For security purposes, have the connections back into the BigCo network from Locations 1 and 3 screened by the BigCo edge routers. Only traffic from the three Class C addresses in use in the TinyCo network will be permitted to pass through the BigCo edge routers.

8. Install firewalls at the TinyCo ISP connections in Locations 1 and 3. If the Internet connection in Location 3 (for use by the traders) were to falter, the Location 3 system would point to the Location 1 firewall for Internet access. But note, in this case, the firewall in Location 1 would have to be configured to translate the Location 3 addresses to an address from the Location 1 address space. Otherwise, the ISP servicing Location 3 would still advertise the path to that network to higher-level ISPs, but the path wouldn't be available.

Preparing for Renumbering

The first step in the BigCo renumbering project will be to request address space from the ISPs servicing Locations 1 and 3. Given that there are more than 400 users who will access the Internet through the Location 1 IS connection, the IS will be able to justify two Class Cs of address space for TinyCo from its address blocks. But because some ISPs allocate standard, smaller address blocks, such as a /25 (128 addresses), TinyCo may have to negotiate for more address space than the ISP normally grants.

Integrating the TinyCo network into the BigCo network won't be much of a challenge, because the TinyCo network will exist as a separately attached network that uses its own address space. The two BigCo border routers that terminate the two WAN connections to the TinyCo network will be reconfigured to use RIP-II on their interfaces to the TinyCo network.

The client machines in Location 3 and the clients in Locations 1, 2, and 4 will need to have their default gateway addresses pointed to their new default gateway addresses. The default gateways for systems in those locations won't change, but their addresses will.

Continuing to use DHCP services for all of the TinyCo network will simplify the problem of propagating default gateway addresses to the client workstations. Changing the address pools for TinyCo's DHCP services will have to be coordinated for the TinyCo network before readdressing begins.

The DNS issues will be fairly straightforward for the TinyCo renumbering project. The existing TinyCo DNS services will have hosts with 10.0.0.0 addresses. These addresses will have to be changed to the public addresses from the new address ranges. In addition, the two new ISPs will need the host name and IP addresses to which they should direct email and other Internet traffic. Both IS connections will be behind a firewall, so the new DNS records for each of the ISPs will be the firewall's single external interface.

Addressing Rollout

This renumbering effort has been designed to minimize the impact on the BigCo network. Hosts in the TinyCo network will come through the BigCo network edge router to access BigCo's main business applications. However, the BigCo network won't be affected by the renumbering in the TinyCo network.

Again, because address space for the TinyCo network will come from two different ISPs, the renumbering could start in any of the smaller offices, such as Location 2 or 4. That said, Location 3 is a good place to start, because it has its own address space and its own Internet access, and it's a relatively small network (about 50 hosts). Furthermore, it has all of the elements that have to work when readdressing it done elsewhere.

The TinyCo network is using DHCP, so the installation, test, and operation of the new DHCP address pool is the first step. Only the largest of the TinyCo offices, Location 1 and Location 3 need their own DHCP servers. Once the DHCP server is using the new address pool, its functions will be tested with the existing 10.0.0.0 address space before using the new address block.

DNS servers for the ISP will add appropriate A records for the mail exchanger in Location 3. In addition, the DNS records for the servers in Location 3 will be changed on the TinyCo DNS. If there are hosts in the TinyCo network that will have to be reached by the users in the BigCo network, their records will also be added to the TinyCo DNS.

Once the network in Location 3 operates properly, addressing can move to the two smaller locations for the rest of the TinyCo network, Locations 2 and 4. Each has only a few hosts, and so can be renumbered from a /27 subnet (32 hosts) of one of the addresses from the Location 1 ISP. Their routes will be summarized in the remainder of the address block, which will be used, along with the second Class C address from the ISP, to renumber the hosts in Location 1.

Administrative Cleanup

The private address space that had been used in TinyCo isn't being retired, as it would be if it were public address space from an ISP, so the administrative cleanup after renumbering is relatively straightforward. As long as the ISPs advertise the network addresses for the two logical parts of the TinyCo network (Locations 1, 2, and 4, and Location 3) properly, they will have proper Internet accessibility. The key is in the word "properly." It's important that the ISPs do their routing announcement jobs properly, because the Class C space into which the TinyCo networks have been renumbered belongs to two different ISPs, and their Internet routing responsibilities cover different parts of the TinyCo network. The TinyCo and BigCo network administrators will have to run network traces (using the traceroute command) periodically on the Internet connections, to make sure that Internet traffic is being routed the way they want it to be.

It may be helpful for the BigCo network administrator to perform the same checks on its Internet connections, to make sure that Internet traffic isn't being backhauled across the TinyCo network and back into the BigCo network to reach the Internet through the BigCo Internet access points.

Both BigCo and TinyCo will be operating their own DNS services. While the TinyCo and BigCo intranet Web sites will be cross-listed on each other's DNSes, few other hosts will be. As in the other case studies, the appropriate A records in each company's DNS service will include comments and additional host records for both the old and new hosts until the old 10.0.0.0 addresses have been completely eliminated.

Future Growth

TinyCo's twofold ISP strategy, and its arm's length attachment to BigCo, may well set a difficult challenge for future growth. Though Location 3 has enough additional address space—assuming it was able to justify getting a full Class C—to triple in size, the other locations may be constrained for future growth, because of their higher demand on their Class Cs. Locations 1, 2, and 4 are numbered from two Class Cs. In addition, Location 1 must summarize the addresses from Locations 2 and 4, and announce them back into the BigCo network. Since all of the address space in the TinyCo network is Class Cs from different ISPs, future growth can be accommodated by getting more Class C space from the respective ISPs.

The only restriction on the use of that space will be that the address space assigned by the respective ISPs can only be used within the locations served by that ISP. Internet routing and reachability would not work properly if the address space were used across the two ISP service areas. The ISP for Location 3, for example, would not advertise addresses from the ISP serving Locations 1, 2, and 4, because they would not belong to its address space.

Summary

This case study has illustrated a way in which a large company, with its own big IP network, can incorporate a much smaller acquisition into that network. Instead of undertaking a wholesale renumbering program, or even extending its address space to the acquisition, this company has elected to attach the smaller acquisition in its own address space.

This arm's length approach has the advantage of keeping the acquisition a separate business entity, in its own address space. The disadvantage is that the big company may find in the future that it might have been easier to extend its address space to the acquisition, as a means of extending its internal routing plan over the whole network.

CHAPTER

19

The Future of IP

During its development, if the inventors of IP had known it would become as widely used as it has today, would they have done anything different? Would they have tried to make it more robust, more adaptable, or more accommodating of a huge and growing Internet? Might they have given more thought to incorporating data management, quality of service, security, and other features into IP, so that it could accommodate greater demands for services and applications unimagined a decade ago? We'll never know, but in any case, IP has proven to be more capable and more robust than its designers ever intended it to be.

The Trouble with IPv4

Saying there's trouble with IP as it stands today doesn't mean that it's not working. It means that its current capability probably won't be adequate to meet the demands of users and network designers in the future.

Take, for example, a relatively simple issue like address space. All of the efforts to conserve IP address space—justifying address space usage, CIDR, and subnetworking—have been driven by the profligate use of IPv4 address space for the past 20 years. The concept of classes of IP address space, to accommodate networks of different sizes, was a terrific idea when it was invented. But in practice, it has been extremely wasteful, stranding large blocks of host addresses in Class A and B networks that can't be used elsewhere.

The Class A address space represents the largest untapped reserve of unassigned addresses. Of the 127 possible Class A network addresses (networks 1.0.0.0 through network 127.0.0.0), approximately half have been assigned. The rest, representing about one billion potential host addresses, have been held in reserve by the IETF, and its successor for address assignment, ARIN.

Fortunately, only a relatively small percentage of the addresses that have been assigned are actually in use, somewhat less than 40 percent. Even allowing for the tremendous growth of the Internet in the past few years, only a third of all of the assigned IP addresses are actually in use.

Address space remains a vexing problem, and given the spiraling growth of the Internet, and future projections of the growth of the numbers of devices that will use IP addresses, it's only a matter of time before ARIN will run out of "fresh" IP space.

Killing Me Softly with New Apps

IPv4 has other problems beyond addressing. New applications, such as streaming video; voice-over IP; Internet radio, music, distance learning, videoconferencing; and all sorts of Web-as-TV applications have put the IPv4 to the test. IP was never intended to be a real-time protocol, yet most new, high-stress Web applications depend on a reliable, constant stream of IP datagrams.

That IPv4 works at all is a testament to the flexibility and robustness of its design, but this can't go on forever. The main problem is that IP is a "best effort" delivery mechanism, not a guaranteed delivery mechanism. That's what TCP is for; but even it can't manage bandwidth or ensure that the pipe between two endpoints on a network will always be available. So, if it absolutely, positively has to get there in the next 2 milliseconds, make a phone call. Circuit switching reserves the bandwidth necessary to guarantee enough bandwidth for delivery. Packet switching doesn't, at least packet switching as we know it today, and as IP does it.

This has not stopped people from trying to make IP connections (which are actually TCP sessions) act like circuit-switched channels. The objective is to get IP networks to deliver Quality of Service (QoS) channels with fixed, reliable amounts of regularly available bandwidth.

The point is to be able to use the Internet as we do the long-distance phone network or like the broadcast airwaves for live video feeds.

These are all fabulous ideas, and they're technically feasible, and to a certain extent, they can be made to work. The only problem is that the idea of QoS is a total mystery to IPv4. IPv4 never promised you a rose garden, nor anything but its best effort to deliver your traffic whenever it was able to do so.

Feelings of Insecurity

Security was never part of the game plan for IP either. Security means a lot of different things to a lot of people, but it often encompasses authentication, encryption, validation, and several other functionalities. Just as new protocols and techniques have been developed to make IP deliver sufficient quality of service to meet some applications, new protocols have been developed to add security to IP communications; for example, the IP Secure protocol, or IPsec, adds encryption and secure key-based authentication to IP communications. Several firewall vendors offer proprietary encryption and authentication capabilities to establish secure tunnels through virtual private networks over the Internet.

But, again, these innovations, while clever and, to a certain degree, remarkably effective, aren't part of IP itself. It would be nice, for instance, to use a computer's IP address as a secure identifier, so that the IP address, rather than an external security mechanism, could identify the source or destination of IP traffic.

Once and Future Solutions

The Internet engineering community believes that the ultimate solution to the shortcomings of IP is a bigger, better, and faster version of IP, which is IP version 6, or IPv6. But implementing the solution is not as simple as just replacing one version of IP with another. For one thing, most network managers can't afford the time to make a protocol change "pitstop," particularly if not everyone is making the same change.

Applications developers, communications system vendors, ISPs, and Internet entrepreneurs dreaming of striking it rich in a buyout or an IPO have already devised a number of short-term solutions to make IP do the things that the Internet expects of it. Some of these solutions actually work fairly well—that is, until something better comes along.

Quality of Service

As far as applications are concerned, the basic problem with IP is that it doesn't have a concept of on-time delivery. Delivering IP datagrams across the Internet in a steady, predictable, and reliable stream is key to making a whole range of new applications possible, including streaming video, IP telephony, and Internet radio. IP must be made to deliver a "virtual channel," illustrated in Figure 19.1, with regularly available bandwidth, like circuit-switched phone lines or broadcast radio and TV frequencies.

There are those who say that such machinations to IP are unnecessary, because the technologies already exist to do these applications perfectly well. The technologies are television, telephones, and radio—but we'll leave that discussion for another time.

There are three techniques that could be used to provide QoS:

Gimme air. Raise the likelihood that there will be enough bandwidth for a QoS-sensitive application by increasing the bandwidth of the Internet, an ISP's network, or a customer's ISP connection.

Clear the airwaves. Prioritize network traffic through bandwidth managers or policy-based routing.

End-to-end. Establish end-to-end mechanisms specifically tailored for QoS, such as RSVP, IP switching, or channel management.

The gimme-air scenario is the simplest to implement, and, on an individual, user-by-user basis, actually works. Internet Web surfers have found that as long as there aren't any serious communications problems on the Internet (always a chancy proposition, but it does happen), faster

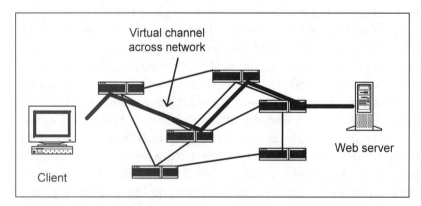

Figure 19.1 An IP virtual channel, with a fixed, dependable bandwidth.

Internet access can make applications work better. Just as a 56Kb modem usually improves the performance of bandwidth-dependent applications, ISDN or DSL access makes them that much better.

Companies, organizations, and Web sites have also found that bigger Internet circuits also make more things possible. Many Web site managers feel that there are few applications issues that a few more high-bandwidth circuits won't solve.

Throwing ISP access bandwidth at the problem may not be enough, however, if bandwidth-sensitive applications have to compete with all of the other traffic pouring out of the same Internet connection. That's why some vendors have focused on the clear-the-airwaves option, managing and controlling access by different applications at each ISP access point.

Bandwidth managers and policy-based routers (hardware devices at the Internet access points) give network managers the ability to control which users or applications have priority in the Internet access pipe. Lower-priority traffic and IP datagrams from less bandwidth-sensitive applications can be shunted aside to make way for those labeled high-priority. For instance, users on an IP telephony conference call across the Internet can be given priority access to the ISP connection, while Web surfers' traffic may be delayed a few seconds to service the priority traffic first.

Bandwidth managers and policy-based routers give network managers a better chance of giving new applications better Internet service. Their chief advantage is that their operation is transparent to IP. Their chief disadvantage is that the control they exercise stops at the ISP connection. Bandwidth management techniques don't extend all the way across the Internet. Individual ISPs may be able to control bandwidth-managed traffic all the way across their networks, but not on the Internet at large.

The Resource Reservation Protocol (RSVP), developed by the IETF, was one of the first efforts to control bandwidth allocation from end to end, all the way across the Internet. In that sense, it's the first QoS mechanism designed to give IP true QoS at the application level. Several major software vendors have announced plans to support RSVP in videoconferencing and voice-over-Internet applications.

There's one big catch to RSVP, however: applications, operating systems, and network routers must be ready to work with it. For example, an application such as a videoconferencing application that required reserved bandwidth would issue a bandwidth reservation request, specifying the amount of bandwidth required and the maximum delay in datagram transmission that could be tolerated. This would be directed across the Internet to the destination system and to all of the intervening routers and switches. The key is that all of the network routers and switches in between would have to recognize and honor the RSVP request, as illustrated in Figure 19.2. Whether they can do continually is another issue, too. In practice, RSVP is a more reasonable proposition in a private network, across VPNs controlled by a single ISP, or by coordination among ISPs.

IP switching, which also goes by the name of *tag switching*, is another version of the same kind of bandwidth reservation scheme. It moves the responsibility for IP network path reservation to the routers. The routers examine traffic flowing through them to identify longer-lived streams of datagrams. Then they set up virtual paths across the IP network (which must be composed of IP-switching routers), so that the traffic is pipelined to the destination. It's more complicated than methods like RSVP, but it puts all of the burden on smart routers that can detect transmissions that need reserved bandwidth.

Except for RSVP, most of these techniques are attempts to add extra capabilities that are transparent to applications. Some of them, such as RSVP and, to the extent that it can be controlled, IP switching, offer a decent chance of adapting the current TCP/IP protocol stack to bandwidth-sensitive applications. However, they imply the cooperation and coordination of many different systems and network elements all across the Internet. Running a streaming video broadcast between a user's PC in New York and a Web site in California assumes that all of the local ISPs involved, all of the potential top-level ISPs, and all of the routers in between can handle whichever IP management protocol is being used. It also assumes that all of them have enough bandwidth to sup-

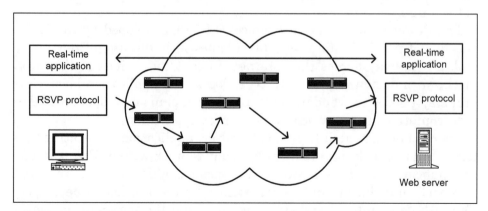

Figure 19.2 An RSVP service reservation request to support a real-time application.

port the application, and that the user's local ISP access channels also have enough bandwidth. Hosting bandwidth-sensitive applications on distributed mirror sites is another way around the problem.

Changing to a completely different protocol stack, and leaving TCP/IP behind, is highly unlikely. It's remarkable that the computing universe was able to fix on TCP/IP as the universal protocol in the first place. Ten years ago, TCP/IP was a "Unix thing." If it hadn't been for the Internet and Windows NT's adoption of TCP/IP, we'd still be in the middle of the old wars among IPX, NetBIOS, TCP/IP, and SNA, as well as whatever new entries other companies dreamed up.

The Version 6 Solution

It may be that the most likely alternative to bringing IP to a new level of capability is creating and implementing a new version of IP. This is not to say that this is the best choice, or something that everyone wants to happen. But maybe it's the only practical way to make IP do all of the things that we want it to do.

With that in mind, the IETF has created the next generation of IP, which, as mentioned, has been designated IP version 6 (IPv6). (Don't ask what happened to version 5. Actually, it was an experimental version of IP, never intended to be used as a production protocol, so version 6 is the next "real thing.") IPv6 is specified in RFC 1752, indicating that it has been specified for several years.

At this date, IPv6 seems destined to play a major role in the future of the Internet. But its future depends on the Internet community agreeing to change IPv4 software to IPv6, which is not exactly a slam-dunk decision. The point is, IPv6 could easily end up on the shelf, watching its aging but still serviceable predecessor hold sway.

The most evident benefit of IPv6 is that it would relieve the problem of the exhaustion of IP addresses. The 32-bit IP address fields of the IPv4 headers permit 4.3 billion possible unique IP host addresses. IPv6 will expand the size of the IP address field to 128 bits. This will raise the number of potential IP addresses to approximately 2^{128} (the number 340 with 33 zeroes behind it). The math works out to several thousand IP addresses for every square meter of the Earth's surface, which ought to hold us for a while.

One word of warning: If you have trouble remembering the dotted-decimal representations of IPv4 numbers, you'll really be in trouble with IPv6 addresses; they're four times as long. However, so as not to make the lengthier IPv6 addresses totally incomprehensible, IPv6 addresses will be expressed as eight hexadecimal numbers separated by colons (:). Thus, an IPv6 address might be expressed in hex as 2C01:45:26:2DE5:60:101:B038:88. It hardly need be said that given the chance for error in typing such an address, DNS will become indispensable, instead of a luxury.

IPv6 addressing also allows for different types of addresses, such as NetWare IPX addresses, and broadcast and group addresses, to be incorporated into the 128-bit address field. Presumably, the size of the IPv6 address field would remove, at least for several generations, limitations on the growth of the Internet in particular and computing networks in general, at least for a while.

The other major benefit of IPv6 is that it will incorporate a number of capabilities that IPv4 does not incorporate, such as improved routing, security, and QoS capabilities. For instance, IPv4 sees all routers as peers, and IP addresses have nothing to do with where hosts actually are in the network. By contrast, IPv6 supports a concept called hierarchical routing. The objective of hierarchical routing is to simplify the job of the Internet's core routers, by allowing them to link IP addresses to physical locations in the Internet. For example, IPv6 addresses within a certain range might be located in Asia, another range in North America, and so forth.

That Security Thing

The security implication for IPv6 is a set of security protocols developed by the IETF, which as mentioned at the beginning of the chapter is called IPsec, for IP Secure protocol. IPsec adds an optional, extension header to the standard IPv6 datagram header, as illustrated in Figure 19.3, to integrate encryption and authentication into the IPv6 datagram. The additional header enables applications to use authentication or encryption, or both, in IPv6 communications.

IPsec is a network-level protocol, dealing with security at the IP level, regardless of what security (if any) has been implemented by higher-level protocols. This means that a Web browser and a Web server could use the Secure Sockets Layer (SSL) protocol to authenticate Web access and the IP layer beneath it could use IPsec to encrypt the transmission.

Another application of IPsec is establishing virtual private network (VPN) channels across IP networks, such as the Internet. As the IPsec protocols are implemented in IPv6, two systems that communicate

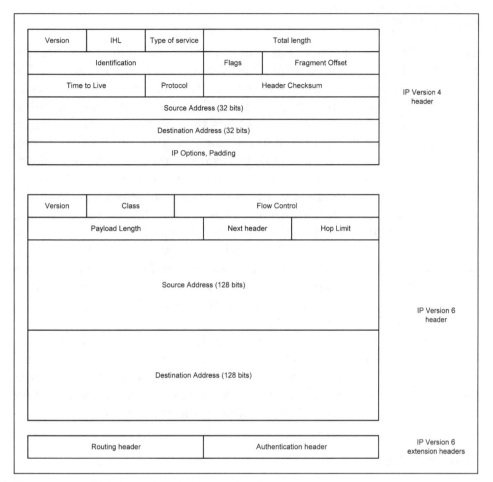

Figure 19.3   The IPv4 and IPv6 datagram headers.

across an IP network establish what are called Security Associations (SA). An SA might include the algorithm it will use for authentication or encryption, as well as the keys for each. SAs are one-way logical relationships, so authenticated communications between two hosts will use two SAs, one in each direction.

IPsec defines two types of SAs: the transport mode and the tunnel mode. The former can encrypt the IPv6 datagram, whereas the latter wraps the IPv6 datagram in a new, additional, IPv6 datagram. The benefit is that the tunnel mode packages the IPv6 datagram in a completely new IP "envelope" that shields it during transmission across the VPN.

IPv6 and QoS

The IPv6 datagram header that was illustrated in Figure 19.3 incorporates additional capabilities for QoS. The two new IPv6 header fields are the Class and Flow Control fields. The Class field replaces the Type of Service field in the IPv4 header, which has rarely been implemented in IPv4 routers. The IPv6 Class field lets the originating application or host designate a priority for the datagram. The idea is to provide a hook in the IPv6 header that will link the routers that handle IPv6 datagrams to higher-level protocols that need priority network-level service.

The Flow Control field gives a host or an application a way to designate a sequence of datagrams or data blocks that require special, sequenced routing through the network. It identifies the stream of datagrams, as well as their order. The implementation of IPv6 flow control depends, of course, on routers that understand how to manage such a flow, and to reserve bandwidth for it. IPv6 flow control accomplishes the same objective as IP switching, by moving the flow control mechanism into the IPv6 header itself.

The QoS features of IPv6 provide the link between the applications and network transport mechanism. An application for streaming video, for instance, might use the RSVP protocol to reserve bandwidth across the network. At transmission time, RSVP would be able to use the Class and Flow Control fields of IPv6 to manage the stream of datagrams.

IPv6 and DNS

If IPv6 is ever widely implemented, it may indeed make life easier for IP network administrators, but it also implies big changes for some key network applications and utilities. For one, the tremendous increase in IP address space in IPv6 would have a significant impact on Domain Name Service (DNS) servers.

Ignoring for the moment the changes that would have to be made in client and server implementations of IP, existing versions of BIND and DNS would have to be modified to recognize the 128-bit IP addresses that IPv6 uses. DNS host name-to-IP address tables would have to be modified to recognize and to accept a new kind of resource record to map host names to much longer IP addresses.

A new kind of DNS resource record, called an AAAA record, would have to be implemented to map host names to IPv6 addresses. (It's called an AAAA record because the current DNS records for IPv4 addresses, called A records, use 4-byte (32-bit) IP addresses.) The IPv6 addresses would be four times as long (128 bits, or 16 bytes), so their resource records would also be four times as long, and be called AAAA records.

If DNS were to use IPv6 addresses, that would mean that other utilities that assign those addresses, such as DHCP, would also have to be modified to handle the longer addresses. Similarly, the Internet Control Message Protocol (ICMP) would have to be changed to understand 128-bit addresses. (ICMP is a protocol that is implemented along with IP in routers and hosts. It generates those "host unreachable" messages, and points them back to the source of IP traffic, if a router doesn't know where to forward an IP datagram.)

Applications including Web browsers, network file and print services, and local DNS services would also have to be modified to use IPv6 addresses. Software vendors say they plan to support IPv6 when there's sufficient demand for it (which translated means whenever Microsoft supports it). So far, Microsoft's research division has shipped a functional skeleton of an IPv6 protocol stack. It works, but it's intended only to enable software companies to experiment with IPv6. By no means does it mean that Microsoft will be undertaking a crusade to convert the world to IPv6. That's for someone else to do.

Getting There

The key issue with IPv6 is how to get there from here. In fact, almost as much of the IPv6 development effort has been devoted to the transition from IPv4 as it has to the new protocol itself. Despite all of the terrific features IPv6 incorporates, there's no groundswell of network administrators clamoring to switch all of their IPv4 software to IPv6, and manage all of the transition issues. In short, it won't happen until there's a compelling reason t do so.

Nevertheless, the IETF has mapped out a transition strategy to get from IPv4 to IPv6. Recognizing that converting both individual systems and whole networks to IPv6 is a complex operation, as well as one that could take years to accomplish, the IETF's strategy assumes that there will be some extended period of time when networks, particularly the Internet, will be implementing both IPv4 and IPv6 systems and that both IPv4 and IPv6 systems will have to coexist and communicate with each other. The transition will be further complicated by network routers, which must also be able to understand and route IPv4 and IPv6 traffic.

There are three key components to the transition-by-coexistence strategy, each of which addresses IPv4 and IPv6 compatibility. The three components, each of which is a mechanism to permit IPv4-to-IPv6 communications, are:

- IPv4-compatible IPv6 addresses
- Dual IPv4 and IPv6 protocol stacks
- IPv6 over IPv4 tunneling

IP addressing is the most obvious problem in a transition scenario, because IPv4 systems will have 32-bit addresses and IPv6 systems will have 128-bit addresses. However, the IPv6 standard defines a special IPv4-compatible IPv6 address type, a special unicast, or single-destination, address that an IPv6 system and an IPv4 system can use to communicate over a network of IPv4 routers. The special IPv6 address contains a standard 32-bit IPv4 address embedded in a 128-bit IPv6 address, with the first 96 bits of the address zeroes. For example, if a system's IPv4 address is 192.57.1.2, its IPv4-compatible IPv6 address would be 0:0:0:0:0:0:0 C039:102. Using that address, an IPv6 system would see a valid IPv6 address, and an IPv4 system would ignore the leading zeroes.

Many systems, particularly network routers and network servers, will have to run dual IPv4 and IPv6 protocol stacks during the transition. A dual-stack system would have both IPv4 and IPv6 addresses for network interfaces, and could handle datagrams with either type of address. A router would probably also need to maintain two different routing tables and be able to handle IPv6 QoS features such as traffic prioritization and flow control.

Network routers that couldn't handle IPv6 addresses or traffic would still be able to handle IPv6 traffic by tunneling. The idea behind tunneling is to encapsulate IPv6 datagrams in IPv4 datagrams so that IPv6 is transparent to IPv4 routers. An IPv6 system, for example, could communicate with another IPv6 system or an IPv4 system using tunneling. The tunneling mechanisms—encapsulation, decapsulation, and managing tunneling—aren't that complicated in themselves; still, they add complexity to a system that is already complex enough. Furthermore, tunneling obscures some of the advantages of IPv6, such as QoS. That said, it could be widely used as a backward-compatibility strategy for IPv6 transition.

Why Me?

It could be argued that the IPv6 transition mechanisms are too good, in that they provide too much compatibility between IPv4 and IPv6 systems. If, the thinking goes, older IPv4 and newer IPv6 systems can coexist so well, why should most users bother using IPv6 at all? Admittedly, the transition to IPv6 may not happen until the life support systems of the Internet start to fail. If we really do run out of IP addresses, and if those attempts to make the old dog (IPv4) perform new tricks fail, and if we absolutely, positively have to watch TV over the Internet, and if, and if, and if . . .

To repeat, the switch to IPv6 won't happen without a compelling reason to do so, or unless a prominent vendor or network provider decrees it. Case in point: Despite its technical advantages, there was little motivation for anyone to take the Universal Serial Bus (USB) peripheral interface seriously; that is until Apple incorporated it in its wildly popular iMac computer. Apple forced the move to USB for iMac users, because the iMac had no other interface, save for an Ethernet port. The iMac didn't even have a SCSI interface (which, ironically, Apple had also made popular on the original Macintosh). One of the most remarkable aspects of the iMac's success has been its wide acceptance and huge commercial impact, despite making obsolete entire generations of Macintosh peripherals. Vendors have been developing serial- and SCSI-to-USB interfaces, though, over a lengthy period of time.

Perhaps it will take just such a shock for IPv6 to get rolling. Its first dose of Miracle Grow would have to come from a vendor of Microsoft's or Cisco's import, or in the form of a decision by a big Internet top-level provider to support IPv6. The commercial risks would be the same as they were for the iMac, but the technological impact would be more far reaching.

Can the Internet survive this kind of drastic change? Of course. Nobody really cares what kind of IP anyone uses, as long as it works, and as long as it's compatible. New generations of applications, as well the evolution of the Internet as a real-time medium, assume and depend on communications along the "circuit-streaming" model. IPv4 was never designed to do that, and eventually, it will have to be modified so that it can adapt to the new demands that will be placed on it.

Bibliography

Books

Albitz, Paul, and Cricket Liu. *DNS and BIND*, 2nd Ed., (Sebastapol, CA: O'Reilly & Associates), 1997.

Berkowitz, Howard. *Designing Addressing Architectures for Routing and Switching*, (New York: Macmillan Technical Publishing), 1999.

Chapman, Barry, and Edward Zwick. *Building Internet Firewalls*, (Sebastapol, CA: O'Reilly & Associates), 1996.

Gilly, Daniel. *Unix in a Nutshell,* (Sebastapol, CA: O'Reilly & Associates), 1998.

Graham, Buck. *TCP/IP Addressing*, (San Diego: Academic Press), 1997.

Halari, Bassam. *Internet Routing Architectures,* (Indianapolis, IN: Cisco Press/New Riders Publishing), 1997.

Huitema, Christian. *Routing in the Internet*, (Englewood Cliffs, NJ: Prentice-Hall), 1995.

Hunt, Craig. *TCP/IP Network Administration,* (Sebastapol, CA: O'Reilly & Associates), 1996.

Microsoft Press. *Windows 95 Resource Kit*, (Redmond, WA: Microsoft Press), 1995.

Moy, John T. *OSPF: Anatomy of an Internet Routing Protocol,* (Reading, MA: Addison-Wesley), 1997.

Pearce, Eric. *NT in a Nutshell*, (Sebastapol, CA: O'Reilly & Associates), 1997.

Russell, Charlie, and Sharon Crawford. *Running Windows NT Server*, (Redmond, WA: Microsoft Press), 1997.

RFCs

RFC 760, "DoD Standard Internet Protocol," J. Postel, 1980.
RFC 790, "Assigned Numbers," J. Postel, 1981.
RFC 791, "Internet Protocol," J. Postel, 1981.

RFC 826, "An Ethernet Address Resolution Protocol," D. Plummer, 1982.

RFC 894, "Standard for the Transmission of IP Datagrams over Ethernet Networks," C. Hornig, 1984.

RFC 903, "A Reverse Address Resolution Protocol," R. Finlayson, T. Mann, J. Mogul, and J. Postel, 1985.

RFC 950, "Internet Standard Subnetting Procedure," J. Mogul and J. Postel, 1985.

RFC 951, "Bootstrap Protocol," W. J. Croft and J. Gilmore, 1985.

RFC 1009, "Requirements for Internet Gateways," R. Braden and J. Postel, 1987.

RFC 1034, "Domain Name System Concepts and Facilities," P. Mockapetris, 1987.

RFC 1058, "Routing Information Protocol," C. Hedrick, 1988.

RFC 1122, "Requirements for Internet Hosts–Communication Layers," IETF (R. Braden, ed.), 1989.

RFC 1123, "Requirements for Internet Hosts–Application and Support," IETF (R. Braden, ed.), 1989.

RFC 1293, "Inverse Address Resolution Protocol," T. Bradley and C. Brown, 1992.

RFC 1338, "Supernetting: An Address Assignment and Aggregation Strategy," V. Fuller, T. Li, J. Yu, and K. Varadhan, 1992.

RFC 1466, "Guidelines for Management of the IP Address Space," E. Gerich, 1993.

RFC 1492, "An Access Control Protocol, Sometimes Called TACACS," C. Finseth, 1993.

RFC 1517, "Applicaibility Statement for the Implementation of Classless Inter-Domain Routing (CIDR)," R. Hinden, editor, 1993.

RFC 1518, "An Architecture for IP Address Allocation with CIDR," Y. Rekhter and T. Li, 1993.

RFC 1519, "Classless Inter-Domain Routing (CIDR): An Address Assignment and Aggregation Strategy," V. Fuller, T. Li, J. Yu, and K. Varadhan, 1993.

RFC 1520, "Exchanging Routing Information Across Provider Boundaries in the CIDR Environment," Y. Rekhter and C. Topolcic, 1993.

RFC 1533, "DHCP Options and bootP Vendor Extensions," S. Alexander and R. Droms, 1993.

RFC 1597, "Address Allocation for Private Internets," Y. Rekhter, B. Moskowitz, D. Karrenberg, and G. de Groot, 1994.

RFC 1627, "Network 10 Considered Harmful," E. Lear, E. Fair, D. Crocker, and T. Kessler, 1994.

RFC 1631, "The IP Network Address Translator (NAT)," K. Egevang and P. Francis, 1994.

RFC 1700, "Assigned Numbers," J. Reynolds and J. Postel, 1994.

RFC 1752, "The Recommendation for the IP Next Generation Protocol," S. Bradner and A. Mankin, 1995.

RFC 1812, "Requirements for IP Version 4 Routers," F. Baker, 1995.

RFC 1878, "Variable Length Subnet Table for IPv4," T. Pummill and B. Manning, 1995.

RFC 1883, "Internet Protocol, Version 6 (IPv6) Specification," S. Deering and R. Hinders, 1995.

RFC 1884, "IP Version 6 Addressing Architecture," R. Hinden and S. Deering, 1995.

RFC 1918, "Address Allocation for Private Internets," Y. Rekhter, B. Moskowitz, D. Karrenberg, G. de Groot, and E. Lear, 1996.

RFC 1930, "Guidelines for Creation, Selection, and Registration of an Autonomous System (AS)," J. Hawkinson and T. Bates, 1996.

RFC 1995, "Incremental Zone Transfer in DNS," M. Ohta, 1996.

RFC 2050, "Internet Registry IP Allocation Guidelines," K. Hubbard, M. Kosters, D. Conrad, D. Karrenberg, and J. Postel, 1996.

RFC 2071, "Network Renumbering Overview: Why Would I Want It and What Is It Anyway?" P. Ferguson and H. Berkowitz, 1997.

RFC 2072, "Router Renumbering Guide," H. Berkowitz, 1997.

RFC 2136, "Dynamic Update in the Domain Name System (DNS)," P. Vixie, Y. Rekhter, S. Thompson, and J. Bound, 1997.

RFC 2138, "Remote Authentication Dial-In User Service (RADIUS)," C. Rigney, A. Rubens, W. Simpson, and S. Willens, 1997.

RFC 2317, "Classless IN-ADDR.ARPA Delegation," H. Eidnes, G. J. de Groot, and P. Vixie, 1998.

RFC 2390, "Inverse Address Resolution Protocol," T. Bradley, C. Brown, and A. Malis, 1998.

RFC 2391, "Load Sharing Using IP Network Address Translation (NAT)," P. Srisuresh and D. Gan, 1998.

Index

A

AAAA record, 288–289
address allocation assignment,
    see IP address allocation
    assignment
addresses, see IP addresses
addressing protocols, 4
Address Resolution Protocol
    (ARP), 223
address space, *see* IP address space
administrative cleanup, after
    renumbering, 246
    large network case study, 276
    medium network case study,
    264–265
    small network case study, 252
Advanced Research Projects
    Agency network (ARPANET),
    18–19, 21
aggregated addresses, 91

all-ones subnet, 55, 121–122
all-zeroes subnet, 55, 121–122
American Registry for Internet
    Numbers, *see* ARIN
American Telephone and
    Telegraph (AT&T), 20, 197
applications, documenting
    existing, 100–101
applications protocols, 4
ARIN (American Registry for
    Internet Numbers),xv, 23
    challenges, 28
    fast-track program, for small
    ISPs, 170–171
    and ISPs, 24–26, 27
    justifying request to, 79–84
    and PI address space, 67
ARPANET (Advanced Research
    Projects Agency network),
    18–19, 21

ASes, *see* Autonomous Systems
Asia-Pacific NIC (APNIC), 21, 22, 23
asymmetric routing, 183
AT&T, 197
   role in InterNIC, 20
authentication
   IPsec, 286–287
   server access, 226, 228–230
Autonomous System numbers, 22, 208
Autonomous Systems (ASes), 46
   and BGP, 198, 211
   and CIDR, 49–50
   and connectivity after renumbering, 188
   need for, 171–172
   organizational ISPs, 207–210

B
bandwidth, 280
bandwidth reservation schemes, 144–145, 282–285
base address, 56
BGP (Border Gateway Protocol), 5, 47
   described, 211
   and transit networks, 196–199
BIND DNS service, 157, 178, 237
Bolt, Beranek, and Newman Corporation (BBN), 12
bootP service, 176, 181
Border Gateway Protocol, *see* BGP
bridged LANs, 65
   transition from, 224–225
browsers, *see* Web browsers
business case, for renumbering, 75–79

address space request justification, 79–84
business partners
   documenting address ranges, 93–94
   NAT for, 130, 133–134
   network joining, 64
bytes, 10

C
Cable & Wireless, 40, 197
CerfNet, 40
Changeover, of ISPs, *see* Internet service provider changeover
CIDR (Classless Inter-Domain Routing), xv, 25, 50–53, 91
   aggregating subnetworks into, 68
   and business case justification, 83
   and future of Internet, 27
   and LAN interfaces, 223
   practical effect of, 58
   and renumbering, 67–71
CIDR masks, 53–58
CIDR prefixes, 53, 54
CIDR subnet mask, 11, 54–58
circuit switching, 291
   packet switching contrasted, 280
Cisco Systems, and IPv6, 291
Class A addresses, 6, 7–8, 52
   identifying, 11–12
   stranding of addresses in, 280
Class A subnetworks, 104–106
Class B addresses, 6, 8–9, 52, 90–91
   identifying, 11–12
   stranding of addresses in, 280

Class B subnetworks, 104–106,
108–117, 120
Class C addresses, 6, 9, 52
and CIDR consolidation, 53, 68
identifying, 11–12
outgrowing, 64–65
route aggregation, 204–205
serial router ports, 219
TWD reclaiming, 70–71
Class C subnetworks, 104–106,
117–121
Class D addresses, 9–10
Class E addresses, 9–10
classful addressing, 13, 52
classless addressing, 13
Classless Inter-Domain Routing,
see CIDR
classless routing, 63
Class values, 155, 156
CNAME resource records, 154,
157–158
.com designation, 19
annual fee for, 21
communications protocols, 3
community string, 89
configuration files, *see* host
configuration files
connectionless routing, 41
costs, of renumbering, 78

D
datagrams, 5, 32–33
Data values, 155
default routes, for IP routing, 42
Defense Communications Agency
(DCA), 20
delay count, 44
delegation, *see* IP address
delegation

Department of Commerce, 22, 23
Department of Defense Advanced
Research Projects Agency
network (ARPANET), 18–19,
21
dependencies, 86
DHCP (Dynamic Host
Configuration Protocol), xix,
xvii, 100, 176, 231
disadvantages, 185–186
hosts, 176, 180–183, 185–186
IP routers, 226–228
linking with DDNS, 149
PC configuration, 182–183
and reduced renumbering need,
61, 244
setup in large network case
study, 271, 275
setup in medium network case
study, 261, 263
setup in small network case
study, 251–252
DHCP servers, 180–181
diagrams, xvii, 246
for business case presentation,
77–78
organizational ISPs, 214
preparing, 86–102
dial-up access, 99
dial-up port pools, 226–227
distance learning, 280
DNS (Domain Name Service),
xviii-xix
as database, 148–149
documenting existing use,
99–100
dynamic, 148–149
and Internet routing, 36
IP routers, renumbering
implications, 227–228

DNS (Domain Name Service)
(*cont.*)
and IPv6, 286, 288–289
as network service, 149–150
operation, 151–154
organizational ISPs, 207–210
origins of, 20
renumbering considerations,
147–160
resetting in renumbering
rollout, 245
role of, 2
root file, 20
services and domains, 150–151
DNS resource records, 154–159
changing in renumbering,
238–239
DNS root file, 20
DNS server updating/upgrading,
154, 231, 237–238
medium network renumbering
case study, 261
in rollout, 243–245
SOA changing, 239–240
DNS zone file, 159, 239–240
DNS zones, 159–160, 239
DNS zone transfer, 160, 239–240
documentation, xvii, 234, 246
organizational ISPs, 214
preparing, 86–102
domain names
naming conventions, 19
registration, 21
Domain Name Service, *see* DNS
domains, 150–151
dot designations (.com, .org, etc.),
19, 21, 150
dotted decimal numbers, 10–11,
285
Dynamic DNS services (DDNS),
148–149

Dynamic Host Configuration
Protocol, *see* DHCP

E
.edu designation, 19
800 number address portability,
169
email addresses, 156
encryption, IPsec, 286–287
Ethernet networks, 9, 14, 32, 105
switch problems with hosts,
184–185
executive summary, 76, 77
Expiration values, 155, 157
Extended Terminal Access
Control and Communications
System (XTACACS), 229
exterior routing protocols, 46–49,
96–97
external WAN links, 89–90

F
Federal Networking Council, 19,
20
firewall rulesets, 243
firewalls
documenting existing, 97–98
medium network renumbering,
256
Network Address Translation
(NAT), 130, 135, 137
and rollout, 242–243
frames, 5
FTP, 19

G
Gantt chart, 233
General Atomics, role in
InterNIC, 21

Ghost, 179
global Internet routing, *see* IP
    routing
Green Paper, 23

H
handshake, 143
hard addresses, 32
hierarchical routing, 286
homed, to ISPs, 187
hop count, 44–45
host configuration files
    readdressing with, 179
    Unix networks, 178–179
    Windows networks, 177–178
host identifier (host ID), 7,
    106–107, 175
Hostname values, 155
hosts, 6, 13–14, 175–176
    and DHCP, 176, 180–183,
      185–186
    documenting existing, 101–102
    Ethernet switch problems,
      184–185
    IP addresses, 35
    multiple interfaces, 183–184
    and NetBIOS, 177–178
    readdressing with configuration
      files, 179
    renumbering, 237
    resource records, 154, 157
    as routers, 217–218
    Unix configuration files,
      178–179
    and Windows Internet Name
      Service (WINS), 177–178
HOSTS file, 176–177
HP Desktop Administrator, 179
HyperText Transfer Protocol
    (HTTP), 36

I
IANA (Internet Assigned
    Numbers Authority), 19–20,
    27
ICANN (Internet Corporation for
    Assigned Names and
    Numbers), xv, 23, 28–29
ICMP (Internet Control Message
    Protocol), changes required
    for IPv6, 289
IETF (Internet Engineering Task
    Force), xvi, 289–290
ifconfig command (Unix),
    178–179, 182
IGRP (Interior Gateway Routing
    Protocol), 63
iMac, 291
interfaces, 31
    LAN, 14, 218, 222–225
    WAN, 14, 218, 219
Interior Gateway Routing
    Protocol (IGRP), 63
interior routing protocols, 46–49,
    96–97
Internet Corporation for Assigned
    Names and Numbers
    (ICANN), xv, 23
Internet, xiv. *See also* IP routing
    connectivity after renumbering,
      187
    future of, 26–28
    history of, 19–23
    IP protocol transparency, xiii
Internet Assigned Numbers
    Authority (IANA), 19–20
    future of, 27
Internet Control Message
    Protocol (ICMP), changes
    required for IPv6, 289
Internet Domain Name Service
    (DNS), *see* DNS

Internet Engineering Task Force
(IETF), xvi
IPv6 strategy, 289–290
Internet Network Access Points
(NAPs), 34, 40, 52
Internet radio, 280, 282
Internet Registry (IR), 19
expanding task of, 20–22
future of, 26–28
and ISPs, 24–26
Internet routing, *see* IP routing
Internet service provider
changeover, 66–67
address assignments, 237
address portability, 168–170
administrative cleanup after
rollout, 246
NAT for, 132–133
and private address space, 93
small network renumbering
case study, 248–254
Internet service providers (ISPs),
xv, xx, 95. *See also* provider-
aggregated (PA) address
space; provider-independent
(PI) address space
ARIN's fast-track program for
small, 170–171
business case for renumbering,
76
changing, and need for
renumbering, 66–67
hierarchy of, 47–48
and Internet Registry, 24–26,
27
Internet routing by, 34–41
multiconnected networks,
190–192
multihomed networks, 190,
192–196, 206–207

organizational (operating as
your own), xx, 201–214
stub networks, 188–190
transit networks, 196–199
transit rights, 49
Internetworking Protocol (IP), 4
InterNIC, 20–22
Intrusion Detection System (IDS),
98
IP, *see* IP protocol
IP address allocation assignment,
233–234
current address usage, 234–237
and IP routers, 220
IP address classes, 5–10. *See also*
Class A addresses; Class B
addresses; Class C addresses
IP address delegation, xiv-xv,
17–28
defined, 18–19
family trees, 23
IP addresses, xiv, 35. *See also*
renumbering; subnetworks
bytes, 10
classful vs. classless, 13
conventions, 10–12
defined, 1–2
documenting available, 94–95
documenting existing, 90–91
fixed, 42
future developments, 27,
279–291
identifiers, 7
identifying, 11–12
in-use percentage: less than
40%, 280
and IP routers, 107–108
as network interfaces, 13–14
nonunique, 68–69
perpetual ownership, 163

role of, 4
as soft addresses, 14, 32
types of things which have, 31
uniqueness of, 1, 17, 163
IP address renumbering, *see*
    renumbering
IP address space. *See also* private
    IP address space; provider-
    aggregated (PA) address
    space; provider-independent
    (PI) address space
  depletion, 15
  expansion in IPv6, 28
  grandfathering, 71
  IPv6, 285
  outgrowing, 64–65, 103
  request justification, 79–84
ipconfig command (Windows), 182
IP datagrams, 5, 32–33
IP header, 37, 38
IPng (IP Next Generation), *see*
    IPv6
IP protocol, 3–5
  development of, 5–7
  future of, 279–291
  future developments, xxiv
  transparency to Internet users,
    xiii
IP protocol version 4, *see* IPv4
IP protocol version 6, *See* IPv6
IP routers, 32, 33–34, 217–218
  authentication server access,
    226, 228–230
  configuration, 34
  connect/not connect decision,
    37–40
  DHCP services, 226–228
  dial-up port pools, 226–227
  DNS implications for
    renumbering, 227–228

documenting existing, 95–96
  interfaces, 218–226
  and IP addresses, 107–108
  lost packet discarding, 5
  network interfaces of, 14
  renumbering, 217–230
  serial ports, 219–221
  and subnetworking, 103
  terminal ports, 225–226
IP routing, xv, 32–34
  asymmetric, 183
  with CIDR, 51
  convergence, 209
  documenting existing, 88–89
  dynamic changes in, 46
  enabling in renumbering
    rollout, 241–243
  future of, 27
  hop count, 43, 44–45
  interior/exterior routing
    protocols, 46–49, 96–97
  Internet example, 34–41
  IPv4 vs IPv6, 286
  link weight, 45
  masks, 44
  NAT for, 127–128, 130,
    132–133
  principles of, 41–45
  role of, 5, 17
  routing table checking, 38–40
  routing tables, 42–44, 45
  top-level, 40–41
IPsec (IP Secure protocol), 281,
    286–287
IP switching, 284
  and QoS, 144
IP telephony, 282
IPv4
  problems with, 279–281
  transition to IPv6, 289–290

IPv6, 5
  and DNS, 286, 288–289
  and future of Internet, 27–28
  and future of IP, 182, 285–288
  and QoS, 145, 288
  transition from IPv4, 289–290
IP version 6, *see* IPv6
IR, *see* Internet Registry
ISO model, 3
ISPs, *see* Internet service
    providers

L
LANDesk, 179
LAN interfaces, 14, 218, 222–225
LANs (Local Area Networks), 1,
    13, 14
  documenting existing, 87–88
  routers for, 32, 218
  virtual, 65–66
large network renumbering case
    study, 267–277
leaded line connections, 13
legacy routing, 63
link weight, 44–45
LMHOSTS file, 176
load sharing, in multihomed
    networks, 195–196
Local Area Networks (LANS), *see*
    LANs
loopback address, 45, 225
loopback interface, 218
loopback tests, 184

M
mail exchanger (MX) resource
    records, 155, 158
management buy-in, for
    renumbering project, 75

masks
  CIDR, 53–58
  IP routing, 43–44
  subnetworks, *see* subnet masks
master DNS server, 21, 22
master root zone server, 152
MBONE multicast network, 9
MCI, 197
medium network renumbering
    case study, 255–265
MetaIP, 237
Metropolitan Area Exchanges
    (MAEs), 40
Microsoft, 289, 291. *See also*
    Windows networks
Milnet, 21
multiconnected networks,
    190–192
multihomed networks, 190,
    192–196
  load sharing, 195–196
  organizational ISPs, 206–207
  primary/backup approach,
    193–195
multiple interface hosts,
    183–184
multiuser applications, 13
music, 280
MX resource records, 155, 158

N
name server (NS) resource
    records, 155, 158
  changing in renumbering, 153,
    238–239
name servers, 151
NAT, *see* Network address
    translation
National Science Foundation
    (NSF), 20, 21, 80

Internet privatization
initiative, 22–23
NetBIOS, 177–178
.net designation, 19
  annual fee for, 21
netmasks, 112
netstat command (Unix), 179
Network Access Points (NAPs),
  34, 40, 52
network addresses, 42
Network Address Translation
  (NAT), xviii
  basic concepts, 128–129,
    134–137
  disadvantages, 137–138
  firewalls as, 97
  need for, 127–128
  positioning, 137
  and private address space, 92,
    93
  reasons for using, 129–134
  and reduced renumbering need,
    61
  and TCP, 138–145
network cabling, 87
network identifier (net ID), 7,
  106–107
Network Information Center
  (SRI-NIC), 19
network interface card (NIC)
  addresses, 14, 32
network interfaces, 13–14, 31,
  218
network protocols, 4
network routers, 31–32. *See also*
  IP routers
  changes required for IPv6,
    289–290
networks. *See also* LANs;
  subnetworks; WANs
  bridged, 65, 224–225

changes required for IPv6, 290
  documenting existing, 86–87
  documenting expansion plans,
    94
  documenting incomplete, 63–64
  expansion, and renumbering,
    71
  joining with business partners,
    64
  large network renumbering,
    267–277
  medium network renumbering,
    255–265
  multiconnected, 190–192
  multihomed, 190, 192–196,
    206–207
  separated, 223–224
  small network renumbering,
    247–254
  stub, 188–190
  transit, 196–199
Network Solutions (NSI), xv, 80
  address assignment spin-off to
    ARIN, 23
  role in InterNIC, 20–21
  Web site, 238
NIC (network interface card)
  addresses, 14, 32
nonunique IP addresses, 68–69
NSI, *see* Network Solutions
NS resource records, 153, 155,
  158, 238–239

O
Open Shortest Path First Protocol
  (OSPF), 5, 256–265
Optimal Surveyor, 89
organizational ISPs, 201–214
.org designation, 19
  annual fee for, 21

OSPF (Open Shortest Path First Protocol), 5
move to, medium network renumbering case study, 256–265

P

PA address space, *see* provider-aggregated (PA) address space
packets, 5
packet-switching networks
circuit switching contrasted, 280
IP routing networks as, 45
partners, *see* business partners
path selection, 211
PDP-11, 6
peering, 40
personal digital assistants (PDAs), 62
PI address space, *see* provider-independent (PI) address space
ping testing, 235–236, 242
planning, of renumbering, 232–233
large network case study, 272–274
medium network case study, 259–261
small network case study, 249–250
pointer (PTR) resource records, 155, 159
primary DNS, 160
printers, documenting existing, 101–102
private IP address space, 65, 167–168

documenting existing, 92–93
NAT for, 130, 131, 132
private TCP/IP networks, 167
project overview, 77
project plan document, 233
provider-aggregated (PA) address space, xix, 172
and connectivity after renumbering, 188
defined, 164–166
evaluating in renumbering project, 233
provider-independent (PI) address space, xix, 170–171
and connectivity after renumbering, 187–188
defined, 164, 166
evaluating in renumbering project, 233
getting, 172–173
organizational ISPs, 204
portability, 168–170
and renumbering, 67
proxy servers, 98–99
NAT for, 130, 131–132, 136–137
PTR resource records, 155, 159

Q

QoS, *see* Quality of Service (QoS)
Quality of Service (QoS)
interim solutions, 144, 282–285
and IPv4, 280–281
and IPv6, 145, 288

R

RADIUS (Remote Access Dial-Up System), 229
Refresh values, 155, 156, 160, 240, 244

Remote Access Dial-Up System
(RADIUS), 229
remote access servers, 35
adding in medium network
renumbering case study, 257,
263
documenting existing, 99
renumbering, xv-xvi
business case for, xvi-xvii,
75–84
diagrams and documentation
for, 86–102
DNS considerations, 147–160
drawbacks, 72
IP routers, 217–230
and IPv6, 71–72
large network case study,
267–277
medium network case study,
255–265
organizational ISP, 201–214
process step description,
232–246
process step overview, 232
reasons for, 62–71
routers, xxi
small network case study,
247–254
Request for Comments (RFCs),
see RFCs
Reseaux IP Européean (RIPE),
21, 22, 23
resource records, *see* DNS
resource records
Resource Reservation Protocol
(RSVP), 144, 283–284
Retry values, 155, 156, 240, 244
reverse address resolution, 159
RFC 760, 5–6, 293
RFC 790, 293
RFC 791, 6, 13, 18, 122, 293

RFC 826, 294
RFC 894, 294
RFC 903, 294
RFC 950, 53, 294
RFC 951, 181, 294
RFC 1009, 294
RFC 1034, 294
RFC 1058, 294
RFC 1122, 294
RFC 1123, 294
RFC 1174, 19
RFC 1293, 294
RFC 1338, 294
RFC 1466, 21, 294
RFC 1492, 294
RFC 1517, 50, 294
RFC 1518, 50, 294
RFC 1519, 50, 294
RFC 1520, 50, 294
RFC 1533, 294
RFC 1597, 294
RFC 1627, 294
RFC 1631, 294
RFC 1700, 294
RFC 1752, 285, 294
RFC 1812, 294
RFC 1878, 295
RFC 1883, 295
RFC 1884, 295
RFC 1918, 64, 65, 92, 167, 247, 295
RFC 1930, 47, 295
RFC 1995, 295
RFC 2050, 24–25, 81, 295
RFC 2071, 295
RFC 2072, 295
RFC 2131, 180
RFC 2136, 295
RFC 2138, 295
RFC 2317, 295
RFC 2390, 295
RFC 2391, 295

RFCs (Request for Comments), 5
list of, 293–295
review and editing of, 19
risks, of renumbering, 78
rollout, of renumbering
completing, 245
DNS updating and testing,
243–245
large network case study,
274–275
medium network case study,
263–264
routing enablement, 241–243
small network case study,
251–252
starting, 240–241
root zone servers, 152
route aggregation, 49–50
organizational ISPs, 204–205
route flap, 209
router address pool, 226
router configuration files, 234
routers, *see* IP routers
routing, *see* IP routing
Routing Arbiter Database
(RADB), 209–210
Routing Arbiter servers, 210
Routing Information Protocol, 63,
88, 256
routing protocols, for IP routing,
41–42
routing tables, 42–44, 45, 234
checking, 38–40
RS232 ports, 225

S
scoping, renumbering projects
large network case study, 271
medium network case study,
258–259

small network case study,
248–249
secondary addresses, 222–225
secondary DNS, 160
second-level domain names, 19
Secure Sockets Layer (SSL)
protocol, 286
security. *See also* firewalls
IPv4, 281
IPv6, 286–287
medium network renumbering,
256
NAT for, 129–130
and private address space, 92
separated networks, 223–224
serial router ports, 219–221
Serial values, 155, 156, 160
Simple Network Management
Protocol, *see* SNMP
site plans, 86–87
small network renumbering case
study, 247–254
SNMP (Simple Network
Management Protocol), xx,
89, 138
and DHCP, 185
SOA (Start of Authority) records,
155–157, 239–240
soft addresses, IP addresses, 14,
32
Sprint, 40, 197
CIDR enforcement, 58, 169–170
Stanford Research Institute
(SRI), 19–20
Start of Authority, *see* SOA
records
changing in renumbering,
239–240
static routes
multiconnected networks,
190–191

organizational ISPs, 204–206
stub networks, 188–189
streaming video, 280, 282
stub networks, 188–190
subnet masks, 11, 54–58,
    112–114, 117
    Variable-Length Subnet
    Masking (VLSM), 58, 95,
    122–124
subnetworking on a byte
    boundary, 111, 114–117
subnetworks, xvii-xviii, 52, 53
    aggregating into large CIDR
    blocks, 68
    all-zeroes and all-ones subnets,
    55, 121–122
    benefits, 103–106
    Class B, 108–117, 120
    Class C, 117–121
    documenting existing, 92–93
    IP addresses, 108–111
    principles, 106–124
    stockpiling, 111
    Variable-Length Subnet
    Masking (VLSM), 58, 95,
    122–124
supernetworking, 50
synchronization message, 141
System Management Server
    (SMS), 185

T
tag switching, 144, 284
TCP header, 37, 38
TCP/IP, 1, 280, 285
    defined, 3–4
    IP addresses, 31
    and Network Address
    Translation (NAT),
    138–145

routing, 33
    Web browser relationship to,
    36, 37
TCP ports, 138–143
technical justification, 77
Telnet, 19
terminal router ports, 225–226
Time To Live (TTL) values, 155,
    157, 240, 244, 245
token ring networks, 14, 32
top-level domain names, 19
top-level ISPs
    CIDR enforcement, 58
    routing by, 40–41
top-level routing, 40–41
traceroute utility, 220, 228
traffic dumping, 198
transit networks, 196–199
transit rights, ISPs, 49
Transmission Control
    Protocol/Internetworking
    Protocol (TCP/IP), see
    TCP/IP
Transmission Control Protocol
    (TCP), 4
transport protocols, 4
tunneling, 290
TWD reclaiming, 70–71
Type values, 155

U
UDP port numbers, 181
unaggregated addresses, 91
Unix networks
    configuration files, 178–179
    hosts as routers, 217
unnumbered serial router
    interfaces, 221
URL, 36–37, 149
UUNet, 40, 197

V

Variable-Length Subnet Masking (VLSM), 58, 95, 122–124
videoconferencing, 280
Virtual LANs (VLANs), 65–66
Virtual Private Network (VPN) services, xvi, 286–287
    dedicated QoS, 145
voice over IP, 280

W

WAN interfaces, 14, 218, 219
WANs (Wide Area Networks), 13, 14
    documenting existing, 87–88
    documenting links, 89–90
    routers for, 32, 218
    serial router ports, 219
Web-as-TV, 280
Web browsers. *See also* proxy servers; security
    and DNS, 149
    IP datagrams, 32–33
    need for protocols, 3
    relationship to TCP/IP, 36, 37
    and TCP ports, 139–145
Web servers
    NAT for, 131
    need for protocols, 3
    and TCP ports, 139–145

White Paper, 23
Whois databases, 234–235
Whois Web sites, 235
Wide Area Networks (WANS), *see* WANs
Windows Internet Name Service (WINS), 177–178
Windows networks, 238
    DHCP-assigned address display, 182
    DHCP configuring, 182–183
    hosts as routers, 217
    hosts files, 176–177
winipcfg command (Windows), 182

X

XTACACS (Extended Terminal Access Control and Communications System), 229

Z

Zero Administration Client (ZAC) suite, 179
zone files, 159, 239–240
zones, 159–160, 239
zone transfer, 160, 239–240